THE BRITISH POLITICAL FRINGE

A Profile

GEORGE THAYER

ANTHONY BLOND
LONDON

To

G.M.T.

(1873-1964)

G.T.A. and E.T.L.

First published in Great Britain 1965 *by Anthony Blond Ltd.,* 56 *Doughty Street, London, W.C.*1. © *Copyright* 1965 *George Thayer. Foreword* © *copyright* 1965 *A. P. Herbert. Printed in Great Britain by Tonbridge Printers Ltd, Tonbridge, Kent, and bound by the Dorstel Press, Harlow.*

FOREWORD

by A. P. Herbert

I am proud to introduce Mr George Thayer, a welcome visitor from the United States, who has written a most interesting and instructive first book. Leaving out the Communist Party, which, he feels, has had enough attention, he has put under the microscope a number of 'groups' or 'movements' on the fringe of British politics. He is not concerned with Nature-Preservers, Anti-Vivisectionists, Round Tablers or Flat-Earthers; but only with groups 'whose primary objective is to alter all or any part of the existing political institutions and attitudes in Great Britain' – from the neo-Nazis to the Irish Nationalists, through the Freedom Group and the Campaign for Nuclear Disarmament.

His researches have occupied two thorough and toilsome years. He has interviewed more than four hundred individuals. He has given us portraits of many who before were merely names in the papers – or the courts; and he has disinterred some fascinating facts. Did you know, for example, that 'contemporary Welsh nationalism was born in 1886 with the establishment of an organisation called the Cymru Fydd (the Welsh Federation) one of whose founding members was David Lloyd George'? Did you know that the 'nationalists' of Cornwall are the only ones in this island who do not want to break away from England entirely? Did you know that there is a gentleman who for years has been known as the 'Prime Minister of Wales'? Or that many brave Cornishmen believe that King Arthur will return, but meanwhile would like Home Rule on the lines of Northern Ireland or the Isle of Man? Did you know that the various neo-Nazi groups dislike each other almost as much as they dislike the Jews? That in 1960 one of them formed a secret élite corps called 'Spearhead', 'a uniformed group of militants who were trained and dressed in imitation of Hitler's Brownshirts'? Do you know the full history of CND?

All this is observed with a neutral eye and a stranger's detachment: so the voice is the more valuable.

In his final chapter Mr Thayer gives us an able summary of his discoveries among the fringe folk. First, he rejects the epithet 'lunatic' commonly applied to any fringe. 'The people who take part in fringe group activities may be eccentric, narrow-minded, intolerant and even mentally unstable, but none that I ever met would qualify as people dangerous to the public safety'.

He does find a kind of pattern of character and behaviour which explains why they are not better loved and more successful. 'The most universal characteristic of all British fringe groups is the tendency to over-state their case'. I noticed a good example of this in the chapter on Scottish Nationalists. Their case is fully and persuasively stated: but one lady wrote somewhere:

> The English Channel Tunnel, which is to cost about £170,000,000, is to be added to the things which Scotland is expected to pay for . . . What Scotland most needs is a deep, wide channel across the Border – and no tunnel.

Over-statement – over-simplifying – and so the loss of a sense of proportion. 'They soon find it difficult to believe that anyone, save themselves, possesses intelligence, reason and understanding.' (But then, on our own pet subjects, do we not all tend towards that state of mind?)

He finds that 'the most devastating criticism levelled at the British political fringe groups as a whole is that they are negative and out of date . . . Most of them are nothing but protest groups'. Thus, no doubt, all 'movements' must begin. 'But' says our author 'they have never understood the value of compromise; and that in 1965 makes them out-of-date'. This disdain of compromise mainly explains the rending internal struggles within a group, or between one like-minded group and another. One lot would stick to the 'pure' doctrine, and does not mind being 'disreputable', indeed, rather likes it. Another, though just as 'pure', they think, would like to be 'respectable', for otherwise they will repel the people who matter. Many leaders are torn between the two. Only the Freedom Group (Mr Martell) and Plaid Cymru (Wales for the Welsh) have successfully dealt with this dilemma.

Many of the rank and file have the 'losers' complex' and have no hope of success. Some leaders do not want to be successful. If they are, they will cease to be the one big fish in their own little pond – or rather, perhaps, the one big frog. If other groups attach themselves there will be rival croakers.

But Mr Thayer finds much virtue in the existence of the groups. Though none of those he surveys have 'any appreciable political power, they do play a role in British society which cannot be overlooked'. For one thing, 'they are a possible source of new ideas. Any group that might develop new ideas – no matter how remote the possibility – should be encouraged to put them forward for evaluation by the public'. One of them may bear fruit – who knows? 'It therefore becomes important that they be encouraged to speak up'. This, I feel, is the right line.

Also, the groups are convenient outlets for rebellious spirits, 'particularly when the penalties for joining them are not too severe'.

Far better for the unusual or restive person to go to the meetings, join the committee, read or write for the 'publication', if only for a year or two, than to express his intellectual discontent with bicycle-chains or coshes.

So I was very glad to read Mr Thayer's tribute to British tolerance in this sometimes provocative corner of life: especially to the tolerance of the English, whose partners in these islands, including Cornwall, throw so many stones at them.

> From time to time they [the authorities] act as if certain fringe groups – particularly Colin Jordan's NSM and the Committee of 100 – were about to take over the reins of government, but such examples are the exception. The Home Office – which includes the police and Scotland Yard – keeps a wary eye on the more volatile fringe groups (most all of whom claim, in a form of fringe group snobbery, that their telephones are tapped) but, at the same time, allow them full freedom to do as they please as long as their activities remain within the law. More important, however, the authorities do more than just tolerate the expression of unpopular views; they actively encourage all people to stand up and say whatever is on their minds. They will not only provide the speaking areas (except under extraordinary circumstances), such as Trafalgar Square, but will at the same time protect the speakers to ensure that they have a chance to air their unpopular views. Freedom of speech, as I viewed it for a year through the 'back door' of British politics, is not some right in which all Britons say they believe but few of whom tolerate or promote at the moment of truth; it is a right that is consciously extended by the authorities to everyone – particularly the political fringe groups – despite the repugnant nature of much of it. It is ironic to think that those fringe groups who most wish to curtail that right are the ones who benefit most from it.

The Courts too – and even the police – get a good mark. 'Undoubtedly, there are some inequities, some free-swinging constables, and some cruel gaolers: however, there have been no signs yet that the fringe groups have been subjected to any more of them than the average British citizen'.

And here is Mr Thayer's verdict on you and me:

> The public's attitude towards its own fringe groups varies considerably. Most Britons agree that, although they do not like what they stand for, they should nevertheless be given every freedom permissible under the law. There are those Britons who are amused by fringe group antics; there are those who find the fringe groups

interesting from a sociological or medical point of view

interesting from a sociological or medical point of view; there are others who are confused by the whole picture; and there are those who find the fringe groups to be a general source of irritation. But by far the vast majority of Britons – those who are aware that there *is* a British political fringe – have come to the conclusion that most, if not all of the groups have little to offer that is relevant to their own problems. They have rejected them and, subsequently, have turned their minds to more important matters.

All this is good to hear. But Mr Thayer does not say – and could not say – that in our *electoral* arrangements we show our famous 'tolerance' or are even reasonably fair. I will take one example – my old *bête noire*, the electoral 'deposit' of £150. If you do not get one-eighth of the votes polled you must forfeit that to the State. Why? As I said in my Letter to the Electors of East Harrow in 1958:

> Why on earth should I, or anyone else, be fined £150 for failure? It is like hitting a man when he is down, is it not? And why is he down? Because he sought to serve the State. It is like the umpire saying to a cricketer: "You are out, Sir. May I add that you are out for a duck? And now you will be hit on the head with a bat".

Now, this undemocratic nonsense does not affect the supporters of the 'great Parties', which have huge funds and insurance schemes. It does affect the Independent and the Fringe-Candidate, very much. At the last General Election, Mr Thayer tells us, 134 fringe-folk (including 36 Communists) were candidates, and they received a total of 348,905 votes – or 1.3 per cent of the total votes cast. 'Only 13' he says 'saved their deposit'. 'Most of the Scottish National Party candidates' he says 'lose their deposits'. The same is true, I gather, of the Plaid Cymru (Welsh Home Rule) candidates.

I do not call this 'tolerance'. The deposit system was created by the Representation of the People Act 1918. Payment of Members (£400 a year) had recently begun, and the object of the 'deposit' was to discourage (a) 'freaks' and (b) people after that £400 – yes, that was said in the House. But what is a 'freak'? You might describe so a man who wanted to introduce a Bill to assert that the Earth was flat. But Plaid Cymru, for example, have a perfectly serious and comprehensive plan to take over Wales and let the Welsh govern it. You may not agree, it may never happen: but no man has a right to call them 'freaks'. A Liberal Member said well in 1917: 'It seems to me that if a man can get *one* vote he is justified in testing the opinions of the electorate'. I was regarded as a 'freak' when I first stood at Oxford University in 1935. I was certainly on the 'fringe' of something or other. For though I said dutiful things about War and Peace and other great 'issues', I said much more about the reform of the Divorce, Licensing, Betting and Libel Laws – subjects not mentioned in any other election address. I advocated the abolition of Entertainment Tax, which did not happen for another 25 years. A 'freak' indeed. But the 'freak' was elected, and one of the official Conservatives lost his deposit.

So before we can be said to deserve Mr Thayer's compliments on our 'tolerance' we must first abolish the 'deposit' system.

I would do more. We are rich in minorities, as Mr Thayer shows. Any sophisticated society is bound to be. We are rightly proud that we protect them while they spout their 'new ideas' in Trafalgar Square, but if we agree with Mr Thayer that some – or even one – of them may in time be a winner, we should surely make it easier for them to be heard at Westminster. I am not afraid of full Proportional Representation, but it will never, I feel, be practical politics in this dear land. But there is a reasonable half-way house – two-Member constituencies in the towns, with the Single Transferable Vote, and single-Member seats in the rural areas, with the Alternative Vote. This was defeated by a few votes only in 1917–18. Sir Winston Churchill was for it. Though this was narrowly rejected Parliament decreed that the scheme should be operated (I believe, as an 'experiment') in University Elections. That is why, I *think,* I was elected – I was never quite sure: for I was second (to Lord Hugh Cecil) on the first count, as well as the others. But I got my quota and was declared elected, by second choices. So the fact remains that under this system this 'freak' did secure the second seat. Nowhere else, under the ordinary 'first past the post' arrangements, would he have had the slightest chance. Who knows? Perhaps, under the same system, some of the fringe-folk might creep in too, do no great harm, and justify Mr Thayer's compliments upon our 'tolerance'.

At all events, my compliments to him, and good luck to his labours!

A. P. HERBERT

AUTHOR'S PREFACE

In writing this book, I have been concerned with describing the British political fringe groups as they exist today. By political fringe groups I mean all those relatively small political parties and pressure groups outside the two-party system whose primary objective is to alter all or part of the existing political institutions and attitudes in Great Britain. I am not concerned here with the thousands of British pressure groups whose fundamental interests lie outside of this objective.

Strictly speaking, the Communist Party of Great Britain is a part of the political fringe but because so much has been written about it I have refrained from discussing it except as it affects other groups. Likewise, I have given the Liberal Party – small in comparison to the Conservative and Labour Parties – the benefit of the doubt and have not considered it a part of the British fringe.

I have approached the subject as an outsider to the entire British political scene and in a spirit of pure enquiry. As far as possible, I have tried to ignore my own political views which fall within the mainstream of American political thought.

This book would have been impossible to prepare without the generous assistance of many people, but I would emphasize that the responsibility for the accuracy and interpretation of all facts is entirely my own. I am indebted to those members of the groups on which I have written who, with courtesy and in a spirit of cooperation, gave up their time to explain the objectives of their own organizations. I am also indebted to those in the House of Commons, Civil Service, British Museum, the Conservative Party Central Office, Transport House, the University of London, and the Wiener Library who so generously assisted me in my research.

I wish to express particular thanks to Tom Driberg, MP, and Miss Elizabeth Chanler for all the advice and help they have given me.

I also wish to acknowledge the kind permission of Curtis Brown Ltd, Macmillan and Company Ltd and the Times Publishing Company Ltd to quote material from their publications.

London 1965 G.T.

CONTENTS

Chapter		page
1	THE NEO-NAZIS	13
2	THE UNION MOVEMENT	33
3	THE LEAGUE OF EMPIRE LOYALISTS	53
4	THE FREEDOM GROUP	66
5	THE YELLOW STAR MOVEMENT	82
6	SPREADING THE WORD	96
7	THE OUTSIDE LEFT	119
8	THE CAMPAIGN FOR NUCLEAR DISARMAMENT	156
9	PLAID CYMRU & MEBYON KERNOW	177
10	THE SCOTTISH NATIONALISTS	189
11	THE IRISH NATIONALISTS	203
12	THE PROTESTANT PARTY	225
13	THE BRITISH POLITICAL FRINGE	238

Appendix

I	ORGANIZATIONS PROSCRIBED BY THE LABOUR PARTY	247
II	ORGANIZATIONS OUTLAWED IN NORTHERN IRELAND	249
III	MINOR POLITICAL PARTY CANDIDATES IN THE 1964 GENERAL ELECTION	250

Index 252

1 *The Neo-Nazis*

'Hitler was Right!'

COLIN JORDAN

Probably the least-read newspaper in Britain, and the one with the smallest amount of news value, is the *National Socialist,* the sporadically-published voice of Britain's National Socialist Movement. Every so often, however, it prints a story that could by any standard be considered a scoop. For instance, in one of its recent issues (undated) it had this to report:

COLIN JORDAN WEDS

Colin Jordan, Leader of the NSM, married Françoise Dior at a National Socialist wedding ceremony at NSM Headquarters in London on Sunday, October 6th, 1963, after register office formalities at Coventry the previous day.

Françoise Dior comes from Nordic stock in the French province of Normandy, settled by the Vikings. She has been a devoted National Socialist for many years, and in recent months, as WUNS [World Union of National Socialists] representative in France has been responsible for gathering together the support which has now enabled the establishment of a thriving young National Socialist movement there.

The ceremony took place in the presence of a private gathering of London members. The couple took their places behind a table draped with a swastika flag and flanked by lighted candles. Each in turn, with hand outstretched over the open blade of a dagger in the manner of our forefathers, made a pledge to the other as follows:

'I, Françoise Dior, declaring myself to be of Aryan descent and free from hereditary defect, do pledge myself in loyalty of body and mind as wife to you, Colin Jordan.'

'I, Colin Jordan, declaring myself to be of Aryan descent and free from hereditary defect, do pledge myself in loyalty of body and mind as husband to you, Françoise Dior.'

Next, each in turn made a small incision in the upper part of the ring finger, and the two fingers were held together for a moment to symbolize the union of the blood. A drop of the blood so-mixed was then allowed to fall on the blank fore-page of a copy of *Mein Kampf* belonging to the couple. The couple joined hands and Colin Jordan announced 'This marriage we declare enacted'.

The gathering gave the NS salute, and the NS anthem 'The Horst Wessel Song' was played. The wedded couple were toasted in Mead, the ancient drink of the Nordic peoples.

In a brief speech in response, Colin Jordan spoke of the NSM's meeting in Trafalgar Square in July 1962, as bringing him on the one hand a month's imprisonment for his speech opposing the Jewish control and coloured invasion of Britain, and on the other hand a partner in his struggle against these evils and for the establishment of a National Socialist Britain, for the British. It was a result of the reports of this meeting in the French press that Françoise Dior came to know of the Movement and came to meet him. He went on to disclose that they became engaged at a height of 14,000 feet over mid-Channel – and thus between their respective countries – during a flight to Paris on the night of September 11th 1963. The manner of their engagement symbolized the spirit and purpose of the World Union of National Socialists, of which the NSM is the British Section, fighting to create the National Socialist World Order of the Whiteman, the only alternative to national decline, racial ruination, and Communism[1]

Colin Jordan's National Socialist Movement is not the only neo-Nazi* organization in Great Britain today. There are also John Bean's British National Party and John Tyndall's Greater Britain Movement. Jordan, Bean and Tyndall have known each other for more than ten years: relations between them have never been smooth. Fundamentally, there are few philosophical differences between them, yet they have found it virtually impossible to work together. Each is so headstrong and so convinced of his own infallibility that none will brook any criticism of his own policies. Because right-wing groups tend to split more over personalities than doctrine, perhaps it is surprising that there are only three such 'major' groups today rather than ten or fifteen.

Whatever differences may exist between Jordan, Bean, and Tyndall, however, all three make it quite clear that they have no love for Sir Oswald Mosley and his Union Movement. In order that there be no confusion, Jordan calls himself a National Socialist, Bean calls him-

* I make the distinction that all neo-Nazis are Fascists, but not all Fascists are neo-Nazis. Neo-Nazis are those people who subscribe to the doctrines of Hitler in particular, while Fascists are those who believe in the general Fascist doctrines of, for instance, the Corporate State, the Leadership Principle, and Authoritarianism, irrespective of how much these ideas might overlap with Nazi doctrines.

self a Racial Nationalist, and Tyndall calls himself a British National Socialist. All three refer to Mosley as a Common Fascist. In retaliation, Mosley calls the neo-Nazis race-baiters. There is no doubt that all four men have a healthy hatred for one another; the three neo-Nazis' hatred of Mosley is clearly defined (and vice-versa); however, the animosities between Jordan, Bean, and Tyndall are less clear.

The high priest of post-war neo-Naziism was Arnold Spencer Leese, an Army veterinary surgeon who spent most of his life in the Middle East. At the age of 50, after he had retired from the Army, he entered politics. From 1929 to 1939 he was the leader of the Imperial Fascist League, a small (200 members) party that was always independent of Mosley's British Union of Fascists. (To Leese, Mosley was a 'kosher fascist'.) The IFL was the most pro-German Fascist group in England at that time – far more so than Mosley's BUFs. It's members were the first to wear jack-boots and black shirts; they discarded the *fasces* in favour of the Nazi swastika (usually superimposed on a Union Jack); and they refused to go to war against Germany to 'fight the battle of the Jew against men of [their] own Nordic race!'[2] The IFL was also the most openly anti-Semitic group during this period. Some people claim, for instance, that Leese became an anti-Semite because of his love of animals and because of his hatred of the methods Jews employed to kill them. Leese felt that all English Jews should be deported to Madagascar; to qualify for deportation, all one needed was one Jewish grandparent. Leese also believed that extermination of the Jews was a worthy alternative to deportation, but he had a suspicion that few people would sanction such a move.[3]

Leese spent most of the Second World War in prison and upon his release published a book called *The Jewish War of Survival* in which he argued that, although the Jews and Freemasons had won a battle with the defeat of Hitler, they could still be routed by a determined policy of anti-Semitism. Other works of his include *Out of Step* ('Events in the two lives of an anti-Jewish camel doctor'), and *The Jewish Method of Cattle-Slaughter* ('legalized cruelty of Shechita'). Until his death in 1956, he published a monthly newsletter called *Gothic Ripples* which was almost exclusively devoted to attacks on both the Jews and the fluoridization of water.[4]

Leese's principal disciple during the early post-war period was a young Cambridge University undergraduate called John Colin Campbell Jordan. To Arnold Leese, Jordan represented the new generation of National Socialists who would carry on the work he had started 20 years before. With any luck, he felt that men such as Jordan would be able to turn the tide against the Jews that had received such a serious set-back in 1945. Jordan was an eager student of Leese's philosophy and readily absorbed all of his mentor's knowledge and experience. If Hitler was Jordan's God, then Leese was his spiritual father. Today, Colin Jordan pays tribute to both men and vows to carry on the National Socialist fight in their names.

Jordan has always been close to Leese's wife, May, ever since she first met him after the war. A Fascist like her husband, she has figured prominently in all of Jordan's political activities: she sits as Vice-President of the NSM, she has given her house free of charge to the Movement, and in many instances she has come to the organization's rescue both financially and spiritually.

From 1947 to 1958, Jordan led a rather nomadic life. While he was an undergraduate, he ran the Cambridge University Nationalist Club, an organization which he himself had founded and which collapsed soon after he graduated. He was also associated for a while with the late Duke of Bedford's British People's Party. He then continued his activities in the Midlands under the guise of the Birmingham Nationalist Club. This, too, was not a very successful venture so he joined the League of Empire Loyalists in 1954. Three years later he was expelled because of his intransigence over what he considered the League's lenient attitude towards the Jews. For a while, Jordan was a door-to-door soap salesman, then he became a mathematics teacher at a Coventry grammar school on the strength of his university education.

In 1958, however, Jordan emerged from obscurity as the leader of a new organization he founded in London called the White Defence League. His headquarters were in the 'Arnold Leese House' in the Notting Hill section just north of Holland Park.

It was at this time that rioting first broke out in the North Kensington area. The influx of Jamaicans, Pakistanis, and Indians into this poor neighbourhood, particularly that area around Paddington Station, was so great and had taken place over such a relatively short period of time that it became virtually impossible to assimilate them with any ease. The riots actually started about a mile to the west of Arnold Leese House in the Wormword Scrubs area, but within weeks had spread throughout the whole area. They were to last all that summer and sporadically into 1959.

Jordan took full advantage of the troubles. He and his men – never more than a few score – played on the bitterness between the old and the new residents of the area. They held street rallies almost every night during that summer and, although only rarely were they able to incite the crowds to irrational passions, they were one of the primary factors which kept the antagonisms from dying down. Jordan published a newspaper at that time called *Black and White News* which was devoted almost exclusively both to 'exposing' the inferiority of the immigrants and to calling for their return to their respective countries. The paper was printed by an old (1918) publishing enterprise called the Britons Publishing Society, owned and run by a friend of Jordan's named Anthony Gittens. At that time, the publishing company was in Arnold Leese House and was able to provide the White Defence League with ready material for their attacks on the immigrants.

Jordan was not the only one to take advantage of the race troubles. Mosley and the men from his Union Movement were also there. The League of Empire Loyalists was similarly involved, as was John Bean, who at the time was leader of his National Labour Party, an organization that had similar aims to those of Jordan and his WDL.

John Edward Bean looks like a model for a Propagation of the Nordic Peoples advertisement. Tall, blond, blue-eyed, handsome in a virile way, and not without a sense of humour, he has been an agitator for right-wing causes ever since his release from military service in 1947. He was a member of Mosley's Union Movement for a short period of time but quit because, he claims, it was impossible to work for Mosley because of his reputation. He then moved on to the Midlands as the League of Empire Loyalists' Organizer: there he met Jordan. He was expelled from the League in 1958 for using the offices of that organization to start his own party. Bean then founded the National Labour Party and, at the same time, began to publish a newspaper called *Combat* ('The voice of Race and Nation'). With his few followers, he, too, became embroiled in the Notting Hill race riots. Although he never found a mass following in the area, he did feel that general white resentment against the coloured immigrants had risen to a point where it might be advantageous to him. During the General Election in 1959, he raised £150 and entered an NLP candidate, William Webster, in the 'red' St Pancras North constituency. Webster lost, but Bean felt that the results were a victory for his party:

Robinson, K. (Lab)	22,256	54.1%
Mitchell, D. B. (C)	15,949	38.8%
Webster, W. (NLP)	1,685	4.1%
Nicolson, J. (Com)	1,230	3.0%

Although the National Labour Party had beaten the Communist Party, Bean could claim no other kudos. Not only did he lose the £150 but Webster quit the NLP and promptly joined Mosley's Union Movement.

* * *

In late 1959, the Labour Party obtained an injunction against the National Labour Party to prevent it from using that name. After consulting with Jordan, Bean decided to amalgamate his party with Jordan's White Defence League. By February 1960, they had organized a new party called the British National Party. Andrew Fountaine, a wealthy landowner from an old Norfolk family, was installed as President. Fountaine had fought for Franco during the Spanish Civil War and had, after the Second World War, stood as a Conservative Party candidate for Chorley in Lancashire. Mrs Leese, Arnold Leese's widow, became Vice-President of the new party; Jordan became the National Organizer and 'The Leader' (the position of power in the organization); and Bean became the Deputy National Organizer. Arnold Leese House was the BNP's central headquarters.

The policies of this new party combined all the old ideas of Arnold Leese with those of Jordan and Bean. The most important overall aspect of their policy was their rigid opposition to democratic principles ('decisions by head-counting'). In its place they wished to substitute a Racial Nationalist Folk-State 'embodied in the creed of National Socialism and uniquely implemented by . . . Adolf Hitler'. In order to achieve this Folk-State, they felt that all coloured immigrants should be returned to their respective countries and that every British Jew should be shipped to Madagascar if there were not enough room in Israel for him. Only in this way could Britain be saved from 'degenerating into a mongrel race'. The BNP looked forward to the day when all Northern European peoples and their white brothers in the Dominions would be joined together in a confederation of White Solidarity in opposition to the onslaughts of the 'lesser' (but numerically superior) races. No other point of BNP policy was considered as important as this one.

The BNP policy also included 'Nation above class', 'recognition of the soil as our greatest asset', and the promotion of 'a truly National Culture'. One of the most vital aspects of their policy, from their point of view, concerned education. As an ex-school-teacher (who was subsequently expelled from the National Union of Teachers because of his activities), Jordan appreciated the value of educating young minds. He knew that a massive re-education in values would be necessary if the Folk-State were ever to be achieved. His educational programme included, among other things, a national curriculum controlled by the Education Minister. What was to be taught in the schools, and what was and was not to be emphasized, was the responsibility of this Minister alone; he, in turn, would be directly responsible to 'The Leader'. All teachers would be required to pass a BNP test of acceptability, and as long as they passed that test and were 'free from hereditary defects', they could teach in the schools. The principal courses offered to the students would be 'The Value of Racial Purity', 'Britain's Place in the Folk-Community', and 'Racial Betterment in Marriage'. These courses, in particular, would supersede in importance all the other courses on the national curricula. Although Jordan and Bean are no longer part of the same organization, this policy was and still is the mainspring of Jordan's educational objectives.

For a group of such small size – there were never more than 200 members and sympathizers combined – the BNP had a capacity for creating trouble. For two years the Party stirred up racial antagonisms under such banners as 'Keep White Solidarity' and 'Britons Awake!' The Party's favourite tactic was to picket the coloured immigrants as they came off the trains. Considering the amount of provocation to which the ordinary citizen was subjected, there were at first remarkably few violent clashes; on occasion, however, the Party could generate enough heat to precipitate localized disturbances.

It was in the summer of 1960 that Jordan formed his 'élite corps' within the BNP itself, called 'Spearhead'. The operation of this organization was so secret that it was not fully exposed until two years later. 'Spearhead' was a uniformed group of militants who were trained and dressed in imitation of Hitler's Brownshirts. Judo, guerilla warfare, the handling of explosives (a combination of weed-killer and sugar), and above all rigid discipline were the keynotes.

During the summers of 1960 and 1961, the BNP held camps in various rural areas of England, the favourite locations being in Kent, the Cotswolds, and Norfolk (on Andrew Fountaine's property). There they practised their 'Spearhead' formations – advancing on imaginary enemies, blowing up mythical bunkers, and 'securing vital bridge-heads'. However, all was not work on these outings. Under a flowering Celtic Roundel, they would attempt to revive the atmosphere of their Nordic past:

> The most enjoyable part of the camp was the opportunity to get away from the cosmopolitanism of the cities and to live in the manner of our forefolk amidst the beauty of our own Northland, England. None will forget the comradship round the campfire ... with songs of our race and nation upon our lips, and tankards of English Ale in our hands.[5]

Nor was their love for things Nordic confined to physical phenomena. One description of their 1960 summer camp, from the *Northern European* (Editor: Colin Jordan), was reported to have begun thus:

At a special camp-fire meeting on the Sun Festival of Lammas – named after the Keltic Sun-God Lugh . . .[6]

Unfortunately for the BNP, the comradeship was to last less than two years. The crux of the split revolved around two issues. First, Bean and Fountaine were frightened of the seditious nature of 'Spearhead'. They were not prepared to take their opposition to the State to such an extreme; nor were they willing to spend a possible 14 years in prison because of it. Jordan, on the other hand, along with John Tyndall, an ex-member of Bean's old NLP, were becoming more impatient with what they called the 'kid-glove methods' of the Party. They were prepared to be far more conspiratorial in their activities than they had been previously. Second, Jordan and Tyndall were both hardening their attitude towards the interpretation of *Mein Kampf*. They saw no reason why they should adapt Hitler's ideas to 1962 when it was perfectly obvious to them that his ideas were valid in any era. They felt that Hitler's policies could and should be faithfully copied so that the spirit in which they were written would not be diluted by a continuing re-interpretation. Bean and Fountaine, however, felt that Hitler's doctrines had to be modified to meet the needs of the day. Bean compared the proper evolution of National Socialism to the evolution of the Liberal Party. 'The Liberals', he said*, 'are the spiritual descendants of the French Revolution, but no one would blame [Jo] Grimond for the excesses of that time, because his party has only accepted the best aspects of the revolution and has discarded the rest.'

The split boiled over in February 1962, at the Party's annual Council meeting. Bean and Fountaine tried to unseat Jordan as National Organizer. Of the twelve members present, seven voted for the Bean-Fountaine coalition and five voted for Jordan. It appeared as if Jordan were finished as Leader. But it was Bean and Fountaine who lost the vote. According to the Party's Constitution, the Principal Officer (Jordan) could not be replaced without his personal consent, which voided the vote. Moreover, Mrs Leese, one of those present, said that the organization could use Arnold Leese House only so long as Jordan was 'The Leader'. She was not willing to accept the removal of her 'adopted son'.

With the headquarters and election apparatus safely in the hands of Jordan, both Bean and Fountaine had no other choice but to walk out. They took both the BNP name and their newspaper *Combat* with them. They also succeeded in drawing the bulk of the membership away from Jordan.

From that moment on, there were two neo-Nazi parties in Great

* In conversations with the author, 1963.

Britain: Bean and his followers representing the more 'moderate' elements, and Jordan and his followers who have swung over to the brink of subversive action.

The new British National Party was reorganized much along the lines of Bean's old NLP. Andrew Fountaine was elected President, and Bean became the Party's Organizer. Bean claims that his new party, in the three years of its existence, has grown to a membership of about 1,000 active supporters and 10,000 passive supporters. He also claims to sell six to seven thousand copies of *Combat* per issue. More realistically, the present membership is around 200 active supporters and perhaps 1,000 passive supporters on the outside. From all indications, *Combat* is sold to no more than 500 readers. They may be given away, but certainly are not sold in greater numbers. Bean has a fairly legitimate claim to 10,000 supporters if consideration is given to those who have or would have voted for him and his party at election time. Since the Party does not contest elections on a nation-wide basis, there is no way of verifying this figure. In all probability his support would be substantially less than he claims.*

Although *Combat* is the major source of BNP propaganda, it is not the medium through which the Party has made its name. Rather, the Party prints small 2 x 3 inch stickers that the commuting public can see pasted on 'bus and underground train windows which ask that Britons consider their own welfare before the welfare of 'one million fast-breeding coloured immigrants'. The sticker goes on to suggest that the immigrants be sent home 'before it is too late!'

Combat itself, by fringe group standards, would be placed somewhere below the literary value of Chesterton's *Candour* and somewhat above Jordan's *National Socialist*. With few exceptions, Bean and Fountaine – who do most of the writing in *Combat* – concentrate on four obsessions: preservation of the British stock of peoples, the 'international conspiracy of finance,' opposition to the Common Market ('a bankers' racket') and, above all, the problems of coloured immigration.

The new BNP's attitude towards the Jews, however, has been modified somewhat. Bean does not approve of gas chambers, 'final

* In the 1964 General Election, Bean stood as the BNP candidate for Southall, a Middlesex town with a heavy concentration of coloured immigrants. He received less than one-eighth of the vote and forfeited his deposit:

Pargiter, G. A. (Lab)	18,041	48.0%
Maddin, Miss B. (C)	16,144	43.0%
Bean, J. E. (BNP)	3,410	9.0%

solutions', or deportations to Madagascar. As far as he is concerned, all British Jews can stay in England as first-class citizens. His only major complaint is with what he calls 'the international financial power in the City and Wall Street' which he says is predominantly Jewish. This 'financial cabal', he adds, has to be broken regardless whether it involves Jews or Gentiles. He sees this concentration of financial power as the basis of most of the world's past, present and future ills. Exactly how it is the basis of such ills is never clearly explained but he and his followers are convinced it should be broken up. Bean would like to see a bill passed in Parliament that would tax all profits gained in take-over bids, property sales, and other transactions of a similar nature. Again, he is not clear what he means by this, but he emphasizes that such a tax bill would apply to everyone in international finance, regardless of his religious background. Because of this view, he says, he is often called anti-Semitic which he thinks is unfair.

If Bean's policy towards Jews has been modified slightly, his views on coloured immigration have hardened. To Bean, a few foreigners here and there are not going to have any impact on British traditions, but the 800,000 Jamaicans, Pakistanis, and Indians* now living in Britain constitute a threat to every white Briton. Through *Combat,* he dwells at length on the mental inferiority of the Negro and on the folly of wasting time acclimatizing him to British customs. Bean sees only one solution: ship the coloured peoples back to their own countries before they dominate the island.

Bean is staking his political life on the difficulties arising out of the influx of these peoples. He realizes that the colour problem, although not yet officially recognized by the Conservative and Labour Parties, is potentially one of the most explosive of all political issues in Britain. In this regard, Bean has often been accused of promoting the slogan 'If you want a Nigger for a neighbour, Vote Labour' as a means of getting votes. In addition to taking advantage of the colour question, Bean is shaping his electoral tactics in imitation of those that Hitler used during his rise to power in Germany. For example, Bean does not believe he needs a mass following to be successful because, he says, Hitler never had one until he was about to come to power; beforehand, he was content with a few extremely loyal followers. Jordan and Tyndall concur in this view and all three believe this strategy is just as applicable today as it was during Hitler's early political life. In addition, Bean is concentrating his party's

* The actual number of coloured people living in Great Britain in 1965 is unknown although informed sources, particularly the Institute of Race Relations, considers the figure of 800,000 an accurate estimate. This would represent 1.5 per cent of the population.

activities in a few constituencies only (similar to Hitler) so that, if he is successful in any one of them, he can use the victory for propaganda purposes to gain more victories. The three constituencies of Deptford, Stepney and Southall – all of which have large concentrations of coloured people – are his future battlefields.

In specific wards, BNP candidates claim they can poll as high as 28 per cent of the votes cast, but the overall share of the votes received in the constituency is usually far less. Bean freely admits he uses unusual methods to get votes. One ploy is to put up a BNP candidate whose name is similar to one of their opponents' names. Because no party affiliation is listed alongside each candidate's name, the BNP candidate can collect more votes than usual because of the electorate's confusion. For instance, in the 1961 London County Council (now the Greater London Council) elections, two of his three candidates in the Deptford constituency received perhaps twice as many votes as they might otherwise have received had their names not been similar to those of two Labour Party candidates:

A. J. Blackman (Lab)	9,702
A. S. Simons (Lab)	9,097
H. C. Shearman (Lab)	8,595
I. H. Davison (C)	4,805
D. P. Jeffcock (C)	4,542
P. S. F. Noble (C)	4,503
R. Simpson (BNP)	1,520
A. Charman (BNP)	1,337
J. E. Stanton (BNP)	838

Colin Jordan, after Bean and his men walked out on him, was faced with yet another reorganization of his political instrument to power. He had few followers – perhaps a maximum of 20 at the time, no newspaper, and not even a name for his organization. He was left with Arnold Leese House and little else.

On April 20th (Hitler's birthday), 1963, Jordan launched his new party, the National Socialist Movement*. Jordan became 'The

* Not to be confused with the National Socialist League which existed from 1937 to 1939. One of its founders was William ('Lord Haw Haw') Joyce, an American who fancied himself as a great English patriot. He used to insist, for instance, that his friends stand to attention at the end of a social evening and sing 'God Save the King'. Joyce, as BUF Director of Propaganda, worshipped his leader, Sir Oswald Mosley. When he was expelled from the BUF in the 1937 purge, he set up the NSL with John Beckett and switched his allegiance to Hitler because, he said, Hitler was fighting the Jews and that was in Britain's interest. In 1939, he went to Germany where he accepted a job as a broadcaster in the Propaganda Ministry. At the end of the war, he was tried in a British court as a traitor and hanged.

Leader', John Tyndall became the National Organizer, and Mrs Leese retained the Vice Presidency. The organization's new newspaper, the *National Socialist*, was duly inaugurated at the same time.

With few exceptions, Jordan has turned his small organization into an imitation Nazi Party. Uniforms, for instance, although forbidden by law, are a subtle variation on the Brownshirt dress: khaki shirt and trousers with thick leather belt and combat boots. Within the confines of Arnold Leese House, armbands*, peaked caps and daggers are sometimes affected. Often their imitation is taken to unusual extremes: many members have tooth-brush moustaches, most click their heels at the slightest opportunity, others can speak German, and few of them smoke (because Hitler did not).

No political party in Great Britain today approaches this one in its extremism of policy and conduct. It is considered to be so far outside the pale, and so lacking in political reality, that most observers have difficulty explaining why it exists at all. Many people interpret the phenomenon of Jordan and his party as more the concern of psychiatrists than the concern of political observers. Jordan pays scant attention to this type of remark; he is convinced he is right and if anyone is wrong, it is his critics.

Although the NSM claims it has a full political and economic policy (basically unchanged from the days of the old BNP), it is overshadowed by its single-minded hatred of Jews. All the other ancillary policies are there: white supremacy, propagation of the Aryan race, loathing of coloured peoples, the scientific justification of the superiority of races, and the total rejection of the democratic process. These points, however, are lost in the smoke they raise around their hatred of Jews.

The *National Socialist* best reflects the lengths to which they take their thoughts. This newspaper, for instance, may concentrate on comparing 'Super-Humanity' ('The crack S.S. Regiment "Leibstandarte Adolf Hitler"') with 'Sub-Humanity' ('Outpourings from the Eastern Ghettoes'); or it may have a column or two on the benefits of racial breeding[7]; or it may have articles on the ritual slaughter of animals; or appeals to free Rudolf Hess from prison; or it may have a list of books for young people that can be purchased at the NSM 'Phoenix Bookshop'[8]. The six-page newspaper is covered with swastikas, skulls, six-pointed Stars of David, and pictures of butchered children (apparently by Stern Gang terrorists). There are appeals to

* These armbands are all home-made and come in two varieties: the ordinary armband with red band, white disk and black swastika and the 'British' armband with blue band, white disk and red swastika. When the swastika is cocked at an angle, it is known by members as a 'swastika rampant'.

boycott Jewish goods, claims that 'Hitler was right!' and advertisements for Christmas cards that show a Jew fleeing from a background swastika and crying *'THITH ITH THE END!'*[9]

Jordan has also carried his beliefs into the streets. Although he was a familiar figure in the Jewish section of London for many months, he first broke into the headlines at his Trafalgar Square rally in July, 1962, when he explained to over 4,000 angry listeners why Britain should be free from Jewish control. Within 20 minutes after the start of his speech, Jordan and his fellow neo-Nazis, lest they be lynched, were spirited away in the back of an unmarked van. But he achieved his primary objective; his name was now known throughout the world.

'Spearhead' was again coming into the news. During the summer of 1961, detectives posing as electricians took pictures of Tyndall and Ian Kerr-Ritchie (NSM Research Officer) drilling eighteen uniformed men in an empty school-house in Culverstone, Kent. In May of the next year, the group was spotted by civilians performing military exercises – a mock attack on a tower at Broadmoor Hill, near Dorking, Surrey. Jordan was directing the operations. In August 1962, one month after the Trafalgar Square rally, 'Spearhead' held a four-day camp at Temple Guiting, Gloucestershire, which was attended by the American Nazi, Lincoln Rockwell (who was smuggled in via Ireland), and an ex-SS officer, Col. Friedrich Borsch.

It was at this camp that the 'Cotswold Agreement' was set up whereby Jordan, Rockwell and other National Socialist parties agreed to bind their organizations together into a 'World Union of National Socialists' with Jordan as World Leader, although there is some speculation that Rockwell is the actual leader. (The day after the election, *The People* came out with a large headline which read: 'THE NEW "WORLD FUEHRER" – ELECTED BY 27 IDIOTS!').

The Agreement aimed to 'form a monolithic, combat-efficient, international political apparatus to combat and utterly destroy the international Jewish-Communist and Zionist apparatus of treason and subversion'.[10] No organization or individual who did not acknowledge the spiritual leadership of Adolf Hitler would be admitted to membership.[11] The Agreement was never implemented since no country, including Great Britain, would allow the National Socialist leaders throughout the world to meet in one place.

During the four-day camp, Jordan put 'Spearhead' through its paces to demonstrate to his distinguished guests the efficient nature of his organization. Uniformed National Socialists under the Leadership of Tyndall attacked sham strong-points, wiped out concentrations of make-believe enemies, and fought off 'counter-attacks' with desperate bravado. Jordan, Rockwell, and Borsch watched the 'attack' through field-glasses from a nearby hill-top.

All this activity irritated the local residents whose peace of mind was disturbed by the shouts of 'Sieg Heil!' which rang throughout the night, and by the continual singing of 'The Horst Wessel Song'. They descended on to the camp and demanded that it be disbanded. The camp broke up in disorder when the National Socialists realized they could not contain this counter-attack. Both of the guests were spirited out of the camp with hoods over their heads, only to be deported a few days later.

Within hours, the NSM headquarters in London were raided by the police. There they found a variety of 'Spearhead' uniforms: peaked forage caps, swastika armbands, jack-boots, and daggers. There were enough bags of weed-killer and sugar stacked inside the building, according to the police, to make explosives with the power of 100 Mills bombs. They also found a can of rat poison that had been labelled 'Jew killer'.

Jordan, Tyndall, Kerr-Ritchie, and Denis Pirie (an NSM Section Leader) were charged under the Public Order Act of 1936 with organizing, training, and equipping 'Spearhead' in such a manner as to arouse reasonable apprehension that they were organized and trained to be employed for the use or display of force in promoting political objectives. All four were found guilty. No appeals were allowed and Jordan was sentenced to nine months in gaol, Tyndall to six months, and Kerr-Ritchie and Pirie to three months each.

By May 1963, when all the officers of the organization had been released (Kerr-Ritchie, the first out of prison, tried to organize a *putsch* while his leader was still in gaol, but was unsuccessful and was subsequently expelled from the Movement), the NSM could look back on over a year of activity that, to them, must have seemed successful on balance.

In the spring of 1964, the second split occurred within the ranks of the neo-Nazis. This time it was between Jordan and Tyndall. It was, unlike the Jordan-Bean split, a division as much over policy as over personalities. There is no question that Tyndall has always hated Jordan, and why he ever joined the Movement at the time of the first schism has never been fully explained. There are some indications that the split occurred because Tyndall could never get over the humiliation of having his fiancée, Françoise, stolen away from him by Jordan. (She is now Jordan's wife – see page 13). The major cause of the split, however, undoubtedly revolved around the differences in outlook between the 'German' faction and the 'British' faction within the NSM. Tyndall represents the 'British' section and has always chafed under the 'foreign' aspects of Jordan's strict brand of German National Socialism. Whether this latest split heralds the beginning of a series of similar schisms is impossible to say now with any certainty. In any event, at this moment in time (1965), there are now three neo-Nazi parties in Great Britain.

My first visit to Arnold Leese House came during the time when Jordan and his wife, Françoise, were on their honeymoon. However, Tyndall (still at that time Jordan's deputy) suggested that if I cared to call, he would be pleased to answer any questions I might have.

Arnold Leese House is a run-down tenement along Princedale Road near Notting Hill. The ground-floor bookstore is shuttered in heavy steel and all the windows are screened with thick wire mesh. Nazi swastikas are emblazoned on the brick face of the building high out of reach from the street. On a clear day, the prison of Wormwood Scrubs can be seen in the distance from the upper windows.

My appointment nearly coincided with a slight scuffle that had taken place on the street in front of the bookstore. Apparently about 10 minutes before I arrived, 'Aryans' and 'Jews' had fought it out briefly with buckets of paint. In the fog, it was difficult to see what had happened and, in fact, I was not aware that anything was amiss until my shoes began to beat a snapping tattoo on the pavement. Treading warily around the larger puddles, I rang the door-bell and was instantly faced by five shouting youths, one of whom was waving a shillelagh. Before I could announce myself, a pair of strong hands grabbed me and I was frog-marched through the door and down the hall to their meeting room. I was told to stay there until 'the situation had been brought under control'. Through the closed door, I could hear Tyndall telling his angry associates to calm down. Apparently he was afraid that if the noise and confusion continued the police might well intervene. He began to bark out crisp orders and his men (most of whom appeared to be under 21 years of age) pounded up and down the stairs to carry out their various assignments. A few of the more burly members were sent into the street to 'maintain security', others were ordered to the roof as look-outs, and still others were told to clean up the paint.

The meeting room in which I was placed was nothing more than a small office behind the bookstore. Three pictures dominated the walls: an old photograph of Adolf Hitler, and two large oil paintings of Arnold Leese and Colin Jordan; all three were shown in Nazi uniforms. Along other parts of the walls were swastika flags, old-fashioned pikes and red, white and black banners. Two bulletin boards near a desk were covered with a variety of items. There was a Christmas card from Lincoln Rockwell, quotations of the day from *Mein Kampf*, a duty roster, orders-of-the-day, and a long list of town halls in Britain which had refused to rent their premises to the organization. One hand-printed leaflet described how 'our beloved President Kennedy [had] been assassinated by an international conspiracy of Communists and Jews'. Above this leaflet was a small wooden trophy. Protruding from it was a life-size plastic nose with an exaggerated hook in it. It was covered with 'warts', and small wire 'hairs' curled out from the nostrils. Above the nose was printed: 'Hampstead 1958', apparently in honour of a successful punch-up.

Tyndall eventually came back and took me to his office on the first floor. He was a composite of all the characteristics I had vaguely associated with Nazis in Hitler's Germany: he had cold, evasive eyes, was blond and balding, and had not the slightest spark of humour. He was suspicious, nervous, and excitable, and moved with all the stiffness of a Prussian in Court.

'Jewry', he said, 'is a world pest wherever it is found in the world today. The Jews are more clever and more financially powerful than other people and have to be eradicated before they destroy the Aryan peoples'. He saw Britain crumbling before their grasp, and gave 10 years as the time it would take before all of Britain was fully under their control. Rather than waste time fighting elections (in which they do not believe), Tyndall said the NSM was content simply to remain in the background to step forward when 'the inevitable economic collapse' takes place. He is convinced that the public eventually will become fed up with the Samuels, Clores, Warburgs, and Wolfsons because, as he warned in his book, *The Authoritarian State:*

> As Democracy drives our youth out on the streets, with limitless spare time to fritter away, the Jew comes forward and seduces them with his cunningly devised amusements, such as comic papers, sex-films, and rock 'n' roll.

Tyndall went on to say he could not understand why Britons have not yet recognized the threat as clearly as he.

I asked him how members were selected and he described a complicated process of weeding the fit from the unfit. The qualities demanded of a good Aryan candidate, he said, were blood that was free from hereditary defect, belief in racial betterment, adherence to the teachings and spirit of Adolf Hitler, and loyalty to National Socialist principles. When I asked him how he could determine an Aryan, he said, 'Oh, I can tell just by looking at him'. Would I pass the test, I asked? 'Yes,' I was told, 'you would be a good Aryan.'

A few months later, I had an interview with Colin Jordan. Some time after his honeymoon and before my talk with him, Jordan and his wife had separated over a few ideological differences. Françoise was also disillusioned by her husband's leadership qualities and, within a month from the time they returned from their honeymoon, she had fled back to her family's home in Paris, accusing her husband of being, among other things, 'a middle-class nobody'. When Jordan consented to see me I was surprised to see Françoise there with him. I met them as they, too, were about to enter the building and, as I followed them up the stairs to his office, shouts of 'Sieg Heil' rang throughout the building, and were closely followed by a clicking of heels and a noticeable stiffening of arms from his few enthusiastic followers.

Providence took Jordan from his office for half an hour so I had a chance to chat with Françoise alone. Françoise is the daughter of Christian Dior's brother and has a large income that is the result of her father's association with the famous fashion house. She has been a Fascist most of her life, and has been a family outcast as a result. Before she met Tyndall and Jordan, she had been married to a French Count. She is a faintly peroxided blonde in her early thirties who may at one time have been quite pretty. The day I talked with her she was swathed in fur and had a gold swastika hanging around her neck.*

With no prompting from me, she began to explain in her broken English all the details of her split with her husband. Squinting her eyes, she said, 'I had to be cruel to Jordan (she often referred to her husband as 'Jordan') to shock him into being a good leader'. She said that he had no conception of the meaning of the word leader and that it was her duty as his wife to turn him into one. The difficult phase was over, she continued, but that there was a long way to go before he was a leader worthy of the name of National Socialism. As she spoke, she would emphasize her remarks with a sharp chopping motion with her hand; her eyes narrowing ever so slightly with each blow.

Jordan finally came back into the room. He had many of the physical qualities of his ex-assistant, Tyndall: blond, balding, suspicious, and humourless. He seldom faced me in response to my questions, more often than not he spoke directly to his wife. He has a stentorian voice which, at times, made conversation very difficult. He conceded that the strictness with which the authorities had viewed his 'Spearhead' activities had forced him to revise many of his future

* On January 7, 1965, Françoise hailed a taxi whose driver happened to be Jewish. He recognized her and shouted: 'I don't want you. I'm a Jew. You stinking Nazi.' He then tore off her swastika necklace. She replied, 'Well, if you are a Jew, what are you doing out of the ovens?' The taxi driver was fined £3 for using insulting behaviour.

plans. From now on, he said, he would concentrate almost entirely on the written word. The *National Socialist,* he told me, was to become the Movement's major focal point. He hopes that by increasing the number of issues to ensure the exposition of 'the facts' he can bring about a new wave of support for his views. However, he feels that the Government will eventually restrict even his literary efforts because of what Jordan claims the authorities call his 'seditious and revolutionary attitudes' in the newspaper. Nevertheless, it is the chance he is taking. He has expanded the *National Socialist* to eight pages and is printing it on fairly high-quality paper. His Phoenix Bookstore recently has been stocked with a wider variety of literature and books: *Race, Heredity and Civilization* (a book that 'presents irrefutable facts in support of White Supremacy and Negro inferiority'), *Prisoner of Peace* by Rudolf Hess, and *The Protocols of the Learned Elders of Zion* are a few of the many books available.

Quite surprisingly, he added that he has been making an effort to counter some of the poor publicity his organization has received in the past. I, for one, have noticed this change only when speaking with NSM members over the telephone. When I first rang them up in 1963, it was all I could do to get them to admit that I had in fact dialled the right number. By 1965, when I last talked with them, they were most courteous – complete with 'Yes Sir!', 'No Sir!', and pleas to visit their bookshop – even though they did admit that the conversation was being recorded on tape. Whether this policy is transitional or permanent remains to be seen. Certainly their telephone manners have not spread to their physical activities nor has this policy softened the attitudes of their enemies.

Jordan went on to say that he planned to use his wife's money to expand his operations. Françoise did not appear to be disturbed by this remark. On the contrary, she seemed pleased that her husband had ear-marked it for such a worthy cause.

He then began a rambling account of his philosophy which, he said, is almost identical to that which he finds in *Mein Kampf.* He reaffirmed his faith in Adolf Hitler, stressing that nothing that man ever said or did has shaken his faith in him. He then talked extensively on the origin of races, the reasons why some are superior to others, the definition of an Aryan, and the scientific basis of it all. His remarks were clouded at times and difficult to follow; in fact, much of it was beyond my understanding. Every once in a while, Françoise would break into his talk and correct some point on which he had slipped. He would nod his assent and continue in his booming voice.

Eventually the interview came to a halt and I said my good-byes. As I was being escorted from the building by one of his followers, I could hear Françoise pounding on her husband's desk, and in a loud voice, giving him some sharp advice on a minor ideological slip which I had failed to catch. There was not the slightest protest from him in reply.

Jordan may be considered a fanatic in the most extreme sense of the word: he holds his beliefs to the absolute exclusion of any other consideration. History, to him, is a thin thread of evidence taken from selected literary works; all the facts and figures that do not fit this evidence are twisted so that they do fit. He does not seem to know the meaning of the word compromise, he does not have a discriminating mind, and he appears to be totally intolerant of criticism and other points of view.

There is another aspect of his character which complicates matters. If Jordan were a fanatic who fought for what he believed with zest and passion, it would fulfil the picture expected of him. But Jordan does not fight for what he believes. In the words of John Bean, Jordan wants to be an 'easy Nazi', letting everyone else do the work while he takes the credit in Olympian isolation. This is one of the reasons why both Bean and Tyndall left him. Jordan has never deigned to soil his hands by fighting for what he wants. He seems to be too vain, too self-righteous, and too aware of some personal inadequacy to allow himself to be more than a focal point for the publicity gained by baiting Jews in Trafalgar Square.

Bean, on the other hand, is not so extreme. The roots of his beliefs are drawn from the same narrow sources as Jordan's and in this respect he is considered a fanatic. But Bean is more than anything else an opportunist whose primary interest is the acquisition of power. He is not too concerned how he gets it, just so long as he gets it. If he can climb to power on the strength of Hitler's basic precepts, then he will do so; but if he finds that he cannot, then he would not hesitate to change them. In fact, the longer Bean remains a part of the active political scene, the more he assumes a character uniquely his own, and the less he looks like a pure neo-Nazi.

Tyndall, unlike Jordan, is willing to fight for what he believes and, if necessary, to go to gaol in pursuit of his ideals. Of the two men, for instance, he alone wears with pride the 'martyrdom' of his previous convictions. Tyndall has often been described as a man with a dual personality: on the one side are the traits of the scar-faced Nazi, with all that that entails, and on the other side of his personality are the characteristics of John Bull – proud of his British-ness and fiercely patriotic in his own particular way. By his own admission, Tyndall plans to build his Greater Britain Movement in a British mould, with no pictures of Hitler and no obvious Germanic traits. It will be interesting to see how he combines the qualities of National Socialism with those of John Bull. At the moment, however, he and his organization are an unknown quantity on the fringe scene although a hint to his future course of action may have been given when he and an associate physically assaulted Prime Minister Kenyatta during the 1964 Commonwealth Conference in London.

Provided these three groups stay within the law, there is a good possibility that they will remain indefinitely on the scene as a constant source of irritation to their opponents who, at this moment, include practically everyone in Britain. There may even come a day when, through their assiduous cultivation of notoriety, they will collectively replace Sir Oswald Mosley and his Union Movement as the group most universally despised in Britain.

1. The *National Socialist,* No. 6, (undated), p. 3.
2. *The Fascists in Britain,* by Colin Cross. Barry & Rockliff. (London) 1961. p. 190.
3. Ibid., p. 153.
4. Ibid., p. 199.
5. *BNP* 1960, *Our First Year.* (No date.)
6. *Observer,* July 1, 1962, p. 3.
7. *National Socialist,* Vol. 1, No. 5, August 1963, p. 3.
8. Ibid, No. 6 (no date), p. 6.
9. Ibid.
10. *Daily Telegraph,* 16th October, 1962.
11. Ibid.

2 *The Union Movement*

'Fascism stands for the building of the highest standard of civilization the world has ever seen.'

SIR OSWALD MOSLEY, Olympia, 1934.

Sir Oswald Mosley is perhaps the greatest demagogue that England has produced in the last two centuries. There is virtually no one who is a part of the British political fringe today, or even within recent memory, who has as many of the advantages and talents as this man: wealth, charm, wit, social position, a superior intellect, hypnotic powers, and Messianic zeal. Within the political fringe, he is in a class by himself. If these minor political sects had their own private monarchy, he would be king.

For over 45 years, Sir Oswald Mosley has been active in the British political arena: as a Conservative MP, as an Independent MP, as a Labour MP, as the leader of the British Union of Fascists, and now as leader of his post-war party, the Union Movement. His political star has long since waned and, at the age of sixty-nine, his career is approaching its end. His place is now being taken by a spate of younger men – the Colin Jordans, John Beans, and John Tyndalls – whose combined abilities will probably never match those of Sir Oswald Mosley.

Sir Oswald Ernald Mosley, Bart., was born in 1896, the eldest son of an old, wealthy Anglo-Irish family. He was educated at Winchester and Sandhurst where he gained a reputation as a good athlete and political loner, qualities that were never to leave him. He fought in the First World War both in the trenches and with the Royal Flying Corps. While training with the RFC, he injured a leg and was subsequently invalided out of the service. The leg never healed properly and ever since he has walked with a limp.

From 1918 to 1930, Mosley's political career was spectacular. The tall, handsome, ex-soldier-hero stood as a Conservative Party candidate for Harrow in the 1918 election and won 83 per cent of the votes in the constituency. At the age of 23, he was Parliament's youngest member. In the Commons, he quickly established a reputation as a hard worker, an independent thinker, and a vitriolic speaker. He once referred to Winston Churchill as '. . . a man who, in a spirit of wanton malice, sets light to a house and then throws stones at the fire brigade'.[1] With his first wife, Cynthia (a daughter of Lord Curzon), Mosley became the centre of the rebellious political elements in and around Parliament; among their friends were Harold Nicolson, John Strachey, Aneurin Bevan, and Sidney and Beatrice Webb. Oswald Mosley had the intelligence, political skill, and magnetism needed to be a great leader, yet, in a moment of pure prophecy, Beatrice Webb, whose admiration for him was qualified only by the most feminine of intuitions, wrote of him at that time: 'So much perfection argues rottenness somewhere . . .' It was a description of him with which all his early political friends were forced to agree in later years.

As a rebel, Mosley was never too close to the Tory Party and its political philosophy. He saw it, and the Liberal Party as well, as parties mired in their own histories, incapable of adequately handling the problems of post-war Britain. Mosley believed that an economic crisis of the most catastrophic proportions was about to take place in England as a result of the war. The Conservative and Liberal Parties – the 'old parties' as he called them – appeared to him to be not only intellectually bankrupt but out of touch with his own generation, and he came to the conclusion that only through a young and more revolutionary party could the impending disaster be averted.

In 1920, he broke with the Conservative Party and remained an Independent MP in Parliament for four years. By 1924, he had decided that the Labour Party was the proper revolutionary instrument through which he, and those who agreed with him, could effect some radical changes. He then joined the Independent Labour Party and within five years had risen to the position of Chancellor of the Duchy of Lancaster in Ramsay MacDonald's government. Mosley was only 32 years old at the time and his quick ascent to Ministerial rank was an unparalleled achievement for one so young. Although he was impatient, impetuous and too ambitious, Mosley's abilities as a politician, a speaker, and a thinker had convinced many people that he was of future Prime-Ministerial calibre.

In 1930, however, Mosley abruptly broke with the Labour Party. The full reasons for the break are still obscure but outwardly it was due to the Party's refusal to implement his solution to Britain's unemployment problem. It is also evident that he resigned because of his impatience with democratic procedures. It was inconceivable to him that the political parties, during an economic crisis as severe as Britain was experiencing in 1930, would not accept radical attitudes to alter the situation. Few people in positions of authority paid what

Mosley felt should have been the proper amount of attention to his many proposals. He wanted the State to intervene actively in industrial affairs; he wanted the labour force to be shifted to areas where they were most needed; he wanted the Government to establish a minimum wage; he wanted credit to be controlled rigidly by the Exchequer; and he wanted the banks to be nationalized. It seemed to Mosley as if even the less-traditional Labour Party were incapable of handling the crisis – as apparently were the Conservatives and Liberals before it.

There was one other major factor, in addition, which played a part in his alienation from both the Labour Party and the democratic system. It was of a personal nature and has been perhaps one of the strongest impulses that has motivated everything Sir Oswald has done throughout his life. He has always been haunted by the belief that he is a Child of Destiny, that he was born to be Britain's Saviour – another Churchill or Wellington – who would one day save his country from a terrible catastrophe. When he turned his back on the Party that had honoured him with such high office, the enormity of his ambitions first became apparent. He had set his sights on a higher goal, outside the scope of ordinary political immortality, to that of perhaps a British dictator or Emperor. Extraordinary times beget extraordinary people, and Mosley felt that the crisis that lay at Britain's doorstep in 1930 would bring an exceptional leader to the fore, namely himself. Under those circumstances, the use of the traditional corridors to power did not seem necessary.

From 1930 onwards, Mosley's political career plunged to depths as low as his position within the parliamentary Labour Party had been high.

Mosley first tried to rally a small group of dissident MP's into his New Party (as opposed to the 'old parties') and succeeded in building his parliamentary strength to a total of five members: Sir Oswald himself, his wife Cynthia, John Strachey, Robert Forgan, and W. E. D. Allen from the Conservative Party. The New Party had its intellectuals as well: Harold Nicolson, who edited the Party's newspaper *Action*, Osbert Sitwell, Peter Quennell, and C. E. M. Joad (who resigned almost immediately because, he claimed, he detected 'the cloven hoof of Fascism'[2]). Mosley also organized a rank-and-file within his party. They were, for the most part, young men who, because of their propensity for violence, had earned themselves the nick-name of 'biff boys'. On the surface, their duties were to act as stewards at New Party meetings but, in reality, they were Mosley's personal janissaries. They were to be the forerunners of his Blackshirts.

From the start, the New Party was plagued with misfortune.

Mosley was ill with influenza during the critical formative stages in 1930; many of the original supporters such as C. E. M. Joad, had detected the influence of Fascism and had resigned; and, perhaps the most crucial of all, the 1931 General Election proved to be a disaster for the Party. All 24 New Party candidates, including Mosley and his wife, lost their contests. It was the last time Mosley was to sit in Parliament.

Sir Oswald Mosley by now was convinced that Britain's salvation lay through the formation of another party built along the lines of Mussolini's Fascist Party. He had been deeply influenced by the apparent successes of Italian Fascism and, despite the Duce's lack of compelling philosophy, saw in the Corporate State, the centralized leadership, the rigid control of the electorate and the Press, and the Government's domination of the country's economic life the necessary ingredients to save his own country from economic collapse, Communism, anarchy, and ultimate ruin. His visits to both Italy and Germany in early 1932 (during which time his closest New Party associate, Harold Nicolson, was to break with him), convinced him that Fascism should be introduced on a serious basis in Britain. Upon his return, Mosley formed his British Union of Fascists which he was to dominate until its collapse in 1940.

Its members were drawn at first from the many independent Fascist groups existing in Great Britain at the time: the British Fascists, the British Empire Fascists, the British National Fascists, the Fascist League, and the Fascist Movement. All of them – with the exception of the British Fascists – were tiny and unstable splinter groups. Only one Fascist organization of note, Arnold Leese's 200-strong Imperial Fascist League, refused to join. In addition, the British Union of Fascists was supported by a fairly large segment of the British people. Exactly how many supported Mosley has never been ascertained but the consensus seems to be that, at the height of his influence, he had the sympathy of perhaps 15 per cent of the population. Fear of the Communists, anxiety over the failure of the economy to improve, concern for the spiralling unemployment, and an increasing disenchantment with the Government's ability to handle the situation, drove hundreds of active supporters into Mosley's camp.

The eight-year history of the BUF can be divided into three periods, the first of which was the formative years from 1932 to 1934 when the character and policies of the organization were first set. It was the period in which all of the men who surrounded Mosley were first to join the Party: Alexander Raven Thomson, Arthur Keith Chesterton, William Joyce, Neil Francis-Hawkins, John Beckett, and W. E. A. Chambers-Hunter among others. It was also the period in which his Fascist policies were first given a public airing.

Mosley's prime concern was, upon achieving power, to re-work the British Constitution along Fascist lines. He believed in a one-party state, the leaders of which would be responsible directly to the electorate. The 'leadership principle' ('*Führerprinzip*') was to replace the 'bureaucracy' and was to legislate by Order under the authority of a 'General Powers Act'. The House of Commons would be retained but the members would be elected solely on an occupational basis. The Monarchy would also be retained but the House of Lords would be abolished in favour of a body of elderly 'experts' who would assist the Government whenever they were called upon to do so. Local governments would be abolished as well, their functions being assumed by a Government-appointed 'leader'. The country itself would be divided into 24 economic 'corporations', the directors of which would be responsible to 'The Leader' in London.

Parallel to the developments in Germany, the British Union of Fascists adopted a policy of anti-Semitism. At first, this involved no more than freezing out the few Jews who had joined the organization; but as time went on it developed to a point where it overrode all other considerations. Mosley never clarified his or his organization's position on the Jews except to say that only those Jews who threatened the national safety should be deported. His apparent equivocation encouraged many people to join the party. By 1934, one of the hallmarks of the members was their pronounced antipathy towards Jews. No one who remained in the BUF after this time was free of it.

The Golden Years of the BUF lasted less than two years, from 1934 to 1936. The rally at Olympia in 1934 gave the public at large its first chance to evaluate this new party. This particular rally still holds the record as the largest indoor meeting ever held in Britain. Over 15,000 people poured through the gates to hear the man who was offering Britain a new path to the future. Instead of a speech by Mosley, however, they were treated to a display of brutality by his Blackshirt followers that Britons were never to forget. Apparently, Mosley seems to have planned the rally as a show of BUF strength; the emphasis lay not with what Mosley had to say but with disciplining the audience. Instead of carrying on in the face of a few hecklers, Mosley would stop his speech and direct the operator of an overhead spotlight to pin-point the antagonist, whereupon half a dozen 'stewards' would seize the heckler and drag him from the hall punching and kicking him as they went. One spectator, personally involved, stated:

> I was anxious to hear Sir Oswald's speech and at first I was fed up with the interruptions. But later I became indignant and when he [Mosley] said 'We are not intimidated by these interrupters', I

interjected, referring to the audience, 'We haven't been intimidated but we are being fooled.'

As soon as I had spoken, six Fascists rushed at me, *picked me up and threw me over the balcony into the body of the hall. This was a drop of about ten feet and I became unconscious for a few moments. Some more Fascists who were waiting below then got hold of me and took me outside the meeting to a yard.* [Original italics]

More stewards followed and when they threw me down again I was surrounded by at least 20 men. I was absolutely helpless and they immediately began to beat me up, smashing me about the head and body.

I saw one of them swing a life-preserver a moment before I was struck with it and I began to stream with blood. Someone trod on my left thumb and I am still unable to use it. When I was hit in the mouth my dental plate was knocked out of my top jaw.

After knocking me about like this the Fascists threw me into the street . . .[3]

Following the Olympia rally, Mosley and his Blackshirts moved their strong-arm activities into the streets themselves, confident that the tide of history was on their side. They had found a mass following in the East End of London, particularly among the poor and over-crowded Cockneys and Irish who resented the Jews who lived among them. The Jews themselves, alarmed at events taking place in Germany, were equally disturbed by the activities of the Blackshirts; one reason being that, by 1936, the BUF had discarded its traditional black shirt in favour of an SS-type uniform complete with peaked cap, jack-boots, and arm-band. The Jewish community, on the whole, believed that the violent activities of the BUF might lead to a British-style pogrom.

The climax of the BUF Golden Age came in October 1936 at 'the Battle of Cable Street'. Mosley had planned a march through the East End of London as a large show of strength. He picked Cable Street, a main street of the Jewish community, as his parade ground. The anti-Fascists, however, were prepared for the intruders and, under the Spanish Republican cry of 'They shall not pass!', had barricaded many of the streets in the area with cobble-stones, old furniture, and automobiles. The police, cast in the role of Fascist protectors, formed flying wedges at the head of the marching column of BUFs not only to allow the march to continue but to clear the streets for traffic. Tempers began to flare, cobble-stones were thrown, clubs were swung, Mosley was hit by a rock, a horse stepped on Fenner Brockway, and it appeared as if there might be serious bloodshed.

At the last moment, however, Sir John Simon, the Home Secretary, ordered Mosley to call off his march. He reluctantly complied. The anti-Fascists were victorious; Mosley had not passed. Back at his Chelsea headquarters, Mosley told his men before he dismissed them that the Government had surrendered to 'Red violence and Jewish corruption'.

Within a month, the Public Order Bill was passed by Parliament which severely limited the activities and appeal of the British Union of Fascists. It forbade the wearing of political uniforms, strengthened the existing law which curbed the use of language likely to lead to a breach of the peace, gave the police powers to ban marches and demonstrations in the interests of public safety, and curtailed the use of stewards at open-air meetings. Mosley and his men, along with Leese's Imperial Fascists and Hargrave's Social Credit Greenshirts, were shorn of their uniforms. With them went whatever influence, appeal, and power they ever had.

From 1936 to 1940, the BUF went into decline. Mosley, in his own version of 'the night of the long knives', purged over 100 Blackshirts from his administrative staff in 1937, including John Beckett, the Director of Publications and, William Joyce, the Director of Propaganda. It was also a period in which many of his associates began to resign, the most noted of whom was A. K. Chesterton, the Editor of the British Union's newspaper, *Action*. By 1938, it became Satanic for anyone concerned with his own reputation to be associated with Mosley or his organization. Those who differed with Mosley either over his attitude towards Germany, the coming war, the Jews, the internal policies of the organization, or some other aspect of the movement all found excuses to leave. By 1940, only the most subservient and hardened followers remained.[4]

Under Defence Regulation 18b, Mosley and his second wife, the former Diana Freeman-Mitford – one of the famous Mitford sisters* – whom he had married in 1935 (Mosley's first wife, Cynthia, had died in 1933), were gaoled – it was called 'preventive detention' – in the spring of 1940 along with approximately 1,200 of their fol-

* Her other sisters were Unity, Jessica, Nancy, Deborah, and Pamela. Both Diana and Unity were sympathetic to the German National Socialist Movement and were early supporters of the BUF. Unity was supposed to have been in love with Hitler and tried to commit suicide at the outbreak of war in 1939. She died in 1948. Jessica's political sympathies in contrast were with the extreme left and the three of them – Diana, Unity, and Jessica – used to engage in political shouting matches in their family's Gloucestershire home. Nancy became a famous novelist (*Wigs on the Green, Love in a Cold Climate, Noblesse Oblige,* etc.). Deborah married the Duke of Devonshire. Only Pamela seems to have led what might be called, under the circumstances, a fairly conventional life. She comes into the limelight only whenever her more provocative sisters make news.

lowers. Mosley's Fascists, however, were not the only ones detained; there were, in addition, Arnold Leese and his Imperial Fascists, Cahir Healy and his Irish nationalists (who were imprisoned on a ship called the *Argenta* anchored in Belfast harbour), and a sprinkling of assorted Greenshirts, conscientious objectors, and pacifists.

Included as well in the net was Sir Barry Domvile, the leader of the pro-Nazi 'Link' which he founded a few years before the war 'to promote better understanding and friendship between the peoples of Germany and Great Britain.' The Link was supported by a magazine called *Anglo-German Review* which carried such articles as 'Spring comes to the Black Forest' and 'Birthday Party at the Goerings'. Although never a large organization, its membership consisted of ex-BUFs, a few members of Parliament (Captain A. H. M. Ramsay, MP, for one), and a number of pacifists from the Peace Pledge Union. When Domvile was gaoled, the Link collapsed but its work was carried on by the British Council for Christian Settlement in Europe under the leadership of William Joyce and John Beckett. It claimed to have 18,000 members although this figure was probably slightly inflated. Similar to the Link, the members of the BCCSE were a curious blend of Fascists and pacifists. Contrary to its title, the organization was pro-Nazi; it was able to draw a few pacifists into its fold only because it claimed to be seeking 'peace'. The Council collapsed in the early war years after Beckett and many of his followers were, like Mosley and his BUFs before them, placed in preventive detention.

As the threat of invasion died down, many of the rank-and-file 18b detainees were released from prison providing that they volunteered for military service. It was the Government's intention, however, that all the top leaders should be detained for the duration of the conflict. But in 1943, Mosley contracted a thrombo-phlebitis infection which doctors felt would be aggravated seriously if he were not released from prison. In November of that year, he and his wife were set free despite the furore it caused in Parliament and the Press. He was freed only on condition that he travel no more than seven miles from his Oxfordshire home, that he report monthly to the police, and that he engage in no further political activities for the duration of the war.

Following this precedent, a number of other leaders were released, the most noted of which were Beckett, Domvile, Leese and Ramsay. On VE Day, all those still in detention were set free and the restrictions imposed upon those previously released were lifted. Many of the ex-BUFs were broken in spirit and took the opportunity to retire from politics. Others, however, particularly Leese, Chesterton and Mosley, were to return to the active political scene.

In 1946, Mosley published a book called *My Answer* in which he attempted to justify his pre-war activities. He sought to answer the many allegations of treason, opportunism, and anti-Semitism which were levelled against him. Although brilliantly argued in part, the book did little to change the public's image of him. The book was not widely circulated primarily because most British booksellers refused to stock it.

Mosley came out of the war convinced that the Western World faced another calamitous crisis. He felt that the old order of capitalism had somehow reeled and staggered to military victory but that it was not economically healthy enough to carry on in the post-war era. In 1947, Sir Oswald published perhaps his most important post-war book. It was called *The Alternative* and outlined his plan to save Western civilization from the collapse that he was certain would take place. It is a pretentious and wordy book, full of such phrases as 'transcending the diurnal politics of normality', 'The Great Negation', 'Doers versus Deniers', and 'Hierarchical Synthesis'; nevertheless, it forms the basis of his post-war philosophy, explaining why he founded the Union Movement and why he has acted as he has since the war.

In the book, Mosley conceded that the narrow nationalism of pre-war Fascism was outdated. What was needed in the future, he argued, was a United Europe that served as a third world force between the Communists in the East and the capitalists in the West. This third force would be able to control the balance of world power and, at the same time, be able to preserve the European values that he felt were being threatened by the two giants from the East and West. Mosley's thesis was practically identical to his BUF policies except that he expanded them on to an international scale rather than limiting them exclusively to Britain. 'The Government' would be elected by all Europeans and would be responsible to them alone; industries below an unspecified size – particularly small shops – would remain in private hands while those larger than the unspecified size would be controlled and owned by the workers themselves along syndicalist lines. The Government would have full authority to direct the economy as it saw fit: production quotas, wages, industrial expansion, and foreign trade would be under their control; tariffs, passports, and certain taxes would be abolished; and income taxes and currency would be standardized throughout the area. Each country's parliament would retain some powers, specifically in the social and cultural spheres. Mosley also conceded that the presence of competing political parties might be beneficial.

In addition, parts of Africa would come under European influence. Colonies there would be abolished and the land would be divided between blacks and whites according to the current ratio of races.

The new black and white states then would be set free but only the latter would be allowed the privilege of joining the European sphere of influence. The new black states would have to strike out on their own. With regard to Asia, Mosley felt that it would eventually be lost to the Communists and that any attempt to delay the process of capitulation to them would be a waste of money.

In later years, Mosley's ideas, as outlined in *The Alternative,* incorporated the acceptance of Apartheid. Mosley has never believed in the integration of races. The only way he sees the different races existing in harmony together is by rigidly separating them. Such separation, he believes, in no way would isolate one race-state from another. On the contrary, he feels they would live side by side in mutual respect. Part of the race problem, he says, stems from the coloured peoples' feeling of inferiority towards the whites who have dominated the world for so long. If racial pride and heritage were built up in these black groups, he feels that there would be less likelihood that they would be for ever dependent on the white man's abilities. Mosley envisions the day when the coloured states, with the help of economic aid from both East and West, will be separate (but equal) partners with their more advanced neighbours.

Mosley believed that his revised political philosophy would only be accepted after an apocalyptic economic disaster had occurred in the West. He estimated that this disaster would take place no later than 1948 or 1949, and would be provoked by the narrow nationalist policies of the world powers, by the abdication of power by the once mighty colonialists and by the 'mongrelization' of the European states by outsiders.

No matter how contentious his ideas, Sir Oswald had made a formidable attempt by the end of 1947 to bring his political philosophy up to date. *The Alternative* was proof enough *to him* that he had given up his past bad habits in favour of a far-reaching plan for the good of all Mankind. What irritated him then, and still irritates him today, is that no one would pay any attention to these new ideas.

The rank-and-file Fascists were fragmented after the war into a series of small and unstable 'front' groups. There were, at various stages between 1945 and 1948, the Briton's Patriotic Society; the British National Party (no relation to the present one) whose purpose was 'to fight vested interests, financial control, and Bolshevism'; the New Order Group; the Union of British Freedom; the 18b Detainee's Fund; the British Vigilante Action Committee; the Imperial Defence League; the Order of the Sons of St George; the League of Christian Reformers; the Gentile-Christian Front; and the largest of them all, the British League of ex-Servicemen and Women, which was run by an ex-BUF named Jeffrey Hamm (who was living in London at the time under the alias of Anderson). Mosley himself had organized a few of his faithful followers into 'book clubs' in order to stimulate the circulation of his own political philosophy.

Many of Mosley's old comrades-in-arms, particularly Hamm, were calling for the return to active politics of their pre-war leader. Mosley resisted their offers at first but by 1948 he realized that if his prediction of an economic collapse were to come true he would need a political instrument to which the English people could turn in their agony. He therefore succumbed to the pressure of Hamm and other ex-BUFs and formed his Union Movement in February of that year.

Mosley surrounded himself with many of his ex-BUF faithfuls. Besides Hamm, there were Alexander Raven Thomson, the pre-war BUF Director of Policy, whom Mosley appointed as Editor of his reborn *Action;* Victor Burgess, the founder of the Union of British Freedom; 'Tommy' Moran, a former Naval boxing champion and founder of the Order of the Sons of St George; Michael Ryan, a crippled Irishman, ex-civil servant, and a shop steward of the Transport and General Workers' Union; and Alfred Flockhart, who was considered Mosley's closest associate at the time of the Movement's formation. In later years, Mosley added others to his inner circle of party confidants: one was Hector George McKecknie, an ex-BUF, who is perhaps the closest man to Mosley at present; another was Robert Row, the current Editor of *Action* (Raven Thomson died in 1955); and the most recent has been Mosley's son Max, a graduate of Oxford and a talented speaker in his own right.

The general public first became conscious of the Union Movement in 1949 when Britain was embroiled with both Jews and Arabs in the Middle East over the partition of Palestine. Mosley and his followers agitated against the demands of the Palestinean Jews with a ferocity reminiscent of pre-war days. By 1950, however, the question of partition had faded from the front pages of the newspapers and all Mosley could show for his efforts was a massive re-opening of old wounds. To escape the notoriety, he retired to County Cork for three years. His temporary exodus from the political scene was further stimulated by the lack of an economic crisis which he had predicted would take place by that time.

For five years, beginning in 1950, Sir Oswald published a literary pamphlet called *The European*, the subject matter of which ranged almost exclusively outside the political field. He felt that the public was putting too much emphasis on a minute aspect of his overall philosophy. He claimed that this pamphlet was his effort to redress the balance. His discussions on Shaw and Wagner, for example, are considered by many people to be of the highest literary merit. They feel that, in future years, when the prejudices and provocations engendered by Mosley have faded, he will be re-evaluated more favourably in the light of those literary efforts rather than on the basis of his political views alone. *The European* died, however, for the same reasons his book failed to sell: it was boycotted.

Mosley's return from exile in 1953 brought no new philosophical or tactical slant to his party's policies except that the date of the 'inevitable' economic collapse had been pushed forward to 1958 or 1959. To prepare himself for the chaos, Mosley began to put up his men in elections on a limited and scattered basis. Most of the elections were local ones and in no case did his men come near to the top of the poll. Like John Bean, Mosley would point to one ward in a constituency that had given his man a 'good' vote and blow it out of proportion to the overall vote; his 'good' vote usually amounted to no more than 2 per cent or 3 per cent of the total vote in the constituency. Most of his candidates stood under the UM label although, on one occasion at least, Jeffrey Hamm stood as a 'Blackshirt'.

The Movement's election material concentrated on the fears of the ordinary citizen: Negro immigration ('Send immigrants back to their own lands to good jobs and conditions in a fair and decent way . . . It's our country, isn't it?'), housing ('. . . young married couples looking for homes and old people kicked out of theirs – in many cases by unscrupulous alien landlords . . .'), Retail Price Maintenance ('Protect [the small shopkeeper] from the monopolies of the giant combines and cut-price racketeers'), and 'Squander-mania' ('We won't spend public money on trips to Russia, China or Timbuctoo').

Mosley decided to put his own prestige on the line in 1959 for the first time since his defeat at the polls in 1931. His policies towards coloured immigrants had hardened considerably during the latter half of the 1950s; the 1958 race riots in Notting Hill, in which his men had played an active part, had convinced him that a crisis – racial, economic, political, or social (it was never made clear) – was about to take place. This seemed to be the opportunity he was waiting for. He entered himself as the Union Movement parliamentary candidate in the constituency of North Kensington, the centre spot of the previous year's race riots. Hopes were high as over 200 UM canvassers began their door-to-door appeal for their leader. The first returns showed that Mosley would win one-third of the votes. Figuring that the other two-thirds would be evenly divided between the Conservative, Labour and Liberal candidates, he was confident of victory. After 28 years in the political wilderness, he felt that this victory would be the crowning justification for all the slights he had suffered in the intervening years.

> Mosley's standard speech [during the election] incorporated a high and a low road. On a higher level, he advocated compulsory free passage back to the West Indies for the immigrants... For good measure Sir Oswald threw in a solution for Africa – complete *Apartheid* for the whole continent...
>
> The low road led through long sordid tales of sexual offences by coloured men, spiced with such nasty remarks as that West Indians provided cheap labour because they could at a pinch live off a tin of Kit-E-Kat a day. These were the arguments of an American Southern demagogue in the accents of a British gentleman.
>
> ... Some of the wizened old men, wan spinsters, and duck-tailed teddy boys seemed intrigued to hear a man of education and breeding clothe in fancy words their fouler thoughts.
>
> Sir Oswald made no use of pseudo-scientific nonsense about race. The *claque* [which surrounded him] frequently seemed bored at the concentration on West Indians and disappointed at the absence of full-blooded anti-Semitism. When Sir Oswald made an incidental reference to the Jasper case, there were eager shouts of 'At last we've got the Yids on the run!'[5]

Mosley's high and low road did little good. When the returns were in, he was at the bottom of the poll. He not only lost, but for the first time in his career, he forfeited his deposit. Sir Oswald had cornered 8.1 per cent of the votes.

After this disaster, Mosley changed the basic tactics of his party. The continual electoral failures, particularly his own, had finally convinced him that the British people were not yet ready for his new social order. Furthermore, he realized that his party alone was incapable of bringing it about. The only hope for his revolutionary political philosophy lay, he believed, in uniting all the European parties with a similar character to his into a supra-national organization. The seeds for unity can be traced back to *The Alternative* where Mosley argued for the internationalization of his pre-war policies; but at the time of writing in 1947, apparently he secretly felt that he could come to power on his own. By 1960, however, after 13 years of failure, he realized this was no longer the case.

Accordingly, he began to sound out the possibilities of a political union among all those political parties in Europe whose views were similar to his, carefully avoiding those groups whose characters were predominantly neo-Nazi. In March 1962, he organized a 'Conference of Venice' (actually held outside the city since authorities would not allow the delegates to use the public meeting halls). Present were representatives from the Union Movement, the Deutsches Reichspartei of Germany, Jeune Europe and Movement d'Action Civique from Belgium, and Movemiento Sociale Italiano from Italy. These groups drew up an agreement whereby they would band together under the name National Party of Europe. The aims of this party were identical to those found in *The Alternative* although this time they were incorporated under the term 'Europe a Nation' apparently to flatter his captive audience. Sir Oswald told me that his conception of a united Europe pre-dated the Common Market by a decade but that no one has ever given him credit for it. He omitted to say that the idea can be traced back at least to the days of the Roman Empire.

Mosley returned from this conference with renewed energy. Three weeks after Colin Jordan held his 'Free Britain from Jewish Control' rally in Trafalgar Square, Mosley held a similar rally in the same place. For violence, it nearly equalled the pre-war Cable Street riot. An estimated 6,000 people crowded into the Square to witness the spectacle. The warm-up speech by Jeffrey Hamm had barely begun before copper coins, eggs and rotting vegetables descended on members of the Movement crowded together at the base of Nelson's Column. To keep the mob at bay, Hamm was forced to swing the microphone in front of him like a scythe. Fist-fights broke out between Mosley's supporters, Communists, anti-Fascists, anarchists, members of the Committee of 100, and the police. The meeting was halted by the authorities before Mosley himself had a chance to speak. By the end of the day, more than 40 people – few of whom, incidentally, were members of the Union Movement – had been booked for various offences against the peace.

From Trafalgar Square, Mosley went to Manchester where the scene was repeated. He then returned to London and once more began to stalk his old adversaries in the East End. This time, however, they were prepared for him and it resulted in one of the few physical beatings that Mosley himself has ever received.

In spite of all the public disorders that took place during the summer, Parliament was in no mood to consider introducing legislation to curb 'inciting racial hatreds and violence.' In an editorial entitled 'Freedom of Speech', *The Times* perhaps best reflected its feelings when it wrote:

> Should incitement to racial hatred or prejudice be made a crime? Mr George Brown thinks so, so do the National Council for Civil Liberties, the London County Council, the Communists, and the members of Parliament who supported the Bills introduced last session by Mr Brockway and Mr Iremonger . . .
>
> The whole development of modern domestic British history is towards a position of political maturity, in which people are left

> to weigh for themselves the opinions, policies, and creeds that are publicly proclaimed before them; treating with contemptuous disdain those that are deserving of contempt; resolving their differences by argument and by constitutional machinery; and refusing to be stampeded by fools, charlatans, and psychopaths . . .
>
> Why should we be deflected from this course by the ranting of a handful of exhibitionists, by the sporadic violence of factions which thrive thereby, and by the honest fury of a few citizens who have lost control of their feelings in public?[6]

Since 1962, the Union Movement has kept itself off the front pages of the newspapers, partly due to an informal agreement between the publishers not to play up the wilder activities of the Movement unless they *were* news, and partly due to a marked loss of momentum within the Movement itself. The formation of the National Party of Europe seems to have had no regenerative effect on any of the member parties, least of all the Union Movement. In fact, its existence is only occasionally mentioned in the pages of *Action*. Nor has it made any noticeable impact on either the British or Continental electorates; they are still not aware of its existence. Also, there are some indications that the Movement is undergoing an agonizing re-appraisal at the moment and that it may soon lurch off on some new tack not previously considered by Mosley. There is no question that Sir Oswald has tired of predicting the date of the 'inevitable' economic collapse since none of his past estimates have proved to be accurate. Because the Movement is in a state of flux, its cohesion – between the intellectuals who surround Mosley and the rank-and-file rabble which follows him – is beginning to weaken.

Mosley's organization has always had a split personality: between the intellectuals and the rabble. It is this latter group, the overwhelming percentage of members, who can be blamed for the Movement's failure to grow, just as much as Mosley himself and his policies. For the most part, the rank-and-file is composed of young and violent racists who join the Movement as an excuse to release their anti-social attitudes. The extremes to which they take their actions are perhaps best reflected by the behaviour of one ex-member, Peter Dawson. In 1961, he publicly assaulted Ghana's High Commissioner and pummeled him to the ground in full view of a group of dignitaries. He later tried to burn down the London anti-Apartheid headquarters. Eventually he was expelled from the organization.*

In 1963, two teen-aged members of the Crawley, Sussex, branch

* It has never been established whether this Peter Dawson is the same Peter Dawson who founded an organization in the early 1960s called 'The British Society for the Removal of Jews to Israel'.

of the UM were involved in a struggle for power which was resolved by one of the two being stabbed to death. The Union Movement disclaimed any responsibility for the murder, stating that the death was the result of factors not connected with UM activities. No doubt this is partially true, for the man convicted of the murder was in gaol less than a year before he also stabbed one of his fellow inmates to death.

Loyalty is not one of the most noted qualities of the ordinary member either. John Bean is a good example: he joined and quit all within two weeks, perhaps a record. Another example is Keith Goodhall who tried to overthrow Mosley himself. He later founded a short-lived sect called the European Union of Fascists, the only post-war British group openly to use the word Fascist.

Those members whom I have seen in the Union Movement are almost wholly those species of man who have sexual, psychological, or physical axes to grind. Most of them have an abject contempt for the society in which they live. Their attitudes bear no relationship to the rebelliousness of the 'Mods' and 'Rockers'; they have not yet reached that level of social sophistication. They are more the misfits, the dullards and the outcasts of society who can think of nothing more constructive to do than to destroy all the icons – the 'Jews', the 'Communists' and, less specifically, 'they' – which they feel are responsible for their own shortcomings and frustrations. Whether or not they belong to the UM is incidental to them; if it did not exist, they would find some other vehicle for their violence. For example, one day I was in the UM bookstore (which also serves as a recruiting centre) on Vauxhall Bridge Road for an appointment with Sir Oswald and, as I was waiting, a huge, blond Scot entered and walked up to the counter. He had pock-marks on his face and neck so deep that I thought they were the result of a losing encounter with a rake. He was so scarred that he could not shave properly and tufts of hair stood out at odd angles. In a voice of suppressed anger, he asked the clerk behind the counter if he could join the organization and, if so, could he wear a uniform and carry a weapon? The clerk explained to him that weapons were not allowed and that uniforms had been banned since 1936. He added that, if he wished, he could wear the Movement's lightning lapel badge. The Scot stood there a moment, staring vacantly at the wall; then he whirled around, cursed, and stormed out of the building.

In spite of his ability to attract all manner of right-wing extremists, Mosley insists that he personally is not anti-Semitic. Judging from what he has published since the war, this is so: he seldom touches specifically on the subject of Jews even though he often uses such words as 'alien', 'foreign', and 'unwelcome' to describe those vaguely-defined groups of whom he disapproves. Many of his non-political friends will also say that, deep in his heart, he is not *really* anti-Semitic. But if there is some doubt about Mosley's true sentiments on this point, there is none about his rank-and-file's. They are the most venomous anti-Semites in Britain and, what is more, they are proud of it.

This split between the 'intellectuals' and the rank-and-file is so fundamental that it has always threatened to tear the party apart. Mosley-ologists see the day when just that will happen. Why he allows his Movement to be dominated by these people has never been explained adequately. Mosley did say at one time that he needed these men to assist him in his quest for power: once in power, he claimed, then he could weed out the disreputable individuals.

The linch-pin between the two groups is Edward Jeffrey Hamm, an ex-BUF, the UM's Secretary, and probably Mosley's most loyal supporter. He is a slightly built man with sunken cheeks, cynical eyes and a sallow complexion. He is an exceptionally talented speaker and organizer. As the Movement's front man, he is the person who actually initiates group activities: he sets up the speaking tours, scouts out possible opportunities, organizes the electoral campaigns, and maintains what little discipline there is over the rank-and-file. In addition, Hamm is Sir Oswald's informal bodyguard; despite his relatively small stature, his opponents treat him with great respect, for he is wiry, shrewd, and possesses considerable courage.

Hamm controls an active membership in the UM of no more than 200 individuals although there are about 1,000 additional inactive supporters throughout the country who work part-time for the party. The relatively small number of members does not reflect the UM's immense nuisance value on the British political scene. All 1,200 or so are zealous workers; when elections occur or rallies are to be organized, the amount of work they can do is formidable. These members are controlled through a network of UM branches that, to an outsider, makes the Movement look larger than it is. Although branches flourish and die with disturbing frequency, there is an average at any one given time of 24 'cells' which stretch from the English Channel to Bannockburn. Closer inspection reveals that, in most cases, a branch is no more than a member's home from which information can be disseminated, and where the local four or five activists can meet.

To keep the Union Movement before the public eye, Mosley still continues to speak on selected occasions at both indoor and outdoor rallies throughout the country. In most cases, his very presence is a provocation; he need not say one word because, to many Britons, he is a living symbol of Naziism, dictatorships, gas-chambers, prejudice, intolerance, and all the other horrors of the Second World War.

On a lesser level, Union Movement speakers can be seen almost every night at selected speaking sites throughout London haranguing the passers-by. These soap-box orations by rank-and-file UM members have been going on for almost 18 years and, for anyone impatient to catch the Sunday afternoon show at Speakers' Corner, they are an interesting week-day diversion. I myself have seen a crowd of approximately 300 people stand in a light rain on Earls Court Road to heckle a UM speaker. As long as Sir Oswald does not put in an appearance, these meetings are relatively orderly in the British tradition of almost unlimited tolerance; but if he shows up, it seems to be the signal for everyone to start breaking up the furniture.

I once watched Sir Oswald speak in public, and there is no question that the power this man commands from his followers stems in part from his personal magnetism and from the sheer force of his personality. Mosley is a speaker of the old school: he appeals to the heart rather than the head, although there is a certain amount of reasoned argument in the contents of his speech. He has the ability to transfix his audience with a voice that is both soothing and compelling. The tone of his voice is not unlike that of a hypnotist's: he carries on at an uninterrupted pitch that has its own special vibration; at precisely the right moment, he will raise his voice to a new pitch – like a car changing gears – and slightly increase the volume and resonance. The effect is similar to that which is produced by Ravel's 'Bolero'. His actions on the podium are fully complimentary to his voice and can physically transfix his listeners with as much ease as his words can their minds: he will stab the air like a dart-thrower, stop the swaying of his body abruptly with his arms akimbo to emphasize a point, raise his fore-finger by the side of his face, pause, catch the proper nuance, and then plunge on into the body of his speech. Every facet of his speech – his actions, words, voice, tone, and content – is combined for maximum effect, and at the climax – a crescendo of words and movements – his audience is on its feet, stamping, clapping, shouting, and chanting '*Mos-ley! Mos-ley! Mos-ley . . .*'

The audience of which I was a part consisted overwhelmingly of white South Africans and Southern Rhodesians who stood and cheered him for well over ten minutes.

After he had left the podium, Jeffrey Hamm then conducted a money-raising effort, which had been carefully planned beforehand. 'First we will start with the five-pound notes,' he said. 'Who will be the first to contribute?' After a few moments' silence, a youth in the back of the hall, wearing the UM Lightning badge (known by opponents as 'the flash in the pan'), produced the first note. Seven five-pound notes were subsequently collected from the audience. And so it continued through the pound notes, the ten-shilling notes, and finally to the loose change.

Mosley then returned to the podium to answer questions from the floor. This, too, had all been planned beforehand. It was designed so that Sir Oswald could expound on various subjects outside the context of his main speech. In this instance, he concentrated particularly on the problems of South Africa and Southern Rhodesia, to the delight of the audience. He appealed to their frustration by saying 'People tell me: "Why don't you pack it up, go home, give up, forget about it? You're out of step, behind the times, and out of fashion."' But, he added by way of reply, 'I need not remind you that it is not even fashionable today to be a man!'

There were a few instances when hecklers rose from their seats to shout at him. Mosley's command of invective was so swift and vicious that his tormenters were quickly reduced to silence.

Sir Oswald himself is a tall, heavy-set, and dignified man with slightly bucked teeth and burning eyes. His most immediately noticeable characteristic, however, is his charm. For a man with such a formidable reputation, he has the ability to put all his guests immediately at ease by taking a genuine interest in their own affairs. Whenever I met him, he was most considerate and courteous.

I asked him, in an interview, to explain his Europe a Nation ideas and he straightaway launched into an explanation so fervent that he gave the impression that the Movement's future rested on my conversion to it. Full of gusto, he stabbed the air with his finger, pounded his fist into his palm, broke out into laughter over some amusing point, and at a vital juncture would ask me: 'Don't you agree? Isn't it logical?' Without waiting for an answer, he would continue, peppering his argument with statistics, supporting data and pleas to reasonableness. This combination of charm, intelligence, wit, and conviction is devastating at close quarters. It is perhaps difficult to understand without actually meeting him why this apparent misfit once had the following he did and why he can still command a small army of loyal supporters. If the only source of information about him were the newspapers, it would be exceedingly difficult to believe how such a man could once have had friends of the calibre of Aneurin Bevan, John Strachey, Sidney and Beatrice Webb, and Harold Nicolson; but anyone subjected to the man personally soon understands why.

However, 35 years in the political wilderness has had its effect on him. His pride is beginning to crack around the edges; he seems very sensitive to slights and the first glimmerings of self-doubt are noticeable. His ordinary self-assurance appears to have been replaced, in part, by a gnawing fear that perhaps, after all those years, he may have been wrong. He seemed resigned to his ostracism; the pride with which he once carried it has worn thin. He gives the impression that he dislikes his squalid surroundings, the furtiveness of his life, and the men with whom he associates. Above all, I noticed that he seemed to miss the company and confidence of great men. His tailored appearance and old-world courtliness and consideration only heightened the mean aspects of his life; but he never apologized for them.

I mentioned that I once knew some of his first wife's relatives in America and his eyes lit up with warmth at the thought that anyone was considerate enough of him to associate his thoughts with him socially. He is obviously accustomed to being treated like an outcast and is always on guard for the usual questions about why he hates Jews. He fends off unpleasant queries with a demeanour that is part Stoicism, part arrogance.

Many members of his own family have rejected him. For instance, I mentioned that I had met one of his nephews (who also lives in London) by chance a few days previously. Sir Oswald replied, 'Oh yes, I know him, but I haven't seen him for over seven years.'

Whether Sir Oswald Mosley has come to the conclusion that his fight is a nearly hopeless one is not known. Certainly he does not admit it publicly and would not admit it privately to me. There are some indications, however, that he wants to close down his political party and retire to his house in France. Provided he can find a face-saving exit from the scene, I think he will probably do so. He is almost 70 years old, much of the fire has left him, and the futility of the last 45 years has left its mark. If and when he retires, it will be the end of an era – an era that most Britons will be thankful to see end.

1. *The Fascists in Britain,* p. 13.
2. Ibid, p. 50.
3. *Fascists at Olympia,* by 'Vindicator'. Gollancz 1934. Mr Jacob Miller; Statement made while in St Mary Abbots Hospital, reported in *News Chronicle,* June 13, 1934.
4. See *The Fascists in Britain,* by Colin Cross. Barry & Rockliff. 1960, for a more detailed account of this eight-year period.
5. *The British General Election of* 1959, by D. E. Butler and Richard Rose. Macmillan. 1960. Description of the North Kensington campaign by Keith Kyle. p. 179–180.
6. *The Times,* August 25, 1962.

3 *The League of Empire Loyalists*

'These people have never really believed that Queen Victoria is dead.'

AN EX-MEMBER

If Mosley and his Union Movement are the most disliked of all the political fringe groups in Britain, then the League of Empire Loyalists qualified, at one time, as the scene's most annoying. For example, at a parliamentary lunch in honour of U Thant on July 5, 1962, *The Times* had this to report:

Ambassadors and Ministers from some 40 countries, MPs and Mayors and Mayoresses from many parts of the country were among the 600 guests who heard Mr Nigel Nicolson, Chairman of the executive Committee of the United Nations Association of Great Britain and Northern Ireland, say in introducing the speakers that one of his duties as Chairman was to 'look under the table to see if Empire Loyalists have crept in.'

If Mr Nicolson's searches had been inadequate, his apprehensions were quickly confirmed. Although a bearded member had been asked to leave during the reception, Mr Macmillan had scarcely started his speech when Miss Avril Walters, the League's Secretary, stood up in a corner of the room and shouted: 'U.N.O. is an anti-British racket, the Empire Loyalists say . . .'

Shouts of 'Shut up!', 'Sit down!' and 'Throw her out!' prevented the . . . guests hearing what she wished to say on behalf of her organization and officials ushered her out of the dining-room. A few minutes later, an elderly man protested: 'Stand by the Empire!' Again, angry diners called on him to be quiet and he, too, was escorted from the room. Mr Macmillan, smiling and unperturbed, observed: 'I am accustomed to certain amounts of interruption.'

Then it was the turn of the grey-haired man, seated not far from U Thant: 'Ought we to enter this Common Market; it is the greatest high treason you ever saw in your life. Only traitors could contemplate it' he said with a wave of his fists in the Prime Minister's direction.

More shouts on a similar theme from the same source prompted

Mr Macmillan to answer back: 'I don't believe you have paid your subscription.'[1]

Such was the League of Empire Loyalists in action during one of their less successful forays into the enemy camp.

The League was founded in October of 1954 by Arthur Keith Chesterton, a cousin of the famous writer, G. K. Chesterton. 'A. K.,' as he is called, has a long history of Fascist and right-wing activities. He was a founding member, in 1932, of Mosley's British Union of Fascists and spent two of his six years in that organization as Editor of *Action*. He was also Mosley's official biographer.[2] However, Chesterton resigned from the British Union in 1938 over a long-standing dispute with Mosley concerning certain questions of policy in the BUF. Whereas Mosley seemed equivocal on the question of whether his Fascists should either fight or stand aside in the coming world struggle, there was no question in Chesterton's mind what had to be done. As the informal leader of the 'patriotic Fascists' within the BUF, Chesterton and his small group of followers left the party to join the military forces of their country.

Having first won the Military Cross as a young man in the trenches during the First World War, and having subsequently distinguished himself fighting (ironically) the Italians in Abyssinia in the Second World War, Chesterton was not so heavily subjected to the post-war accusations of having been a pre-war Nazi sympathizer as was Mosley. Generally speaking, Chesterton's public position at the end of the war was one of past mistakes having been partially if not wholly rectified by his patriotic actions during his country's gravest crisis.

Chesterton held a number of jobs after the war before he founded the League. For a time he was Deputy Editor of *Truth*, a right-wing review edited by the father of W. Austen Brooks, the League's present Deputy Chairman. He then worked for the United Central Africa Association, a group organized to promote the establishment of the federation of the Rhodesias and Nyasaland. For a short time, he was a journalist for the Beaverbrook newspapers.

In 1953, Chesterton branched out on his own. Having a small income, he began to publish his own newspaper, *Candour*, which eventually became the unofficial voice of the League of Empire Loyalists. In the following year, the League itself was founded. Its formation came about at the right psychological moment since Britain was in the throes of shedding her Empire. Most of the members who joined the League at that time, and in later periods as well, were right-wing Conservatives who were opposed to their country's course of action. Many of them came from a rather limited but nevertheless distinguished section of society. For example, some of the current members of the League's General Council include The Earl of Buchan, Field-Marshal Lord Ironside, Lt-Gen Sir Balfour Hutchison, Brigadier A. R. Wallis, Group Captain R. T. Leather, and Air Commodore G. S. Oddie. The League also attracted a few pre-war Fascists but their numbers were never large. The only one of note, besides Chesterton, was W. E. A. Chambers-Hunter, Mosley's BUF organizer in Aberdeen. He, too, is a current member of the League's General Council.*

Since the League's inception, however, it has had only four active leaders: Chesterton himself, whose only titles are Founder and Policy Director; W. Austen Brooks, the full-bearded son of the Editor of *Truth;* D. S. Fraser Harris, the League's current Chairman; and Leslie Margaret Campbell Greene, a relative of both Graham Greene and Sir Hugh Carleton Greene (Director-General of the B.B.C.). Miss Greene is now married to an American, Richard B. von Goetz, who is also a member of the Empire Loyalists.

To all members, the League was a respectable base from which they could oppose the more liberal tendencies of post-war Governments. Although this situation has changed, the League seemed to be

* One source of recruits was the late Duke of Bedford's British People's Party. This organization was founded in 1939 by John Beckett, an ex-BUF, who first achieved notoriety in 1930 when as an MP he stole the Mace from the House of Commons (the Serjeant-at-Arms stopped him at the door). Beckett founded three other political parties as well, all of which were short-lived: the National Freedom Rally – which was loosely associated with the BPP, the British Council for Christian Settlement in Europe (q.v.), and the National Socialist League (q.v.).

The aims of the British People's Party were best reflected in the character of the Duke of Bedford, the Party's Chairman. He was, all at the same time, a pacifist, an appeaser (he wrote pro-Hitler articles in *Peace News* before the war), a Social Crediter, a 'Christian Socialist' (after breaking with the Church of England), and an anti-Semite. Some of his associates in the Party were: Admiral Sir Barry Domvile, the founder of the pro-Nazi 'Link'; H. St John P. Philby, the Middle East expert, father of 'Kim' Philby, and BPP candidate for Hythe in 1939; and Laurence Housman, a pacifist. The Party was never well-received by the public and died with the Duke in 1953.

During his later life, the Duke was also the Major financial benefactor of the United Socialist Movement, a Glasgow-based sect with similar views as the Duke's. Its founder was Guy A. Aldred, for many years the Editor of the Movement's paper, *The Word* ('To rouse the people, combat fascism, and to speed Commonweal'). Aldred died in 1963 but his organization continues on, still committed to its late leader's vague policies of anarchy and 'Social Revolution'. Two anarchists in particular, Rudolph Rocker and Emile Armand, were frequent contributors to *The Word.* Aldred himself was a prolific writer. Among his many works are: *Socialism and the Pope* and *Armageddon Incorporated: the True Story of the Jehovah Witnesses.*

– at least for the first four years of its existence – a natural haven for the less sophisticated right-wing Tory reactionaries.

The aims of the League have always been quite clear. Their literature lists seven primary objectives but they can be reduced to three essential points. First, the League believes that the sovereignty of Britain should be maintained at all costs. Any tendency towards world government or international alliances that requires a partial relinquishing of British sovereignty is an anathema to the League. The UN, NATO, SEATO, CENTO, and the Common Market are all 'monster plots to rob Britain of her independence and strength.' According to Austen Brooks, these alliances are 'international cabals' capable of destroying British sovereignty. Possession of the Bomb is considered by him as absolutely necessary to ensure the maintenance of Britain as one of the world's strongest powers. The Empire Loyalists are opposed to American influence in Britain because its immense wealth and power have robbed England of the power and independence she might otherwise have. Their opposition to Communism is total but, at times, this message is lost in their enthusiasm to rid their country of 'Yankee domination'. What the Empire Loyalists would really like to see is Britain return to her 19th-century position of strength where few nations ever dared question her authority.

Second, and complementary to the first point, the League believes that, instead of liquidating her Empire, Britain should continue to build one along the lines of Rhodes and the old East India Company. Loyalists are aghast at the thought that Britain is now 'throwing away' her colonies. They have never reconciled themselves to the rise of nationalism, be it black, brown, or yellow. They cannot believe that Kenya, the Rhodesias, Tanganyika, or any other British colony for that fact, are able to govern themselves properly without the white-man in control. Nationalism has always meant to them a selfish craving for power by a few foreign extremists who want to turn those countries back on the road to savagery and nihilism for their own ends. What makes Loyalists furious is the thought that this nationalism is being encouraged by 'an incredibly naïve and uninformed Colonial Office.' Austen Brooks again expressed League feelings succinctly. He said to me, 'This business of handing over Africa to the black man is as much a betrayal of the blacks as it is of the whites. There is no evidence that the black man is capable of governing a modern state in the Nuclear Age.' All that the white settlers have done in Africa and Asia is seen going for naught as the black, brown, or yellow man selfishly claims such achievements as his own. Whitehall, added Brooks, is betraying its own country in its rush to break up the Empire under the pressure from 'public opinion.'

The third major point concerns coloured immigration. The League, similar to Mosley, Bean and Jordan, is concerned over the number of coloured people that are living in Britain. Despite the fact that the Commonwealth Immigration Act of 1962 has substantially reduced the influx of immigrants, the Empire Loyalists, along with these other groups, continue to raise their voices in opposition to these foreigners. 'England is a white country', says Brooks, 'and should remain one. A large influx of people of alien culture just aggravates our problems. Everyone talks about integration but where do you see it? Nowhere. It doesn't exist. I do not feel that 800,000 coloured people can be assimilated into our society.'

Emanating from these three official points of policy are lesser aims of an unofficial nature. For instance, the desire to re-create the England of yesterday has turned many members into absolute Monarchists. These people feel that the present governmental structure should be altered so that the Monarch would have the powers to rule as 'implicit in our Constitution.' It is not clear exactly at what point in English Constitutional history the ideal power relationship between Monarch and Parliament existed. Apparently it lies somewhere between the reigns of Kings Henry VIII and Charles I. Nevertheless, they would like to see the monarch rule *in fact.* Many Loyalists believe the Crown should have the actual power to appoint or remove Minsters, rather than perform the function as it does today under advice from the Prime Minster.

Most Loyalists feel that the present party structure is too confining, with its strict discipline and centralized power. They would like to see the individual MP given more freedom of action and expression. Rather than have the MPs responsible solely to an 'oligarchic cabal' in Smith Square, they feel that they should be directly responsible to the Crown. Loyalists see the present party system in such shambles that it is incapable of producing a decent Prime Minister. Harold Macmillan, for instance, is considered by many Loyalists to have been one of the worst Prime Ministers Britain ever produced. During his term of office, *Candour* suggested many ways in which he might be removed from 10 Downing Street. Some of them were: 'To the gallows with Macmillan' and 'Empire Loyalists say "Hang him!"'

The League is not a political party*; rather, it considers itself primarily a right-wing pressure group. Because it cannot benefit from

* However, the League still contests elections sporadically. In 1957, Miss Greene stood as an Independent Loyalist in the North Lewisham by-election. She received less than 2,000 votes and lost her deposit. In the 1964 General Election, the League was even less successful: three Independent Loyalist candidates together could muster only 1,046 votes.

the free publicity given to participants in elections, and because it eschews violence as a means of attracting attention to itself, it has developed a technique of using what its members call 'unorthodox methods' to put its message across to the public. Loyalists believe that if they can invade an opposition function and heckle the speakers, such as they did with Macmillan and U Thant, they may influence a few people in the audience who are the type of people they want converted to their cause. They feel that if they can sufficiently embarrass, confuse, and irritate their opponents, the resultant publicity eventually will swing a large section of the public over to their point of view.

Some of their efforts have made history. On one occasion, for instance, a few Loyalists dressed up as bishops and Orthodox clergy and invaded the 1958 Lambeth Conference to express their displeasure over what they called the Church's 'fawning behaviour' before Archbishop Makarios. Austen Brooks, the image of a cleric with his flowing beard and pendant pectoral cross, began the League's assault with an unscheduled 'My Lords, Bishops and Spiritual Guests . . .' speech that most of the visitors thought was part of the Conference. His denunciation of Makarios (who was not present) brought thunderous cheers from the prelates who, upon completion of his impromptu speech, surged forward to congratulate him. By this time, the Church of England hierarchy began to realize that this was slightly more than mere trifling un-ecumenical noises from the lower clerical orders. Brooks and the rest of his 'bishops' were dragged by their cassocks from the hall.

On another occasion, the League voiced a quiet disapproval of the United Nations. A small ceremony was held in 1958 at the Tower of London to raise the UN flag symbolically over all of England. As the blue banner fluttered to the top of the flagpole, a Loyalist, dressed as an ordinary seaman, stepped forward and promptly pulled it down again and ran the Union Jack up in its place. The dignitaries were not certain whether this was part of the show; in any event, no complaints were made.

The League has spent most of its time seeking publicity in this manner. For instance, being pro-Bomb, they made a habit of harassing the Aldermaston marches – posting themselves along the line of march with anti-CND posters, the most common of which said 'Empire Loyalists say keep Britain's Bomb!' On other occasions, the League could be more subtle. During an anti-Apartheid march in the autumn of 1963, for instance, the League carried a banner proclaiming: 'Remember Cato Manor where the police were hacked to pieces!' Eventually, the anti-Apartheid marchers realized the uncomplimentary nature of the statement and the LEL banner-carriers were forced to flee amid screams of laughter and snorts of rage.

At one time during their brief history, the members of the League beamed their message to the nation over a 'pirate' radio station. They would cut into the end of a regularly scheduled BBC programme and explain their policies in hurried and garbled phrases. This operation ceased after a few months' trial because of the efficiency with which Scotland Yard could trace the source of the pirate broadcasts. In due course, however, (and according to Austen Brooks, quite incidentally) the use of the pirate transmitter was lost to the League because the owner resigned from the organization.

In the short span of four years, the Empire Loyalists had earned themselves the reputation as the political scene's most effective nuisance. They would heckle unmercifully the more liberal British politicians such as Iain Macleod, Michael Foot, Barbara Castle and Harold Macmillan. Their well-timed interruptions could send many politicians into fits of pique at their audacity. They were equally adept at harassing the pacifist leaders as well. For instance, in 1961, the Rev. Michael Scott chose to go to gaol rather than pay a one pound fine that was the result of his participation in a minor disturbance by the Committee of 100. To the intense annoyance of both Scott and the Committee, the League paid the fine in order 'to prevent his enjoying a second spell of martyrdom.'

Yet the very successes of the Empire Loyalists proved to be their undoing. Before 1956, Chesterton and his League were of little interest to Britons. To those who were aware of their existence, the League appeared to be a haven for right-wing reactionaries and sentimental old cranks. League policies seemed so quaint that they were written off as harmless by the major party politicians. It was felt that as long as this type of person existed, it was best to have him and his friends all under one roof so that they could be watched.

By 1958, however, it was apparent that no one was watching too closely. The success of their public actions had brought them the publicity they were seeking. It also brought them a small wave of supporters. The League's jingoistic programme had successfully reached the consciousness of many right-wing individuals in the nation. Because most of the new members came from the Conservative Party or its fringes, the situation became intolerable to the Tory hierarchy in Smith Square and Whitehall. The Party were faced with the situation of having, on the one hand, its front-bench Ministers being heckled by the intrepid Empire Loyalists, and on the other hand, of having many of its back-bench MPs, rank-and-file faithful, and Party contributors in open sympathy with this group. The amount of sympathy for the League from within the Tory Party was never so great as to be even a minor threat to Party unity; nevertheless, it was exceedingly annoying to many that such a situation existed.

The explosion between the League and the Tories actually occured during the Conservative Party Conference in Blackpool in 1958; The Loyalists had become so over-confident with their past two years' successes that they invaded the Conference headquarters in force to heckle the main speaker, Prime Minister Macmillan. They very nearly succeeded in breaking up the meeting. Hardly had the Prime Minister begun to speak before the Loyalists went into action: blowing bugles, shouting down the words of Mr Macmillan, and arguing with the more moderate Tories around them. Conservative Party patience finally snapped at this moment, and the stewards were ordered to clear the hall of the offending Loyalists. Those who escaped with a black eye or a swollen jaw were fortunate. One Empire Loyalist was beaten unconscious in the corridors.

Ever since that time, the Conservative Party has not been amused by Loyalist antics. Pressure was applied to many sympathetic members either to leave the League or to face the political consequences. By the end of that year, continued association with the Empire Loyalists meant political death to any Tory who still had political ambitions left. Members began to fade as fast as they had joined.

From that moment on, the League of Empire Loyalists has been in decline. The fall in memberships, begun at that time, has never recovered; the slight influence they ever exerted over the reactionary elements was lost; and the respectable label of the League was replaced by the brand of an outcast. Although flashes of the inspired heckling of old would now and then find their way into the news, more often than not the reports reflected an increasing shrillness in their attacks. Their interruptions at functions, such as those reported at the lunch given for U Thant, became more of an affront to all political sensibilities and less of an attempt to embarrass through barbed criticism. The backlog of sympathy in the ranks of the reactionaries began to fade as the less-inspired attacks by the League lapsed into tasteless exhibitionalism.

This fall from grace also coincided with the establishment of The Freedom Group, a conservative organization run by an ambitious ex-Liberal named Edward Martell (see next chapter). This group had, from its inception, all the ear-marks of respectability. Many ex-members of the Empire Loyalists saw the opportunity to continue the promotion of their ideas under a more sophisticated banner and switched their allegiance to Martell. If any of these men stayed in the League of Empire Loyalists, they did so surreptitiously. Martell inherited some of the right-wing people who did not wish to offend the Conservative Party whips, as well as those other ex-members who, if they were not Tories, did not wish to be associated with a discredited organization. Chesterton and his Loyalists were left with a small band of reactionaries who were not particularly concerned about such fine points. From a group of several thousand strong in 1958, the League has been reduced in size to an estimated 100 individuals in Britain at present. There are perhaps an additional 100 members throughout the rest of the world.

As is almost always the case in a crisis of this sort, the League at that time was plagued by internal schisms. Besides having many of its members leave to join Martell's group, Chesterton found that competitors were springing up with alarming rapidity. Major General Richard Hilton resigned to form his Patriotic Party; R. C. Gleaves left to form his Greater Britain Campaign; and Peter Godfrey-Bartram resigned to organize his Heritage Party.*

One of the primary reasons why there was such a quick exit of members from the League was the increasing indication that the character of the organization was predominantly anti-Semitic. This charge had been levelled at Chesterton and a few of his followers ever since the League was founded, primarily because some of the original members, including Chesterton, had been associated with Mosley in the British Union of Fascists. The suspicion that the League was anti-Semitic, however, never reached the public consciousness until the newspapers began to take an interest in its affairs. The publicity, which the Loyalists so assiduously had sought, inevitably brought them under close scrutiny and criticism from the Press. The speculation alone – on the possibility of the League being anti-Semitic – was enough to convince many members that the time had come to resign.

Chesterton and Brooks deny that they or their organization are anti-Semitic. Any direct accusation of that nature will find the accused and the accuser face-to-face in court. They have become very sensitive to criticism since their fall from grace. Brooks pointed out to me that the Empire Loyalists have never sanctioned prejudice of this sort. What individual members think is one thing, but such thoughts, he added, have never become part of the League's policy. There seems to be some basis of fact in this statement since many

* Godfrey-Bartram's Party was still-born. The only report ever received on Gleaves' organization was from *The Daily Telegraph* (24.4.62) when his Campaign held a sparsely-attended anti-CND rally in Trafalgar Square: ' "You are here to keep Britain great," [Gleaves] said [to the small crowd]. "We are here to feed the pigeons," said a disgruntled voice'; since that moment, nothing has been reported on either Gleaves or his Campaign. Hilton's Party is the only one that has survived. Today, its sole function is to contest the seats of the more liberal Cabinet Ministers and MPs (with whom it does not agree) in every General Election. So far, Hilton has not been successful.

openly racist members of the organization have been purged in the past.* Nevertheless, the feelings still persists today that the Empire Loyalists are anti-Jewish.

One of the reasons it persists is the peculiar distinction Brooks, for one, makes between some Jews and other Jews. When I asked him his reaction to the general charge of anti-Semitism levelled against his group, he pulled out the Little Oxford Dictionary and looked up 'anti-Semitism' and quoted the definition to me as being: 'Opposing Jewish influence in politics, etc.' He went on to say: 'If opposition to Jews in politics is anti-Semitic, then we are anti-Semitic. But we are not anti-Semitic in the sense of being opposed to Jews as Jews'. Brooks went on to say that he is just as opposed to Protestants and Catholics if they believe in 'internationalism'.

During my interview with Brooks, the League's pretty secretary, Avril Walters, who was typing behind her desk at the far end of the room, would occasionally leap from her seat and shout 'Hear, Hear!' at whatever statement of Brooks' pleased her. She would stab in the air with a long black cigarette holder for emphasis; then would sit down again and quietly resume her typing.

Another reason why there are allegations of anti-Semitism is the nature of the material to be found in *Candour*. This newspaper seems to have two major pre-occupations, the first of which is an obsession with Jewish financial power. According to *Candour,* this Jewish financial power is so great that it transcends local boundaries to become an international threat to Western Civilization. In some inexplicable way, Jewish money, Wall Street, The City, and the Kremlin are all linked together in a common conspiracy bent on dominating the world. How this actually works is not clear, but the syllogism usually runs as follows: The money powers in New York and London are predominately Jewish; the United States is actually run by a 'secret government in New York'[3]; British Jews financed the Bolshevik revolution; therefore, the Western money powers are sympathetic to Communism, and are in secret alliance with them to destroy Western civilization. Quoting at random from *Candour:*

> There are some readers who have still to be convinced that the dominant Money Power is to be recognized as a supranational body operating from New York, holding absolute sway over Washington and working closely with Moscow . . . We have produced abundant evidence in support of our contention that such a cabal exists . . .[4]

* Including, among others, Colin Jordan of the National Socialist Movement, who resigned because the League refused to accept his motion to exclude Negroes and Jews from membership; and John Bean, leader of the British National Party, who was expelled for trying to start his own party while still a member of the LEL.

> [The Jew] it is who is the perennial law-breaker, the eternal sower of discord among the nations. The responsibilitiy of the Gentile, in the main, is to secure control over the actions of his own fifth columnists, who cringe at the feet of Jewry and hasten to do its bidding.[5]

The newspaper's second pre-occupation is with the colour question. Because *Candour* writes so much on this subject – be it concerning Britain or South Africa – the League is naturally accused of being racist. One point on which the League will not disagree with anyone is its official pledge to '. . . protect the European character of British stock against floods of coloured immigrants.'[6] Although this presumably refers only to Britain, the policy is extended to include the acceptance of Apartheid in Africa. Negroes there should be walled off from their white neighbours to live their own separate lives; and according to the Loyalists, Negroes in Britain should be sent home to join them for the same reason. When I mentioned to Brooks that this sounded like intolerance to me, he said, on the contrary, it was not intolerance or prejudice but simply common sense.

Candour puts the blame for this state of affairs as well on the Jews:

> The Jewish interest in the business of nation-smashing and race-mixing is manifold . . . most ominous of all, there is the belief that if nations and races can be progressively obliterated, there will die in the Gentile spirit that survival sense which might otherwise resist Jewish world domination.[7]

> Financial Jewry, with the Western European empires out of the way, will ruthlessly attack European nationalism everywhere, and allow nothing to stand in the way of the foul programme of racial integration which it has devised for the enslavement of mankind[8]

If allegations of intolerance and increasing opposition to League activities were not enough to deter the future growth of the Loyalists, one development has arisen that could spell the end of the organization altogether. In April, 1961, the chief financial benefactor of the Empire Loyalists, Robert Key Jeffrey, died in Chile at the age of 91. Jeffrey was an expatriate Englishman who made a fortune mining nitrates in Chile. For most of his later life he lived as a recluse on a remote estate on the Chilean-Argentine border. He was famous for his personal eccentricities, the most noted of which was his dietary régime. This consisted mainly of a staple diet of walnuts, porridge, and salads. He is supposed to have kept his bathtubs full of walnuts against a possible shortage.

In seven years, Jeffrey contributed approximately £70,000 to the

League. For an organization of such relatively small size, this kind of benefaction put it in the wealthy class of fringe groups. Two years before his death, Jeffrey made Chesterton his only heir to a fortune estimated at a quarter of a million pounds. However, fifteen hours before he died, he made a new will, signed only with his thumb-print, that did not mention Chesterton. This thumb-print will left the entire estate to his long-time nurse who claimed to be his daughter. Chesterton was slightly dismayed at this development and dispatched a trusted Loyalist to Chile to fight the will in court. After three years, a Chilean court decided that the thumb-print will was legitimate and awarded the fortune to Jeffrey's nurse. The League, however, has not given up; it claims it plans to continue the legal fight.

The trickle of contributions to the League since Jeffrey's death has not been able to support League activities in the manner in which it was accustomed. Only Brooks and the League Secretary, Avril Walters, are still paid full-time. The few branch offices are now run on a voluntary basis. It was *Candour,* however, that suffered the most since it was the League's most expensive operation. Soon after the funds stopped flowing in from Chile, the paper was being published as an 'Interim Report'. Most of this is being financed by Chesterton personally. Chesterton has gone to great lengths to keep his paper alive, for he knows that the League would cease to exist without it.

Finances became such a serious matter by 1963 that Chesterton sent Austen Brooks to the United States in a last-gasp effort to raise money. While in America, Brooks appealed to as many potential sympathizers as he could find. Among those he saw were Gerald L. K. Smith ('A thoughtful Christian gentleman'), General Edwin A. Walker, Dan Smoot, and Senators Eastland, Holland, Talmadge and Thurmond. On the whole, his appeals went unheeded and the few contributions he received barely covered the cost of his trip. While in New York, Brooks was quoted as saying: 'The same rule applies on both sides of the Atlantic – that, with few exceptions, the more money people have the less ready they are to give any significant help to those fighting to save Western civilization.' One local American millionaire was heard to retort: 'If the British people won't find the money for *Candour,* they don't deserve to have it!'

The future of the League looks just as bleak. If they are ever awarded the money from Jeffrey's will, they will remain a part of the political scene for some time to come as a Victorian-oriented anachronism. *Candour* may flourish again – its pages probably becoming more hysterical with time. But no amount of money can return the League to its brief days of glory in 1958. The majority of former members realized that, no matter how much they detested what was going on in the world around them, they had to make some adjustment to it. The few Loyalists who are left – Chesterton, Brooks, Greene and the others – still have never been able to come to terms with the 20th century. England's fall from pre-eminence, the apparent 'mongrelization' of the British stock, the rise in selfish nationalism, and the 'sell-out' by Whitehall are all aspects of contemporary life that are so repugnant and wrong to a Loyalist that they see the whole world trembling on the brink of ruin. The only way Britain can be saved from this chaos is for her to renounce the new and untried methods and re-apply the solutions that worked so well in her Golden Age. Until she does that, the League feels that whatever values, standards, achievements and power that England can still claim as her own, is soon to be drowned in a vortex of alien greed and evil. Much in the manner of Edward Martell and his Freedom Group, the successor to the League as the foremost proponent of right-wing Conservative thought in Britain, Chesterton long ago came to the conclusion that the 20th century was 'an absolutely dreadful age'.[9]

1. *The Times*, July 6, 1962.
2. *Oswald Mosley, Portrait of a Leader*, by A. K. Chesterton, 1936.
3. *Candour* Interim Report, June 1963, p. 3.
4. *Candour*, April 14, 1961, p. 113.
5. *Candour*, April 21, 1961, p. 122.
6. LEL policy statement and application form. (undated).
7. *Candour*, January 13, 1961, p. 9.
8. *Candour*, February 10, 1961, p. 42.
9. *Candour* Interim Report, June 1963. p. 7.

4 The Freedom Group

'When our membership reaches one million, then perhaps the Conservative Party will listen to us!'

EDWARD MARTELL

As the left wing in Great Britain has its militant anti-capitalist groups, all vying with one another for the privilege of precipitating the destruction of capitalism, so the right-wing has its own militant anti-Socialist groups all bent not only on halting and ultimately destroying the 'leftward drift' of the nation but, in addition, encouraging the growth of private initiative and enterprise. The most noted of these organizations, as it is constituted today, is the Freedom Group which has been active on the British political scene, in one form or another, since 1955.

The Freedom Group has many advantages over its Socialist counterparts: by fringe group standards, it has a huge membership (estimated at 190,000 in February 1965 and climbing at the rate of approximately 1,000 per week); its members are unusually loyal and once in tend to stay in; it is a wealthy and efficient organization; it has virtually no competitors in its field; its objectives are clear-cut; and, above all, it is considered to be respectable.

The man most responsible for the formation and growth of the Freedom Group is its Chairman, Edward Drewett Martell, at 56 (1965) the driving spirit behind all the Group's multifarious activities. He is physically a small man, heavy set, with blue eyes, black slanting eyebrows, thinning white hair swept straight back, and a mouth set in a permanent goblin's grin. He has a penchant for baggy suits, he walks at a trot, and he eats his meals as if they were wasting his time. Full of energy, constantly talking, always hospitable, he gives the impression of high-speed self-confidence – obviously a man who loves to tangle with difficult problems and all manner of adversaries. He is a Methodist, a non-smoker, a teetotaller, and an excellent snooker player.[1] He is no relation to the brandy family.

Martell began work at the age of 16 in his father's coal business but moved on two years later to Fleet Street where he was to spend the next ten years of his life. He worked for a variety of organizations: the *Saturday Review, World's Press News, Burke's Peerage,* and then for the sports section of the old London evening *Star*. When war broke out in Europe, he joined the Royal Armoured Corps where he attained the rank of Captain. He never went overseas but spent most of the war years printing Army leaflets on War Office presses.

After the war, he started a chain of bookshops, called Everybody's Bookshops. It was a flourishing business but, with the increase of his other activities, he liquidated all the stores save one in Baker Street (renamed the Baker Street Bookshop) which he has retained, he says, because of his love of Sherlock Holmes stories.* At the same time, he became involved in the political activities of the Liberal Party of which he was a member at the time. He stood as a Liberal candidate in the 1946 by-election at Rotherhithe and was placed second behind the Labour Party candidate. He stood again in the 1950 General Election at North Hendon, this time coming third out of four candidates, but saving his deposit. In the slack years, he turned his attention to raising money for the Party, for which he showed surprising ability. However, as the Liberal Party moved leftwards, Martell became alienated and eventually resigned in 1951. For the next three years, Martell was, in his own words, 'in the political wilderness'. By this time, he realised that his personal political creed was more in tune with the Conservative Party's philosophy. He altered his allegiance accordingly, although he did not formally join the Conservative Party until 1963.

It was in 1954 that Martell's organizational and publicity-making genius first became apparent when he organized 'The Winston Churchill 80th Birthday Fund'. Through his recently acquired newspaper, the *Recorder,* he advertised for donations: over 300,000 people responded. They contributed a total of £259,000 some of which was presented to Sir Winston Churchill himself in the form of a cheque, and the remainder of which was split among various Churchill interests such as Bristol University, the Churchill House for the Elderly, and Churchill College, Cambridge. 'The whole business', said Martell, 'had to be above suspicion. There were never less than two people opening an envelope.'[2]

Freedom Group activities actually began in 1955 with the establishment of a small organization called the Free Press Society. The name 'Freedom Group', however, was not adopted until 1963 after five additional organizations had been founded by Martell: The People's League for the Defence of Freedom, founded in 1956; the Anti-Socialist Front, founded in 1958; the *New Daily,* founded in 1960; the National Fellowship, founded in 1962; and finally three limited liability printing establishments known respectively as Tileyard Press Ltd. (authorised Capital: £500,000), Sapphire Press Ltd. (authorised Capital £160,000), and Westbourne Press Ltd. (authorised Capital £2,000) which are known collectively as 'the printing shops'. The

* Sherlock Holmes lived at 221b Baker Street.

term 'Freedom Group' is an umbrella name for all these six organizations together.

Membership in any of the specific organizations (with the exception of the *New Daily* and the printing shops which have no 'membership') entitles a person to belong to the Freedom Group. A member need not, however, subscribe to all Freedom Group policies, only those of the group or groups within it that he has joined. On the other hand, a person can join the Freedom Group as such, subscribing to the policies of all the organizations under the umbrella. Membership requirements are nothing more than filling out a form, indicating a willingness to work part-time for the organization when called upon and, in some cases, contributing money as well.

According to its literature:

> The Freedom Group is loyal to the Crown, asserts the independence of Great Britain and the Commonwealth, and holds firmly to the belief that Britain's right to world leadership has not yet been superseded. It advocates a return by the nation to Christian principles, upholds integrity in public and private life, and condemns expediency.
>
> It is anti-Communist and anti-Fascist, and also anti-Labour until the Labour Party discards in its entirely nationalization, government by rigid control and the undemocratic block vote by the unions. It not only opposes nationalization, but also State interference in industry and commerce. It upholds the individual and advocates free enterprise. It resists to the limit the tendency of the trade unions to become a State within a State. It exposes and fights monopolies and restrictive practices on both sides of industry. It advocates a return to belief in the personal responsibility of all citizens in good health, and the restoration to parents of the care and upbringing of their children. It advocates equality of opportunity, opposes the excesses of bureaucracy, fights high taxation and advocates limiting the social services to those who need them by bringing all State aid for the fit, but lazy and indolent, to an end.
>
> The Freedom Group has no plans for developing into a new political party. To do so would be to risk splitting the anti-Socialist vote. It sees itself rather as a watchdog and ginger group, working to influence the Conservative Party to return to first principles, and calling upon it to abandon its tendencies towards a form of pink Socialism.[3]

To complement the broad statement of aims above, the Freedom Group also provides its members with a policy primer called *A Book of Solutions,* written by Martell, which lists proposed remedies for

191 'problems of the day'. Originally the book was issued exclusively to members of the National Fellowship, but is now obtainable by the Group as a whole. In addition to the book, the Group issues a General Election Policy that concentrates on immediate electoral problems of the day, and which can be found from time to time in the *New Daily,* particularly around election time. Both are the foundations upon which the Freedom Group policies are built.

The 191 solutions cover a wide variety of subjects and, on balance, are considered by most people to be level-headed suggestions:

> If it is permissible for such a ruthless dictatorship as Communist Russia to be a member of the United Nations Organization, there can be no logical or legitimate reason why Communist China should not be allowed to join. [p. 24]
>
> It should be compulsory for all new cars to be fitted with anti-dazzle yellow headlights, as in France. [p. 55]
>
> A decimal system should be introduced at once based on ten pennies to the shilling with ten shillings as the chief money unit instead of the pound. [p. 72]
>
> There should be no restrictions of any sort on broadcasting hours. If people do not want to listen or watch they have only to switch it off. [p. 86]
>
> The present Covent Garden fruit and vegetable market should be closed down . . . The Market should either be re-sited in a more suitable spot – The South Bank, for instance, is a possibility – or preferably London should have a number of area fruit and vegetable markets. [p. 90]
>
> The death penalty should be abolished . . . [p. 96]
>
> Stripes at Zebra Crossings should run the other way. [p. 102]

According to Martell, the critics of the Freedom Group policies in general and his 'solutions' in particular fall into three categories: the left-wing of the Labour Party, trade union leaders, and the left-wing of the Conservative Party. Martell claims that these groups single out only those 'solutions' which seem contentious to them. There are two in particular which seem to annoy the left-wing groups more than any other. The first is called 'Voting Tests' and reads in full:

> Nobody should be eligible for inclusion on the Electoral Register unless he or she is able to pass a simple test. This would simply consist of giving his or her name and address, the name of the Member of Parliament for the division and his Party, the name of the Prime Minister, the name of the Leader of the Opposition, and of the President of the United States of America.

Those who have insufficient knowledge to give the answers to such simple questions are unfit to play any part in choosing the Government which is to run the country.

One critic, Anthony Wedgwood Benn – the former Viscount Stansgate, Postmaster General in the current Labour Government and an old Martell foe – refers to this policy as nothing more than an intelligence test.[4] Other critics, perhaps not so politely, occasionally call it 'an intellectual poll tax'. Martell, however, feels such minimum standards are necessary if the British democratic system is to function properly.

The other policy to which his enemies seem to take exception is his proposal to reform the trade unions. It is a nine-point programme and perhaps is the cornerstone and main *raison d'être* of the Freedom Group. Martell would like to see a Royal Commission established to enquire into the causes of industrial disputes; the closed shop, he feels, should be illegal; picketing should be restricted; and the practice of 'contracting out' should be replaced by 'contracting in'. In addition, he feels that trade unions should not have the power to expel a member if he refuses to disclose his earnings; that restrictive practices should be declared illegal; that agitators deliberately fostering strikes should be liable to charges of conspiracy; that all legal privileges of the unions should be brought to an end; and that strikes themselves should be illegal except where the majority of workers involved are in favour of one.

Martell says that labour unions have been 'Sacred Cows' in Britain for too long and that any criticism of them has been received in the past with embarrassed silence by the Conservative Party and by cries of 'Fascism' from his left-wing opponents. Yet, he points out, a significant number of influential publications are slowly swinging over to his point of view, including among others: the *Daily Telegraph,* the *Yorkshire Post,* and, in a qualified way, *The Sunday Times, The Times* and the *Economist.*

Martell adds that his critics never mention those Freedom Group policies with which they agree, in particular, the policies of advocating top-level salaries for Ministers (for the Prime Minister: £50,000; the Chancellor of the Exchequer, £40,000; etc.), of abolishing the 11-plus examination, of restricting the ownership in monopolies, of excluding ex-criminals from jury rosters, and the policy of restricting the building of office blocks until basic housing needs have been met. He says that if his critics are not concerned with his contentious policies particularly those on trade union reform and voting tests, they tend to single out those aspects which amuse them: for example, the suggestion that schoolgirls learn judo for self-protection and that diplomatic relations be broken with states still practising slavery.

Martell, however, is familiar with criticism and pays scant attention to it. He is convinced that he is on the proper course and that his critics should not be concerned about Freedom Group policies but their own. In response to Anthony Wedgwood Benn's accusation that Freedom Group policies could lead to Fascism, Martell replied:

> If Mr Benn would face reality he would know that most Fascist tendancies are on the left these days. The dictatorships of the Soviet Union, Albania, Bulgaria, Czechoslovakia, East Germany, Hungary, Poland, Rumania, China, North Korea, North Vietnam, Yugoslavia, and Cuba, controlling the lives of over 1,000 million people, are all left-wing. Less than 25 per cent of the total come under the right-wing dictatorships of South Africa, Portugal, Spain, Taiwan, South Vietnam, South Korea, Pakistan, Saudi Arabia, and Sudan. We deplore all dictatorships whether of Left or Right. Mr Benn and his friends are apt to be soft to those on the Left. Why?[5]

Unlike the left wing, Martell is convinced that the world is turning right – 'back to eternal values' – and will eventually repudiate leftish ideas that, he says, are unsuitable for the future. He accepts the term 'radical right' as a description of the Freedom Group's position because, he says, the Group's place in the political spectrum is to the right of the Conservative Party, and that it is advocating radical reform in order that the Party return to the 'basic conceps' of individual freedom, enterprise, and initiative. The Conservative Party, he declares, has strayed off its ideological path and has come to the point of doing nothing more than preserving the *status quo* as it finds it. He points to history as an example: when the Labour Party held office from 1945 to 1951, he claims it pushed the country left – with nationalization, special treatment for the trade unions, 'suffocating' bureaucracy, etc. – and he says it will continue to do so every time it takes office. When the Tory Party took over in 1951, he continued, it did not take the country back to 'first principles' but preserved the country as it found it when the Labour Party left office. This, he says, is wrong; the Conservative Party should reject those alien ideas of Labour Party Socialism and replace them with the basic Conservative Party philosophy. Otherwise, the drift of the country will be steadily left as each Labour Party Government comes to power, only to be 'wrongly' preserved by the next Conservative Party administration. The basic concepts to which he feels the Conservative Party should return are, in fact, those policies which are outlined in the *Book of Solutions*.

*   *   *

The six organizations comprising the Freedom Group all have specific functions independent of the others yet, at the same time, all of them are mutually complementary. They all bear the stamp of Edward Martell's organizational and publicity-making abilities as well as his own personal philosophy. The oldest of the six is the Free Press Society which was established in 1955 to 'safeguard the freedom of the Press and prove to the powerful printing trade unions that they alone (as they believe should be the case)* do not possess the right to run printing machinery'. It grew out of a seven-week press strike in 1955 which Martell, as owner of a press, defied. Despite pressure from the unions, he kept his non-union workers on the job and his presses running full-time. While all the other newspapers were shut down, Martell brought out the *Daily Special* of which he was able to sell 70,000 copies a day to the news-hungry public in and around the London area. This strike marked the beginning of a public coolness between Martell and the printing unions that has lasted up to the present day. Since that time, the unions have periodically pulled their men out of his shops, they have tried to boycott his newspaper, and they have even tried intimidating his employees. None of these tactics, however, has ever been successful primarily because working conditions, pay, and benefits in his three printing shops are generally better than those found in most union shops.

Martell believes that no man should be forced to join a union to get a job. He makes it his policy to hire good men, regardless of background, colour, or whether or not they belong to a union. Martell says that the choice of joining a union is a private one for each individual alone to make and should not be a prerequisite for holding a job. All his men are free to join whatever union they like, but few do.

Originally, the Free Press Society was the name under which his major propaganda organs, the *Recorder* and the *New Daily,* were published. However, it became a separate entity in 1963 at the formation of the Freedom Group proper. The function of the FPS today is to foster freedom within the printing trade and to attempt to break the apparent domination of the printing business by trade unions. Its primary function today is to offer its services to the public at large as a freelance printer during a strike. For instance, it printed over 20 journals during the 1956 printing strike and over 60 journals during the 1959 Press strike. Among those journals printed were *The Listener* for the BBC, *TV Times* for ITA, the *British Medical Journal,* and the *Pharmaceutical Journal.*

The three printing shops: Tileyard Press near Kings Cross (also the site of the Group's headquarters), Sapphire Press in Stoke New-

* Original brackets.

ington, and Westbourne Press in Brighton are the only public companies within the Freedom Group and are the only official sources of the Group's financial structure. Whether the presses are actually subsidized by donations from members is not known, but Martell claims they make money. Only 14 months after becoming a public company, for instance, Tileyard Press Ltd. reported net profits of £17,705.

Martell claims that all his presses combined comprise the largest open-house printing works in the country. Besides printing the *New Daily* and *The Recorder,* they turn out a variety of job-shop orders for the general public. However, most of his job-shop work is for the internal consumption of the other groups under the Freedom Group umbrella. Besides printing his own stationery and envelopes, he prints membership cards, Group policy statements, election campaign statements, campaign index cards, constituency index cards, Master Index cards, canvassing cards, referendum sheets, and questionnaires, as well as a bewildering variety of form letters, brochures, pamphlets and donation slips. He has even printed his own private postage stamps in preparation for Post-Office workers' 'go-slows'.

In addition, he prints a limited number of pamphlets of general interest to the public, most of which complement the Group's over-all philosophy. Some of the titles are: *Unnatural Belief* ('How the Profumo Scandal was born'), *ABC of the Common Market,* by Paul Minet (who is the Managing Editor of the *New Daily*), *Stop These Attacks on the Royal Family,* and *Sealed Documents of the Mau Mau Oaths and Ceremonies.*

The *New Daily* ('The only Daily Newspaper in Great Britain independent of combines and Trade Unions') remains his major publishing-printing preoccupation. It is the Group's main propaganda outlet and, without it, Martell would not have the organization he has today. A sixteen-page newspaper, published six days a week, and with a circulation that normally fluctuates between 45,000 and 48,000 per day (it sometimes runs as high as 90,000), the *New Daily* perhaps best reflects the character of the organization as a whole. It splits its news into two distinct categories: general world news and Freedom Group news. The general news tends to be sketchy and to have a flavour of yesterday's scoops about it. Most of the headlines are devoted to trade union activities: 'Rail Pay Talks End at 5 p.c.', 'The Prime Minister and the closed Shop', and 'Liverpool Dock Strike to Continue' are typical examples.

Freedom Group news is particularly stressed, says Martell, to keep his supporters in touch with Group policies and activities. The newspaper demands full reader participation, in keeping with Martell's desire to have as many members as possible take an active part in Group affairs. Around election time, at least two campaigns are being waged at any one given moment and the readers are asked to join in and help. Exhortations such as 'You can Help', 'It is not too late . . .', and 'If you are with us return this form *today*' help to stir up an active sense of purpose in the reader. Before the last General Election, Martell ran a campaign to 'Keep the Socialists Out' and a subsidiary effort to 'Make them Come Clean'. He and his associates also attempted to unseat Harold Wilson himself in his constituency of Huyton*. They were not successful: Wilson tripled his majority. Headlines which accompanied these efforts were considered to be quite original: 'Beware! Wilson is Playing it Oh So Softly Softly' and 'Make Not Victory out of Grim Defeat' are two examples.

The *New Daily* also runs competitions among its readers, some of which are serious ('. . . a definition of National Greatness . . .' suggested by Admiral Sir Reginald Plunkett-Ernle-Erle-Drax, KCB), and some which are not so serious ('Imagine that the current meat crisis has become so acute that the Government has legalized cannibalism. Whom would you choose for your meal and how would you cook him (or her)? . .').

Martell also serializes the Bible in his newspaper because, he says, no one else does and because both he and his supporters wanted some religious content to the paper. He started with Genesis in 1961 and plans to work his way through both Testaments. At this writing he has reached Job: 16, and he estimates that it will take until 1973 to reach Revelation: 22. At that time he will begin on *Pilgrim's Progress*.

The only other propaganda outlet is the *Recorder*, a weekly magazine, over which Martell gained control in 1954. According to the Group's own definition: 'Its contents consist mainly of extracts from the *New Daily* . . . making up a record of current affairs and the Freedom Group's activities'. It has a circulation of 9,000 per week, carries little or no advertising and, therefore, loses money. In fact, neither this weekly nor the daily newspaper make a profit and are subsidized by contributions from the National Fellowship.**

* At one point, David 'Screaming Lord' Sutch, a pop singer, considered standing in Huyton as well. He planned to campaign as the National Teenage Candidate and promised, if elected, to demand legislation making it an offence to victimize anyone with long hair (his hair hangs down to his shoulders) and to secure knighthoods for the Beatles. He was ineligible to stand because he failed to produce in time the necessary £150 election deposit.

** Shortly after the 1964 General Election, Martell increased the price of the *New Daily* from 3d to one shilling, over twice the cost of any other daily paper in Britain. There has also been some speculation that he would like to sell out; so far, there have been no takers.

The National Fellowship is perhaps the most important organization within the Freedom Group. The Fellowship is a 'gathering together of all men and women of goodwill to bring influence to bear upon the Government, and upon the Churches of all denominations, to use the power which is in their possession, and in their possession alone, to restore Britain's greatness by leading a return to sane government and a national morality based upon Christian principles'. On the surface, the National Fellowship is composed of people who are concerned about the current state of political affairs and who are willing to spend their time and money to change it. But, from the start, it has been more than that. In effect, it has been and, to some extent, still is the primary source of Freedom Group funds. Without these wealthy, distinguished and/or titled people (at one point, the Freedom Group letterhead listed 106 Sponsors of the National Fellowship in the left-hand margin on both sides of the Group stationery), Martell would be powerless. In the early days of his organization, before the National Fellowship itself was founded, these powerful men loomed large; but since Freedom Group coffers have subsequently been filled by its large number of members, these donors have tended to take a back seat. Nevertheless, the National Fellowship is still comprised of those men who can afford to provide substantial financial support to Martell when he needs it.

These financial benefactors have been superseded in large part by the Master Index, Martell's semi-secret list of all members who subscribe wholly or in part to Freedom Group activities. At the time of writing, there are over 190,000 names on the list. Martell's goal is to have one million names on it. This list includes both wealthy and non-wealthy supporters all of whom are asked periodically to contribute to either the Freedom Group in general or to the specific organization to which they belong. All appeals take the form of a long letter, some of which run to four pages. With each letter, Martell encloses a return envelope and a donation form. Part of the success he has had with this type of appeal is due to the intimate nature of the letter which frankly lays bare the needs of the Group, explaining why money is needed and how and when it will be used. His psychology seems to work, for he never has been short of financial backing. In fact, Martell claims he can lay his hands on £20,000 to £30,000 worth of donations in less than a fortnight. For instance, during the 1955 Press strike, he appealed for £10,000 to keep the *Recorder* going and quickly amassed £20,000.

Martell claims that all money sent to the Freedom Group is in the form of donations and that no strings are attached. However, in order to raise money to finance his 1964 election campaign, he sent a letter to the wealthier members of the National Fellowship asking that they loan him £2,000 apiece at 10 per cent interest. He said he would back these loans by his 'personal guarantee', that is to say, he would ensure payment out of his own 'resources'. What he meant by that he refuses to disclose, for he is not a wealthy man. Undoubtedly, part of the answer lies in the National Fellowship itself where some of the sponsors, Sir Bernard Docker being one of the better known, are enthusiastic backers of many Martell projects.

One of the sidelights of Martell's legerdemain is the way he can make a profit by doing nothing more than advertising the aims of his organization in the national newspapers and, in the same advertisement, appealing to the public both to join the Freedom Group and to help pay for the advertisement itself. He showed me an example of how he does it. He put an advertisement in *The Times* on May 5, 1964 which cost £525. In less than five weeks time, he had received £522 6s. 6d. in contributions asserting that, in the following three or four weeks, donations would more than cover the cost. He also signed up 164 new members in the process. Confident of the profits he would receive from *The Times,* he then bought space in the *Financial Times* on May 13, 1964 at a cost of £1,550; within three weeks he had signed up 201 new members and had collected £1,875 in donations. He then placed an advertisement in the *Daily Telegraph* on June 11, 1964 (cost: £1,300) and although the returns were too sketchy at the time of my visit, he had signed up 381 new members and had collected well over half of his costs. From past experience, he knows that each advertisement will pay for itself and, in addition, bring both money and new members into the Group. He then was planning to buy space in both the *Daily Mail* and *Sunday Times* before he started the process all over again.

Another way he makes money is by concentrating his appeal on one particular group of people. His Master Index is cross-indexed into economic or social groups, i.e. Stockbrokers, Barristers, Big Business, Kelly's Handbook of Titled Classes, Architects, etc. (he even has one category known as 'Door-to-Door') so that when he wants to write to, say, all 17,000 stockbrokers in Great Britain, he pulls out his files, writes his four-page letters, encloses his donation form, and sends them off. This is particularly effective whenever the Labour Party comes out in print with some truculent statement concerning the economy. His indexing and mailing system is so efficient that his appeal is usually in the hands of his potential donors before the incident has died down.

Martell has been offered £60,000 for his Master Index with its elaborate indexings, cross-indexings, and references, but he has turned down all comers. Although the list is supposed to be secret, many of the names are well known to the public. *Time & Tide,* in a 1963 article on Martell, stated that they checked many of these names to see if they were still current and found that every one of them was genuine. As far as can be ascertained, Martell does not pad the list. Since his organization has grown so quickly, he has no need to.

Another method Martell uses to make money is his 'Readers Dividend' scheme whereby Martell profits from the readability of the advertisements in the *New Daily*. For example, if a house is being advertised for sale in his newspaper and the 'Readers Dividend' is listed at, say, 5 per cent, then the seller of the house refunds to the buyer 5 per cent of the purchase price, which represents, in effect, the cost of the advertisement to the seller. This refund is then split between Martell and the buyer. If the house remains unsold, the advertisement costs the seller nothing, or, if it is sold through any other media it still costs him nothing. But if the paper was responsible for the sale, all parties are pleased: the seller because he sold the house, the buyer because he bought the house and received a refund as well, and Martell because he made some money with no larger an outlay than a few column inches in his newspaper.

The National Fellowship, although only one part of the Freedom Group, perhaps best reflects the type of person who joins the organization. Members are almost exclusively drawn from the more conservative sections of the Tory Party, particularly from the Upper and Upper-Middle classes of society. Many of his supporters are drawn from the fixed-income groups as well – the pensioners, government workers, and the military. Martell inherited many of his early supporters from the League of Empire Loyalists when it began to disintegrate in 1958. Contrary to what some people believe, most of these early converts were not Fascists or near-Fascists, but tended to be those individuals who wanted to cloak their right-wing views in a mantle of respectability. There are, undoubtedly, some Fascists or near-Fascists in the Freedom Group but they are a small minority who have not exerted any influence over the organization to date.

The names most often seen on National Fellowship literature in particular, and on Freedom Group literature in general, are those of both titled persons and ex-military officers; for instance: Sir Adrian Boult; Air Chief Marshal Sir Philip Joubert De La Ferte; Lord Moynihan, OBE, TD (an ex-Liberal like Martell); Viscountess Bertie of Thame; Emily, Lady Coote; The Lady Studd; Captain Henry Kerby, MP; Dr Donald Johnson, MP; and the Earl of Mexborough. The vast majority of names, however, are neither titled nor military. Most members are simply those upper-class people who, for a variety of reasons, find themselves to the right of Conservative Party policies.

* * *

The remaining two organizsations within the Freedom Group are The People's League for the Defence of Freedom, and the Anti-Socialist Front. They, too, have specific functions to perform, yet are, at the same time, mutually complementary to all the other groups.

The People's League for the Defence of Freedom was founded in 1956 'to organize public support for a policy which will afford protection and help for all citizens whose standard of life or freedom is threatened by the growing abuse of power by trade unions . . . to seek by all constitutional means to reform the law as it affects trade unions in order that they cannot become a State within a State . . ., to curb the power of all kinds of monopolies, cartels, and price rings whose activities hold the public to ransom . . ., to subject all expenditure of public money to rigorous and continuous scrutiny and to campaign for the progressive reduction of rates and taxes and the elimination of bureaucratic waste.'[6] Despite this rather lengthy list of aims, the primary objective of the PLDF is to oppose all trade union strikes except those in the printing trade (which are handled by the Free Press Society). It concentrates particularly on public service strikes where PLDF members, by picking up the services where the strikers left off, can often weaken the strikers' bargaining leverage.

In 1958, during the London bus strike, the People's League operated 70 of its own buses to carry the commuting public to and from their work. Since that time, the League has not been called upon to use them again, but it still keeps 21 buses 'somewhere in the country' ready to defy the unions in the event of another strike.

In January, 1962, during the Post Office workers' 'go-slow', the League organized an Emergency Delivery Service. It issued its own postal stamps and set up a nation-wide chain of Receiving Centres to handle the material. The Postmaster-General, however, would not allow the League to handle letters since such matters are a Crown monopoly; but he hinted that it was perfectly legal to deliver packages, not a Crown monopoly. Before the ban on letters went into effect, approximately 100 had been delivered by zealous members of the League, complete with the PLDF postal stamp and frank. They are now collector's items; most of which are in the possession of the British Museum. Despite the ban on letters, Martell's group was the only organization in Britain delivering any postal material during the strike.

Every member of the League, and there are supposed to be 50,000 of them, pledges some form of service to the organization in the event of a 'national emergency'. As is done in the other organizations, some pledge their time, others pledge money, and still others their cars, vans and lorries. Each member is indexed on a 'Register of

Members' so that when a certain service is needed, those who are willing to participate can be quickly located. Martell claims that, in the event of a General Strike, this Register would be placed at 'the immediate disposal of the Government'.

In 1964, Martell again printed his own postage stamps in anticipation of another proposed Postal 'go-slow'. The 'strike' was called off and Martell apparently faced a loss on his stamp-printing costs. Undaunted he advertised the stamps for sale in the *New Daily* at 16 shillings a set (the face value) and sold them all at a handsome profit. Four months later, the 'go-slow' actually took place and Martell printed up another batch of stamps and was back in business.

Martell is also in the process of setting up an organization called the General Service Agency which will handle some, but not all, of the League's activities. It is planned that the GSA will become an inter-Group employment agency; it will, in addition, handle the 30 or 40 'hardship cases' that come into the Freedom Group each week; and finally, it has been proposed that the GSA run a hostel for all members of the Freedom Group. Whether the GSA will remain a part of the People's League or will become the seventh distinct entity under the Group's umbrella is not known at the moment.

The last major organization within the Freedom Group is the Anti-Socialist Front, founded in 1958. Its principal aim has always been to 'keep the Socialist Party out of power while it remains tied to nationalization and controls'. The Front first went into action during the 1959 General Election and provided a fairly large cadre of workers willing to help the Conservative Party win that election. It was in 1964 before the General Election, however, when defeatism had set into the Tory ranks, that the A-SF actually came into its own. In April 1964, perhaps at the very nadir of Conservative Party fortunes since Suez, the Front launched its 'Keep the Socialists Out' campaign in the belief that, with proper organization and a revival of Party spirit, the Tories could, as Martell put it, 'kill the death wish' and rally to conquer the Labour Party at the Polls in the autumn. This campaign was fought in conjunction with those complementary campaigns noted previously, such as the effort to 'Make them Come Clean' and the attempt to unseat Harold Wilson himself.

Martell offered the services of his organization to all Conservative Party candidates in their fight against the Labour Party. He concentrated particularly on 159 constituencies where the Tory majority was less than 8,000. Of these 159 seats, no less than 27 of them were held by Tory Ministers. Martell's anxiety over the fortunes of the

Tory Party were heightened by the large numbers of Liberals standing for the first time in these constituencies, thus threatening to split the anti-Socialist vote that much more. He wanted to offset these disadvantages as much as possible.

Over the course of the preceding two or three years, Martell built up, in conjunction with his Master Index, a listing of all his supporters according to constituency. Each constituency was broken down into various groups: those who had cars and would be willing to take people to the polls, those willing to canvass, write letters, lick envelopes, and contribute money. All this information was carefully indexed by Martell so that when a constituency asked for help (and over 100 constituencies asked for and received help prior to the 1964 election), he could say to them: 'Here are so many names of people willing to canvass, so many people willing to drive, so many to write letters, lick envelopes, etc.'. However, he did not stop at that point. The previous year, in 1963, he began a concerted effort to infiltrate his supporters into positions of power within local Conservative Parties. He used the same methods the Communists use to gain control of a trade union. Martell realises that less than 10 per cent of all constituency workers are 'activists' and that it is this small minority which actually runs a constituency. These people, in turn, determine which candidate is selected, how the local campaign is to be run, and how efficient is the constituency organization. Martell knew that, if his men could gain control of the majority of constituencies, they would, in the long run, determine who sits in the House of Commons. His efforts have met with considerable success for one basic reason: the very people who work at constituency level tend to be conservative Tories – the little old ladies in flowered hats and the moustachioed ex-colonels in retirement that so often are pictured as the stereotyped Tory – and they are exactly the people who tend to support Martell. All constituency parties, however, are not run by right-wing groups and with those in particular Martell used a different tack. In effect, he used the leverage of his organization (money, efficiency, zealousness, etc.) as bait to get his supporters into positions of control. Instead of *offering* his services to these local parties, he would say to them, in effect: 'I have a ready-made organization to help you win your campaign – complete with canvassers, drivers, writers, volunteers, etc. What are you going to do about it?' Usually, his organization was much larger and better organized than the local party's (there was and still is, of course, some overlapping among those who are loyal to both the Party and Martell). He also knew that the constituency, particularly if it was a vulnerable one, would be willing to listen to his terms. Martell claims today that when he gave his services to a constituency, he was not asking for anyone to subscribe to his views alone since the primary objective was to keep the Socialists out of office; but the net effect has been, so far, that many constituencies have been influenced by Martell's brand of Conservatism.

This, of course, brought Martell into direct conflict with the Conservative Party Central Office. The prospect of having hordes of Martell supporters pounding the constituency pavements, unleashing the Freedom Group's policies against trade unions, boxing matches (it feels they should be outlawed), zebra crossings, and voting requirements has often plagued the sleep of Party officials in Smith Square. They realized that a mass acceptance of Martell's support would, in fact, involve official recognition of him and that such an acceptance, they claim, would turn the flank of both the Party and its policies. As one Cabinet Minister once described Martell: he 'is like some great big dog who comes bounding into the drawing-room after rolling in something not quite nice'.[7]

The Conservative Party Central Office worked out a compromise in 1964, hoping to nip Martell's ambitions in the bud. It sent a letter to all constituency chairmen suggesting that if Freedom Group members were taken on that they be taken on as individuals, hoping thereby to minimize the effect of having a Martell label on any one constituency. Under those conditions, many candidates jumped at the chance to have some militant workers, including (according to Martell) a number of Cabinet Ministers as well.

Unfortunately for Martell, his efforts to revive the Party were not successful and it went down to defeat. (He is now starting a campaign to 'Throw the Socialist Out'.) However, it is impossible to assess at this moment how badly or how much better the Conservative Party would have done without his help. Nor is it possible to assess how effective his infiltration tactics have been. Defeat within the Tory Party generally sparks an internal re-appraisal of structure and policies and it undoubtedly will have its effects on the constituency parties. Whether or not Martell will benefit or lose from this re-appraisal it is too early to say; but the Central Office and the Tory Party hierarchy can be certain that Edward Martell and his Freedom Group will be around for many years to disturb their sleep. Such discomfiture, says Martell, is wholly unnecessary; for, he adds, 'if the Conservative Party were doing its job, there would be no need for us'.

1. *Time & Tide,* 12–18 September 1963, pp. 4–7.
2. Ibid.
3. *The Freedom Group's Campaign to keep the Socialists Out.* p. 14–15. Tileyard Press, 1964.
4. The *Guardian,* June 5, 1964.
5. *New Daily,* June 10, 1964.
6. Sponsors of the National Fellowship, aims of the PLDF. 1962 p. 9.
7. The *Spectator,* No. 7096, June 26, 1964, p. 842.

5 The Yellow Star Movement

'If the Germans want to introduce the Yellow Star for Jews in Denmark, I and my whole family will wear it as a sign of the highest distinction.'

KING CHRISTIAN X OF DENMARK, 1943.

In opposition to the Fascist or neo-Nazi movements of Mosley, Jordan, Bean and Tyndall stand several organizations known collectively as the 'anti-Fascists'. Although there were a few 'anti-Fascist' groups prior to 1940, their post-war re-emergence on to the British political scene has been relatively recent.

Their revival began on July 1, 1962, when the National Socialist Movement held its 'Free Britain from Jewish Control' rally in Trafalgar Square. In front of Nelson's Column stood Colin Jordan, the NSM's leader; he was shouting into a dead microphone. His face red, and his arm and finger extended in accusation, he was goading his hostile audience with his explanation of how every facet of English life was controlled by Jews: when an Englishman dressed himself in his Montague Burton suit, he shouted, it was a Jewish suit that he put on; when he put on his shoes, they were Jewish shoes sold by a Jew named Charles Clore; when he took his lunch at a Lyons' Tea-shop, he was drinking Jewish tea and eating Jewish food because it was owned by the Salmon and Gluckstein families; when he watched television, smoked a cigarette, borrowed from the bank, went to the theatre, or bet on the horses, it was done only at the sufferance of Jews. It was the Jews, he went on, who encouraged coloured immigration, degraded English morals, and were responsible for the British dead in the Second World War. Britain, said Jordan with a scream, must be freed from this Jewish control over their lives. 'Hitler,' he declared, 'was right!' This statement signalled the start of a four-hour riot. Copper coins and fruit were hurled towards the plinth. The crowd began to chant 'Belsen, Belsen, Belsen . . .' and 'Auschwitz, Auschwitz, Auschwitz . . .' Fist-fights broke out; brickbats were thrown; and a thousand people tried to claw their way past the police. The spectators had been goaded into a fury.

Watching this performance from the steps of St Martin-in-the-Fields above the Square was the Reverend William Sargent, the Vicar of Holy Trinity Church, Dalston. Pinned to the stock beneath his clerical collar was a large paper Yellow Star of David. Around him were a few hundred sympathizers, both Gentile and Jew, who had drifted to his side to show that they, too, were appalled at the scene taking place in the Square below. Reflecting a few years later* why he had taken his solitary stand, Sargent said, 'I suppose I wanted to show that someone was willing to say he stood for a decent alternative to what Jordan was advocating.' For that one afternoon, he said, 'I was a Jew.'

It was also the afternoon that the Yellow Star Movement was born.

Concern for the welfare and rights of English Jews can be traced back to the time when Jews first came to Britain; but it was not until 1760 that the Jews themselves first organized a body of men to protect and foster the interests of their own people in England. In that year, the London Committee of Deputies of the British Jews was founded, better known today by its informal title of the Board of Deputies. It was originally established to represent all British Jews in the Court of George III. Since that day, it has taken part in all movements affecting the political and civil rights of Anglo-Jewry. For example, it was instrumental in beginning the long 19th-century struggle for religious equality; it assisted Baron Lionel de Rothschild to become the first Jew to sit in the House of Commons (1858); it backed the passage of the Public Order Act of 1936 that subsequently curbed Fascist activities in Britain; and it is, among other things, currently helping to promote the passage of a bill to make incitement to racial hatred a criminal offence.

The senior members of the Board tend to be unknown (except for its current President, Sir Barnett Janner, MP) but solid citizens from all walks of life. None of the famous Jewish names – the Clores, Wolfsons, Sebag-Montefiores, or Warburgs – appear on its list of directors. Nevertheless, in 200 years, the Board of Deputies has become the principal spokesman for all Jews in Britain and the Commonwealth primarily because its members have gained the reputation as sincere and dedicated individuals. Currently, the Board speaks with a voice that is respected not only by the Jewish community but by the Government as well.

In 1936, the Board set up their Jewish Defence Committee in direct response to growing anti-Semitic sentiment in Britain and throughout the world. The principal offenders in England at that time were Arnold Leese and his Imperial Fascist League, and Sir Oswald Mosley and his British Union of Fascists. The Defence Committee hoped to check their outbursts of exploitation and intolerance by exerting effective control over its own people. Historically, and indeed up until 1962, its attitude had always been to ask all British

* In conversation with the Author, 1964.

Jews to ignore their antagonists in the hopes that they would soon disappear from the scene. Whenever the Fascists or any other antagonist would appear in the Jewish sections of London, the Jews were told by the Defence Committee to close their shops, stay in their homes, and avoid brawling with the trouble-makers.

With few exceptions – the Cable Street riot of 1936 being the most notable – this policy was successful. It succeeded in keeping the disturbances from developing into something far worse. During the 1949 difficulties in Palestine, for instance, the emotions of the Jewish community were successfully held in check by the Board of Deputies, and the antagonistic Fascists were denied the ingredients with which to foment public disorders. Likewise, in the 1950s, neither Jordan, Leese, Bean, nor Mosley were able to cause any significant amount of trouble. Because of the Board of Deputy's authority over the Jewish community, and because of the apparent success of the Defence Committee's policy, many Jews were convinced that that was the only way they, as a group, could effectively combat their antagonists.

However, by 1962, many people – both Gentiles and Jews – were not so convinced that what amounted to a 'do-nothing' policy was right. They could look back to the 1930s and see that the Committee's policy had not, in fact, brought about the decline of the Fascists. By 1936, Fascism had been curbed in England, but not crushed. The critics of the Committee could look back only as far as the war itself to realize that a 'do-nothing' campaign had not prevented six million Jews from being exterminated. Worse still, they realized that the post-war Fascists had not learned anything from history. Mosley, Jordan and Bean were still flogging the same scapegoats and (with minor variations) advocating the same 'solutions'.

The critics were also concerned, particularly in the 1950s, by the apparent revival of sympathy for Fascist ideas; or if that were not readily measurable, at least it was clear that Fascist activities were increasing in volume. This renaissance of intolerance was taking place, to the incredulity of all, despite the efforts of the Jewish community, the Board of Deputies, Parliament, the Press, public opinion and a ruinous war to curb it.

One of the greatest faults of the past, according to critics of the Board of Deputies, was that nothing better was offered to Fascist doctrines. Seldom did anyone ever make any effort to outline an alternate and more decent programme. Moreover, even fewer people made any concerted effort publicly to refute the Fascist accusations. At times, it even seemed as if the Board of Deputies, as the major spokesman for Anglo-Jewry, had no plausible answers to them. And what irritated the critics most was that, after a world war and six million Jewish dead, the Board still gave the impression that to fight

Fascism openly was beneath its dignity. It was obvious that most members of the Board eschewed violence and that they were reluctant to debate with the hated Fascists in public, but their critics felt that that was no reason to retain their old 'do-nothing' policy by hiding their heads in the sand and hoping their antagonists would disappear.

William Sargent, for one, felt that there should be a 'middle way' between on the one hand doing nothing to stop Fascist activities, and alternatively meeting them head-on in a street brawl. In the two years that he had lived in Dalston (a predominantly working-class Jewish area), as vicar of Holy Trinity Church, he devised a plan that was extremely simple in design, imperfect in many ways, yet a plan that has turned out to be highly successful in peacefully combating Fascist troublemaking not only in his neighbourhood, but throughout London as well. He knew that the Fascist's most potent weapon was the street rally. Through the judicious use of mob psychology, these rallies were the means through which the Fascists hoped to arouse the British people to irrational behaviour and passions. He also knew that, in ordinary circumstances, there was no danger of Fascist philosophy, coldly analysed, gripping the immagination of the traditionally democratic British. Nor could the Fascists ever hope to achieve through their written word what they could with their calculated and provocative spoken word. Sargent knew that if the Fascist street rallies could be stopped, or at least neutralized, without having to resort to oppressive legislation or physical force, the Fascists would lose their greatest asset.

It occurred to him that when a Fascist, like Mosley, Jordan or Bean, advertised in advance that a speech was planned for a Jewish area, the residents of the area should occupy the good speaking sites in that area before the intruders arrived. This relatively simple plan, he felt, could be effective because he had one crucial factor working in his favour. He knew that, in the interests of preserving the peace, the police had a vaguely defined policy of allowing only one speaker to occupy a given speaking site at any one time. The police would *not* allow, in most cases, groups of say, Fascists and Communists to stand on their platforms in a close circle to trade insults, for they were afraid that such a situation could easily degenerate into more than a mere shouting match. An opposition speaker could certainly set up his stand down the street and no one would stop him if he were not breaking the law. What constituted 'down the street' was never clearly defined, but it usually meant far enough away to keep the antagonists out of earshot.

This rule did not apply, however, to the speakers at Marble Arch (a Sunday afternoon institution), or to such special areas as Trafalgar Square (where prior permission for its use had to be granted by the

Minister of Works). But, on the whole, the rule applied to the many informal speaking areas throughout London – Portobello Road, Ridley Road, Bethnal Green, Charing Cross ('Revolutionary Corner'), Earl's Court, Manette Street and so on. It was enforced particularly strictly in those areas where serious disturbances might occur, most of which happened to be Jewish areas. Since no prior permission was needed to speak at these informal sites, the police were also inclined to follow a policy of first come first served. As long as the speaker caused no great disturbance, he was free to claim sole rights to an area for as long as he wished to speak.

Freedom of speech has always been encouraged in Britain to an extent that many outsiders fail to understand or appreciate. Britons generally feel that the best medicine for a heretic is to let him speak his mind, knowing that he will probably either be laughed to death or that his heresy will be accepted and become respectable. The job of the police has always been to foster freedom of speech, regardless of the repugnant nature of much of it; and the rules of behaviour governing it are still very much in force today, to be applied equitably to both friend and foe.

When Sargent said he felt that *all* the good speaking sites should be occupied beforehand, he meant just that. In one area it might be only a single key site; in other areas it might mean having five or six speakers strung out along the road. By taking every good site before the Fascists arrived to start their trouble-making, the intruders would be forced to hold their rally at secondary sites, mostly in dark and forbidding areas that would be fairly free of noisy traffic. The secondary sites were seldom places where too many people would go out of their way to hear a speech, particularly a Fascist speech.

Sargent felt that, once the primary sites were secure in his or his friends' hands, the Fascists, many of whom had come across London to the rally, would tend to be confused. In the first place, they would not be sure where they could find their leader; and they would not know immediately either where he was speaking, or even if he had decided to continue his rally since it had to be held at poor speaking sites in the area. If the Fascists were thus split and disunited, Sargent reasoned they would be less inclined to start trouble. Most of all, Sargent was convinced that such tactics would not only take the steam out of Fascist harassments, but provide at the same time to the general public, through the medium of the anti-Fascist speakers, an effective and decent spoken alternative to the alien and hated doctrines and accusations of the Fascists.

His plan was by no means fool-proof. He knew that if the Fascists were looking for a fight, there was little he or any ordinary citizen could do to prevent it except by properly disciplining the local residents in advance. He also knew that if the Fascists held a 'snap rally' as they call it, there was little he could do to stop it. But snap rallies draw few people and cause little trouble. He also knew that if the Fascists themselves decided to adopt his policy of occupying the sites in advance, so as to ensure that their own speakers had the platform when they wanted, there was little he could do. If that happened then the old policy of asking everyone to stay in their homes would have to be revived. But in spite of these drawbacks, Sargent felt the overall plan was sound and could survive on its own merits.

Three weeks after Jordan's rally in Trafalgar Square in 1962, Sir Oswald Mosley held a Union Movement rally in the same place. His rally did not last half as long as Jordan's, but the violence which accompanied it was far more severe. It took the police over twelve hours to restore order in the area.

Sargent was back on the steps of St Martin-in-the-Fields with a few hundred supporters, all of whom were wearing a cardboard Yellow Star of David. Before the day was over, more than a thousand people had taken a stand with them. It convinced Sargent that an anti-Fascist movement could and should be set up at once.

Sargent wanted the Yellow Star Movement to be an informal body with no hierarchy of leaders, no formal members, no rigid rules, and no literature. He felt that the organization would be most effective if, in times of peace, it lay dormant and blossomed forth only when the Fascists decided they wanted to stir up trouble in the Jewish areas. He felt that the YSM could best serve both Jewish and Gentile interests by simply providing a decent standard around which all anti-Fascists could rally in times of trouble.

The organization was duly inaugurated in late July, 1962, with both Sargent and Harry Green, a 71-year old tortoiseshell goods manufacturer, as nominal leaders. The Secretary of the Movement was Olga Levertoff,* a journalist, ballet teacher, and an ex-Communist whose Rabbi father had been converted to the Anglican priesthood. According to Green, the Movement grew very quickly. In less than two months he was claiming the YSM had 8,000 followers.** Most

* Olga Levertoff was also the guiding spirit behind the Daily Peace Picket, a pacifist organization founded in 1959. It was never formally associated with the CND although many of its members were. The chief complaint of the DPP was the re-arming of Germany which Levertoff, among others, felt was a suicidal policy. The DPP, however, never succeeded in arousing much sympathy for its cause and has since faded from the scene. Miss Levertoff died in 1964 from complications arising out of a beating she received at the hands of some Fascists.

** A very difficult figure to verify in so loosely organized a movement as this. They may have had, and might still have, 8,000 sympathizers, but in all probability their active supporters have never numbered more than 1,000 people.

of this support came from the Association of Jewish ex-Servicemen and Women ('AJEX'), the largest and most influential of the Jewish veteran organizations in Britain today. Other supporters included young Jewish trouble-makers who were quick to seize the opportunity to scrap with an 'approved' opponent.

At the same time in 1962, another anti-Fascist organization was formed called the London Anti-Fascist Committee. It was started with the help of Sargent and a few Jewish members of the old London County Council (now the Greater London Council). The leaders were mainly public figures in London politics; one of them was Fred Tonge, a London County Councillor and the treasurer of the Labour Party-proscribed Labour Research Department; and another was a Communist from the East End, Solly Kaye. The main purpose of the Committee was to raise money for anti-Fascist activities and to pressure Parliament into passing a bill making it a crime to incite a person to racal hatreds. The actual anti-Fascist work, however, was done by one of the subordinate committees, the North and East London Anti-Fascist Committee*. This committee adopted all of Sargent's anti-Fascist techniques, particularly the policy of occupying the proposed speaking sites before the Fascists could start any trouble. They also adopted his administrative ideas: no rigid leadership structure, no formal membership, no literature, and no publicity. At first, it appeared as if there were two groups doing the same thing; in fact during the month of July 1962 when both the YSM and the North and East Committee (to use its short title) were founded, there was virtually no difference between them.

The main reason why the North and East Committee was founded at all was due to the rise of a faction within the YSM called the 62 Group. This organization, which has never been more than 400 strong in the London area, is the hard-core, militant wing of the anti-Fascist forces in Britain today. It was set up in 1962 in exact imitation of the now moribund 43 Group, a war-time anti-Fascist organization. The members of the 62 Group are secretive, disciplined, fanatical, and inclined to violence. Their leaders, most of whom are graduates of the 43 Group, are the most intransigent anti-Fascists in Britain today. Curiously enough, most of the leaders are also fairly well-known figures in the Jewish community; but because of the nature of the organization they govern, they are very sensitive to publicity and refuse to discuss their activities at all. In fact, few of

* Originally, there were four such committees, covering all London, whose job was to undertake anti-Fascist activities like those of the North and East Committee. But because most of London's Jews are concentrated in the North and East sections of the city, this committee was the only one to survive.

them will acknowledge that the 62 Group even exists.

The primary aim of the 62 Group, indeed its only aim of any importance, is physically to crush the Fascists in Britain. Its members do not believe in the legislative process, and they are seldom concerned about the Jewish community's reaction to them. In most instances, they act as if they had lost all reason. Every member of the Group, whether he be one of its leaders or one of the rank-and-file Jewish toughs, lives for the day when he can personally crack the skull of a neo-Nazi or Fascist. They do not believe simply in striking back in self-defence; in most cases, when their blood is up they go looking for a fight. They have raided Mosley's headquarters; they have beaten up reporters on the pretext that they were asking too many questions; they precipitated a *mêlée* at Caxton Hall when they heard that Jordan was holding a secret NSM meeting there; and, on one occasion, they ransacked the home of a writer who was doing some research on atrocities in war-time Germany reportedly committed by people other than Germans.

It was obvious to Sargent by August that Green and Levertoff either could not or would not control this element within the Yellow Star Movement. He knew that the Green-Levertoff leadership was never too concerned over the intricacies of his 'middle way', and were thus inclined to give the 62 Group its head. The violent activities of this organization (whose leaders were most willing to use Green and the YSM as a cover for their activities) began to infect the more flexible rank-and-file of the YSM proper until they, too, became difficult to control. Even Green and Levertoff – never known to be members of the 62 Group – were not immune to this faction. They began to swing the Movement away from Sargent's 'middle way' approach to the violent approach of the 62 Group.

Initially, the YSM *had* pursued the policy of denying the Fasicsts an opportunity to speak unopposed. For instance, they held a marathon rally on Ridley Road in the late summer of 1962 that lasted 31 hours. Over 120 people spoke on behalf of the YSM and they succeeded in keeping Mosley from speaking there. But as the weeks went by, more and more of the confrontations turned into scuffles and eventually into riots, most of the latter being initiated by members of the 62 Group. Green and Levertoff did little or nothing to control them. One Mosley rally in the East End in August, for instance, was turned into a full-scale riot that had to be broken up by mounted policemen. Several Fascists were severely beaten and Mosley himself was punched and kicked to the ground.

By September of that year, only two months after the formation of both organizations, there was a clear division between the two. On the one hand, the moderates had tended to collect around the banner of the North and East Committee while the extremists, with Green and Levertoff providing the leadership, were concentrated in the Yellow Star Movement. When Sargent realized that the YSM was beyond his control, he quietly resigned and turned his attention to developing the North and East Committee.

When I talked with Harry Green, I began to understand why he was less concerned about a 'middle way' and more interested in encouraging the use of violence to combat the Fascists. The first impression I had of Harry Green was that he was too fragile physically to be involved in violence. In his seventies and thin-boned, he looked as if one slight encounter with a brickbat would be fatal. He is also obviously intelligent, fairly successful in business, polite, and almost dapper. It was not the picture I had in mind of a street-fighter. His hatred of Fascism and anti-Semitism is so deeply rooted and so deeply felt that it seethed just below the surface of his personality. In fact, he was so overcome by his hatred that he was barely able to keep his emotions under control. When he talked about the YSM and what he, as leader, was trying to do, his eyes, his voice and his actions reflected nothing but frustration and outrage. He told me of the many indignities he and his family have had to endure their whole lives. He had had his house painted with swastikas and with such words as 'Hang Jew' and 'Go home Yid'. He has received hundreds of anonymous threatening telephone calls and obscene letters. He claimed he has had to change his bank account on numerous occasions because the Fascists harass his bankers so much that they would rather not be bothered with his account. He has been physically beaten, spat upon, and publicly taunted. His wrath was so volcanic that it seemed as if the pent-up anger of all Jews, at the thousands of years of injustice they had suffered, had suddenly burst forth in this one man.

'Give us money,' he said, 'and we'll smash Fascism all over the country. You can't beat Fascism with fine carpets on the floor; you have to get out in the streets to nip it in the bud.' His anger boiled over on those he thought had betrayed the YSM and on those he thought were trying to cash in on what he considered their successes. 'Sargent,' he said, 'never faced the threat of violence and made no allowances for it. When it did arise,' he continued, 'Sargent abdicated his position as leader by refusing to lead.' I asked Green if there were ways of defeating Fascism other than through violence. 'No,' he said, 'there isn't. You can talk about it all you want, pass bills in Parliament, and offer a better way of life, but it is in the streets where it is beaten, not anywhere else. We're the ones who do all the dirty work; we're the ones who suffer the beatings; and we're the ones who take the blame; but it is us who have beaten the Fascists! Give us the money,' he repeated, 'and we'll smash them for good.'

'Look at all those other organizations,' he continued, 'like AJEX, the North and East Committee, the Council of Civil Liberties, and the Board of Deputies. When we presented our petition to Parliament in an effort to stop the Fascists from inciting people to racial hatreds, they all jumped on the band-wagon and claimed credit for it. But it was *us* who collected the three-quarters of a million signatures, not them.'*

His anger knew no bounds, but he saved most of it for the Fascists from whom he had suffered enough. The bonds of restraint had burst within him, and he was determined, despite his age, to pay back every insult he had endured. To him, words and laws seemed a waste of time; they had not worked in the past, they were not working at present, and he saw no reason to believe that they would work in the future. From now on, he said, if he were hit by a Fascist, he was going to strike back twice as hard.

From September 1962 to the present, the YSM has reflected solely the attitude of Green. Sargent's 'middle way' has been forgotten. The organization has become more violent with time and no one seems to have made any effort to control it. The current active supporters of the Movement consist not only of the trouble-makers of the 62 Group, but other professional anti-Fascists as well: Communists, Trotskyists, and anarchists. Seldom do they turn down the challenge of a fight with the Fascists.

On balance, the Yellow Star Movement has failed to crush Fascism as it said it could; in fact, it has succeeded if anything in strengthening it. Fascism thrives only on publicity and public unrest, and the YSM has provided its enemies with the ingredients for both. Whenever the Fascists want publicity or wish to aggravate racial and religious tensions, they need only announce a public meeting to know that the YSM will be there to fight them. After the battle is over and the cuts are being sewn up, it is the Fascists who reap the rewards of publicity and unrest while the whole Jewish community suffers from the abuse that is directed towards the YSM. Not that the Fascists are free from abuse – they never are – but they thrive on any publicity, good or bad. The bulk of the Jewish community knows from bitter experience that it cannot afford just *any* publicity.

The YSM has also succeeded in splitting the Jewish community in two. Many Jews, with emotions similar to Green's are secretly delighted that their own people have finally declared open warfare

* The petition was presented to a group of MPs in November 1962. It never reached the stage of becoming a bill for two primary reasons: 1) Many MPs thought there were adequate safeguards under the existing laws, and 2) they also thought the proposal was an infringement on the freedom of speech. This was the first and last attempt by the YSM to use the legislative process as a means to their ends.

on the Fascists. They never believed that the 'do-nothing' policy of the Board of Deputies was the correct one, but they never had the will to change it. There are others, however, particularly some of the leaders of the Board, AJEX, and the World Jewish Congress, who feel that the poor publicity from YSM activities has discredited the whole Jewish community. They, like the Fascists, would like to see both the Yellow Star Movement and 62 Group disappear from the scene. These organizations irritate many moderate Jews not only because they feel compelled to apologize for their activities but because they are powerless to stop them.

The North and East London Anti-Fascist Committee, on the other hand, has little or nothing to do today with the discredited YSM. There is only a slight overlapping of memberships and certainly very little similarity in outlook between the two.

Since it was founded in 1962, the Committee has developed Sargent's anti-Fascist techniques to an extraordinary degree of efficiency. Morris Levy, a borough councillor for Stoke Newington, an ex-Communist and ex-member of the International Brigade, and the Committee's informal Secretary-Treasurer, told me that if Mosley, Jordan or Bean came into the North and East areas of London to start trouble, he could have 1,000 anti-Fascists in the streets to occupy the speaking sites in 15 minutes. Levy, in many ways one of the developers of the anti-Fascist tactics along with Sargent, has set up a chain-letter type of telephone communications system whereby every member in his area of London can be reached in a few minutes. All he has to do is pick up the telephone and make one call. Before he reaches the street in front of his home, all anti-Fascists in the area have been alerted. Once notified, some members rush out to occupy the good speaking sites; other members guard streets, homes and synagogues; and still others keep an eye out for paint daubers. When the Fascists arrive on the scene, all the good speaking sites have been taken and there are no crowds, no trouble and no sympathy.

Although Levy and his co-leaders have developed a very high degree of efficiency and coordination within their organization, it is not by any means kept at this constant pitch of readiness. Levy pointed out to me that the Committee practically ceases to exist when the area is peaceful. As long as the Fascists leave them alone, verbally and physically, they see no need for it.

Levy would give no hint of the number of the Committee's active supporters, but judging from the success they have had, it seems to be quite formidable when need be. They have been so successful, in fact, that the disruptive activities of the Fascists in the Jewish sections of London have dwindled to insignificance.

The change of mood within the Jewish community towards anti-

Semitic outbursts has had its effect on the Board of Deputies and the other Jewish organizations as well. It has, for instance, transformed the Board from a rather aloof body of elders with fixed ideas into an organization much more in tune with the wishes of its own people. In many respects, it still retains vestiges of the old 'do-nothing' policy, because the leaders still do not like to see Jews take to the streets to defend themselves. But, in other ways, the Board has considerably hardened its attitude towards the anti-Semites. It no longer feels, for instance, that anti-Semitism is something with which it must live in the future as it has done for so long in the past. Rather, it has decided to fight Fascists every time they attack the Jewish community.

Accordingly, the Board of Deputies has turned part of its headquarters in Tavistock Square into what looks to me, as an outsider, like a military command post in the last stages of a siege. This is particularly true in those areas of the building which are occupied by the Jewish Defence Committee. Such words as 'operations', 'communications' and 'action' can be seen on bulletin boards and memoranda; the employees seldom walk down the corridors – they trot; telephones are constantly ringing, facts and figures are produced with remarkable speed, and there is a constant hum of voices arguing, ordering and analysing the day away.

This 'battle atmosphere' has spread to other organizations as well, particularly to the World Jewish Congress and AJEX. Between the three of them, there exists an intelligence network that would do credit to DI 5 (the successor to MI 5). If some point of information is not available in one particular set of files, they need only make one or two calls to find it. When I expressed my interest to a member of AJEX in learning about anti-Fascist activities, within days members of the other two organizations could quote almost verbatim my previous conversation. One man whom I had just met began our conversation by reciting to me the number of Fascist organizations I had visited and the number of interviews I had had at each.

These organizations employ men who do little else but scan newspapers for signs of anti-Semitism; news cutting agencies are also employed to catch what they might miss; contacts within Parliament, Whitehall, and Scotland Yard, among others, are assiduously cultivated for the information they might reveal; and all three anti-Fascist organizations (and not surprisingly, the 62 Group as well) are reported to have, at least in England, good contacts deep within most Fascist organizations. The information they collect from these sources is processed, analysed, coordinated and acted upon. It eventually ends up in their files on anti-Semitism that collectively are so large that they constitute a library in themselves. There are rows upon rows of books, pamphlets, reports, and cuttings on anti-Semitism, and many people who have ever seen the combined total of this literature are often led to the conclusion that some sections of the Jewish community must find it difficult to believe that anyone could be free of anti-Semitic feelings except a Jew himself.

In fact, there exists within these three organizations in particular a militant attitude so strong that it has produced a form of xenophobia that sees a Fascist under every bed. It was once described to me as *'There goes another potential anti-Semite! Quick! Get his name!'* For example, an official of AJEX told me in the course of a conversation that he was building a file on Martell's Freedom Group. I asked him if he thought they were anti-Semitic. 'No, I don't,' he said, 'but we've been keeping our eyes on them for years!' Many officials of these organizations have keyed themselves so much to the danger of Fascism, real or imagined, that they have become virtually incapable of interpreting any situation except in the light of it being either pro-Jewish or anti-Jewish. The abolition of Resale Price Maintenance, for instance, they believe to be a plot to run Jewish shopkeepers out of business; because Martell's Freedom Group feels that unions exercise too much power, its efforts to reform union practices are often interpreted as a conspiracy to deprive Jewish trade unionists of their rights; the refusal of Parliament to pass a bill against incitement to racial hatred was interpreted as indicative of the political Parties' indifference to Jews, and not as an infringement on the freedom of speech. 'After all,' said one AJEX official, 'there *are* laws against yelling "Fire!" in a crowded theatre.' Although this blindness is by no means universal throughout these organizations, it exists to such a degree that it is easily noticeable. More often than not, their general attitude seems to be: if they are not for us, they must be, *ipso facto*, anti-Semitic.

The tolerant sections of the Gentile community sometimes grumble that this attitude often indicates a reluctance by the Jewish community to accept the slightest criticism. Whenever it is given, they say, there are screams of *'ANTI-SEMITISM!'* from the Jewish quarter regardless in what spirit the criticism is given. I asked a member of the Board of Deputies about this apparent intolerance to censure and he replied: 'How would you feel if a third of your own people were butchered in one war?'

The result has been that a number of anti-Fascists have unconsciously adopted the militant and intolerant attitudes of the very groups they seek to destroy. In most cases, it has only tended to aggravate the situation. Ever since the end of the Second World War, British Jews have been arguing among themselves about the best ways to go about thwarting the more obvious expressions of anti-Semitism.

When they began to act more decisively in the late 1950s, they in fact went too far. They have only succeeded in keeping the problem before the public to a degree that was not possible before. They have tended to blow up the problem out of proportion.

Only the North and East London Anti-Fascist Committee seems to have grasped the key to effectively combating its foes without exaggerating the problem. Because the organization is almost non-existent in quiet times, the public is not reminded day after day (and thus eventually bored) that there are intolerant people in Britain. By rising up *only* in times of stress, they can enlist the aid of the vast majority of Englishmen – William Sargent being a good example – who are both tolerant of the Jews and sympathetic to their problems. So far, few of the other groups seem disposed as yet to imitate them.

6 Spreading the Word

'. . . In this war, we know, books are weapons . . .'

FRANKLIN D. ROOSEVELT, 1942.

The combined amount of literature produced by political minority groups in Great Britain is indeed prodigious. Every minority sect – rich or poor, large or small, 'left' or 'right' – has its own 'publishing company' from all of which pour a seemingly endless stream of newspapers, magazines, quarterlies, pamphlets, posters, and stickers. There is no way to measure accurately the number of titles published by these many sects over any given period of time, but if it could be measured, it probably would compare favourably with the output of Her Majesty's Stationery Office. The readership of this literature, however, is miniscule if compared, for example, to the readership of one mass-circulation national newspaper. In fact, the combined readership of *all* political minority publications is probably not much larger than the readership of one good weekly review. This leads many people to the conclusion that the consumption of political literature *per capita* is highest among members of minor political parties. In all probability this is true, for there were very few fringe politicians whom I visited whose libraries are not huge by ordinary standards.

Lack of volume sales, however, has never hindered any minority group from going into the propaganda business. Its founders have something to say and are willing to bear the financial burden of saying it. In effect, all minority groups must publish their own literature not only because their very reason for existence is to put across a point of view, but also because they have no other choice. They have no access to the public through the media of radio or television; for the most part, the national newspapers ignore their unorthodox views; and open-air meetings are usually considered to be a waste of time. The only remaining avenue through which they can reach the public mind is their own literature.

Publishing fringe literature (and, for that matter, founding and maintaining a fringe group itself) has never been a stable occupation. It is, in fact, emphemeral to an extreme. Groups may flourish for years, particularly after the initial momentum has been created, but their publications in particular come and go with alarming frequency. Their readers tend to be a fickle group who, in the end, determine whether one publication lives and another one dies. Many periodicals, however, do not die a clean death, but go through a moribund-rejuvenation cycle that can drive many observers of the fringe scene to the point of distraction. Others flourish from their first issue to become a mainstay in many respectable homes; the vast majority, however, pass through a brief period of glory (mostly the result of curiosity) and then slide into oblivion struggling for life long after they should have been mercifully put to sleep. I doubt if the average life-span of such fringe publications is more than two years, yet many of them, long since judged worthless by their contemporaries, continue to remain on the scene, if from nothing else but habit.

Because of (or, perhaps, in spite of) the political instability of the fringe groups in general and their literature in particular, two organizations exist in England which give some sense of stability to the field of minority party literature. One is known as the Britons Publishing Society; it publishes and sells a wide variety of right-wing literature. The other is known as Collet's Bookshop and is the centre in England for radical left-wing literature.* Between the two of them, no communications exist. In fact, they hate each other with mutual passion. But within their own individual political spectrums, each caters to the needs of every sect: in Britons, for example, it is possible to find literature ranging in philosophy from the mildly Conservative to the rabidly anti-Semitic. Likewise, in Collet's, literature can be found that ranges from bland Labour Party literature to openly revolutionary tracts.

In neither case do these organizations descend into the political arena to take up one view to the exclusion of another. They are withdrawn from active political involvement; their job has always been to supply their side of the political spectrum with the staple (and usually more expensive) publications that form the cornerstone of their own customers' philosophy. Each organization is a reflection of the streams of thought on their side of the spectrum and, as the sects change their emphasis, so do Britons and Collet's switch their stocks of goods.

The Britons Publishing Society was founded in 1918 by Henry Hamilton Beamish, a bizarre Rhodesian who spent his entire adult life in a worldwide crusade against the Jews. Well educated, the son of an Admiral, an early friend of Hitler, he travelled continuously throughout the world during the 1920s and 1930s preaching his anti-Jewish creed. He believed that the Jews, ever since the time of King

* The only large group of parties within the political fringe which have no central literary clearing house are the nationalists. Because of their geographical separate-ness and their desire to appeal almost exclusively to those people within each area, they have no need for one.

Solomon, had been involved in a giant conspiracy to take over the world – first, to concentrate as much of its wealth in as few Jewish hands as possible and then to turn all non-Jews into their slaves. Their vehicles for world domination, he believed, were Communism and capitalism and, to a lesser degree, Freemasonry, black magic, and the Christian religion. The only solution to this threat, he felt, was permanently to isolate all the world's Jews, preferably on some remote island.

His anti-Semitism, however, differed slightly from the anti-Semitism of, say, Jordan, Bean, and Tyndall. He believed that Jews were superior to Gentiles; that they had exceptionally fine brains, particularly in money matters and political manipulations; that they had unusually large genital organs which Gentile women found irresistible; and that they were infinitely more clever and resourceful. It was for this reason that they had to be isolated from the rest of the world. The current view of the Jews, on the other hand, is that they are 'racially' inferior – 'pests' to use Tyndall's word – and unworthy of the name human; therefore, Jews must be banished for the opposite reason: they are not fit to live in a world of 'clean, all-white Aryans'.

Beamish formed the Britons Publishing Society in order to publish what is now the handbook of all anti-Semites, *The Protocols of the Learned Elders of Zion.* It was from this book that he formed most if not all of his anti-Jewish attitudes. *The Protocols* has an obscure history; anti-Semites claim that it contains instructions to the Jewish people from their 'Elders' on the conquest of the world. The 'Elders' are supposed to be a secret and self-perpetuating body of Jewish leaders who are the direct spiritual descendants of King Solomon, the man who was supposed to have devised the original plan. Anti-Semites point out that the book recommends the use of all known forms of subversion to undermine both the Christian religion and Western civilization: the perversion of Justice through the use of perjury; the denigration of the clergy; the debasement of currency through economic and political manipulation; the weakening of morals through the sale of pornography; the masquerading of Jews as Christians who secretly take orders from their 'Elders'; the 'promotion of false theories'; and the physical destruction of Gentile cities, etc. Jews themselves claim the book to be a forgery drawn up by Czarist police at the end of the 19th century during one of their many pogroms. A Swiss court upheld this opinion in 1935, but its decision by no means settled the matter to everyone's satisfaction, particularly the anti-Semites.

Beamish died in 1948, but his work was carried on by the current owners of the organization, Antony and Joyce Gittens. Since the end of the Second World War, the Society has had a tendency to skip from site to site. For years it was located in Great Ormond Street; then it moved to 48 Princedale Road; then a few doors down to 74 Princedale Road (Arnold Leese House); and now it is located on Westbourne Grove in 'Beamish House', a first-floor loft over a steamy restaurant.

Today, the Society is run by four people: Antony Gittens, who is in overall charge; Joyce Gittens, his wife; Timothy Robertson, a young, non-paid assistant with a rather suspicious disposition whose duties are obscure; and a printer who runs the Society's Clair Press. Britons publishes approximately 80 titles, most of which are 'staple' books, reprinted year after year; few of them are new. In BPS terms, a 'book' can mean anything from a 300-page dissertation to a 12-page tract. Most of their books tend to be short, rarely running to more than 100 pages.

Since detailed accounts are not published, it is not possible to find out which books are the money-makers. However, Joyce Gittens did say that the Society makes money from two sources: from the publication of its books and job-shop work. The jobbing work seems to be the more lucrative operation: the profits from these special orders undoubtedly cover the overheads. Britons prints restaurant menus, posters, and letterheads, etc., as well as publications for some of the right-wing groups. In the past, for example, it has printed *Northern European* for its Editor, Colin Jordan, and *Candour* for A. K. Chesterton and his League of Empire Loyalists. Its books, however, remain its most important operation and its most substantial investment.

The Protocols (cost: 7/6) remains Britons' fastest-selling book. Over 500,000 copies of it have been sold since 1949 and it is now in its 83rd edition. (The favourite book of the neo-Nazis, *Mein Kampf,* however, is not sold by Britons.) Another of Britons' best-sellers is *Race, Heredity and Civilization* (1/6), by Professor Wesley Critz George, said to be 'an effective answer to those who advocate race mixture'. Over 100,000 have been sold since it was first published in 1961. Another steady seller is the 64-page *Hidden Government* (5/–), by Lieut-Col J. Creagh Scott: over 7,000 copies have been sold in six years. This book explores 'the Jewish part in the Bolshevik revolution'.

It is noteworthy that the largest market for the 80-odd titles that Britons publishes is not in Britain but in the United States. Other sales are scattered through the northern European countries and the white Commonwealth.

The subject matter of Britons' literature gives a good indication of the current streams of thought among right-wing groups in Great Britain today. In addition, it is indicative of the wide variety of groups that align themselves, or have aligned themselves in the past (but no longer exist) to the right side of the political spectrum. Britons' books can be broken down into four subject-matter classifications: the first is a polythematic grouping of War, Peace, the Jews, Freemasonry, Communism, Zionism, and World Government.

Together, they comprise approximately half of all the books published by Britons. Anti-Semitism, anti-Freemasonry, anti-Communism, and the international organizations through which Jews, Freemasons, and Communists operate to further their own ends form the foundations upon which most right-wing parties are built. Beamish's view that all Jews (and, *ipso facto,* Communists, Capitalists, and Freemasons) are instruments of the Devil has been inherited practically verbatim by the current group of Fascist and neo-Nazi organizations. They have, as noted, changed the emphasis: the Jews are no longer superior but inferior; the Jews are considered a race and not a religious group; and Jews are of impure blood who, if allowed to remain free, will sully the purity of the Aryan peoples; and so forth. But the basic belief that the Jews plan to conquer the world has not changed.

How anti-Semitism came to be associated integrally with Fascist and neo-Nazi groups is difficult to say. Part of the answer no doubt lies in the influence of Hitler. Arnold Leese was the first man in England to tie anti-Semitism directly to his Fascist theories. Mosley was the next to pick it up until, today, it is endemic in all Fascist and neo-Nazi organizations. The anti-Semite's perspective of the Jews perhaps best illustrates the axiom that people will believe what they want to believe. For instance, it is indisputable that some Jews took part in the Bolshevik revolution and that some Jewish money (perhaps even a great deal of money) is influential in The City and Wall Street, but anti-Semites take such facts to the point of excluding the possibility that non-Jews are (or were) involved in the same activities as well. It explains, for instance, why Victor E. Marsden, the translator into English of *The Protocols,* was convinced that Lenin was a secret agent of the 'Elders', and why the John Birch Society is convinced that Dwight Eisenhower is a Communist (because he was nominated for President by East Coast politicians who, in turn, are 'controlled by Wall Street').

In addition to *The Protocols,* one of the better-known books in this category is *The Nameless War* (7/6), by the late Captain A. H. M. Ramsay, MP, a one-time member of the BUF and the Link. It describes the role of the Jews in the causes of the Second World War. At the end of the book, Captain Ramsay suggests that the phrase 'anti-Semite' (the meaning of which, he says, could be stretched to include hatred of Arabs as well) be replaced by the term 'Jew-wise'.

Other books are *Too Much and Too Many Roosevelts* (3/6), by the American, Gerald L. K. Smith ('one of the powerful figures behind American affairs'); *Grand Orient Freemasonary Unmasked* (17/6), by Mgr George E. Dillon, D. D. ('This deadly occult order is here shown to be the secret power behind Communism'); *The Struggle for World Power* (21/–), by George Knupffer*; *Admiral to Cabin Boy* (8/6), by the late Admiral Sir Barry Domvile, founder of the Link; and *Where Communist Power Lies* (6d), by A. K. Chesterton.

The second category, Race and Race History, is of considerable importance to right-wing political groups in Great Britain. Practically every member of such organizations – whether he be in Mosley's Union Movement, Jordan's National Socialist Movement, Bean's British National Party, Chesterton's Empire Loyalists, or Tyndall's Greater Britain Movement – is disturbed that the 'predominantly Nordic' blood of Britons is being (or might be) mixed with that of 'lesser' peoples: Pakistani, Indian, Jamaican, African, Jewish, and so on. The range of intellectual interest in race (the physical interest is well known) extends from the serious study of genetics and racial biology to the measuring of members' skulls with calipers. Head-measuring was Arnold Leese's specialty and was one of the many tests prospective candidates for his Imperial Fascist League had to undergo before they were accepted. This tradition has been inherited by a few of the neo-Nazi organizations; the formulas used to determine what constitutes a passing or a failing grade, however, are not for public consumption.

Wesley Critz George's book, *Race, Heredity, and Civilization*, remains Britons' best-selling book in this category. The book begins with the statement: 'Because of the friendly feelings that I have for Negroes, especially many Negro friends whom I hold in esteem and affectionate regard, it is with reluctance that I call attention to weaknesses common in the race . . .' It also dwells briefly on the dangers of integration and mixed breeding, suggesting that the breeding of humans is not far removed from that of animals. Other books offered by Britons on the subject are *The Biology of the Race Problem* (6/6) also by Professor George, *Race and Reason* (25/–), *Apartheid in South Africa* (3d), and *A Survey of the Racial Issue* (6d). All of

* Knupffer is the founder of a new sect in Britain called The Right Party, a group of small size and no influence which has ties with some right-wing organizations in the United States. The party is anti-Communist, anti-Capitalist, anti-Income-Tax, and anti-Foreigner. It is pro-OAS, pro-Salazar, pro-Franco, and pro-Absolute Monarchy. The May, 1963, issue of its magazine, *Right,* stated: 'We do not seek to put ourselves forward: we come forward because no one else with complete knowledge does', Whether it intends to become a pressure group, to contest elections, or both, is unkown at the moment.

them are well-selling books by Britons' standards.

There is another organization in Britain which, in a sense, competes with Britons for the race-conscious audience. It is called The Northern League and bills itself as a 'cultural organization'. Whereas Britons handles a general line of books on race, the Northern League tends to concentrate on subjects relating to the glorification and preservation of the 'Nordic Aryan peoples'. They view people biologically, almost as if they were plants and animals. Like the Britons Publishing Society, the Northern League does not descend into the political arena but stands aloof, offering its theories and publications on race to whoever is interested.

To give it its full title, The Northern League for North European Friendship and Co-operation was founded in 1958. Originally the organization was based in Scotland but recently, for reasons never made clear, the World Headquarters has been shifted to Amsterdam. The British section of the League claims 3,000 members, most of whom are professional people: in particular educators, biologists, anthropologists, doctors, and geneticists. The world-wide membership, generally of individuals of the same calibre, is reported from good sources to be approximately 12,000, most of whom live in Northern Europe. As is implied in its title, the objectives of the League are to protect, foster, and bind together the true Nordic Aryan people and their heritages. Its badge of identification is 'a Fylfott (or tryfoss), a three-armed sun-symbol older than the swastika or sun-wheel'.

Most, if not all, of the Fascist and neo-Nazi groups in England have some association with the League, either through the purchase of their publications *Northlander* and *Northern World*, or through dual membership. Since the League is not involved in factional differences between the various groups, it can benefit from each group's interest in Race and Race History literature.

Articles in the League's bi-monthly booklet *Northern World* tend to exalt all things Nordic. For instance, the cover of the July-August 1959 issue shows the picture of a blonde, blue-eyed young woman: 'A Typical Swedish Beauty from Stockholm'. The contents include 'Who Really Discovered America' (the Vikings), by Patrick J. N. Bury*, 'The Study of Blood Groups as an Aid to History', 'Nordic Elements in Afro-Asia', and an editorial entitled 'Annihilation by Assimilation'. The League's newspaper *Northlander*, tends to dwell

* P. J. N. Bury and his brother A. J. P. Bury (an ex-member of the Union Movement) were founders in 1959 of a quarterly literary magazine, *Resurgence*, which enjoyed some success among left-wing intellectuals until it was discovered to be predominantly Fascist in outlook. Some of its past contributors included members of the liberal-conservative Bow Group.

on more topical issues. For example, to quote from an article on 'How the National Press Distorts Racial News in America' in the December, 1963, issue:

> Here is an experiment the reader can do, if he wishes to convince himself of the actuality of such news manipulation: from newspapers gather 40 or 50 action shots in integrated basketball games; shots in which a White and a Negro player are leaping to make a basket. Note the number in which the Negro is above the White – you will find, in all probability, that it far exceeds those in which the White player is above the Negro.
>
> Dozens of shots are taken by press photographers at basketball games; the best are supposedly selected for publication. Is it not strange that the 'best' shots should almost invariably be those in which the Negro player is elevated above the White? ...
>
> Such photographs, appearing in endless succession, could be well calculated to induce in the White observer, an unconscious acceptance of Negro domination.

In addition, *Northlander* has a column devoted to news which might be of interest to its overseas readers: for instance, news concerning the establishment of a 'Dutch-South African Working Committee' whose aim is to 'stop giving distorted views and . . . provide the public with facts and figures'; and news concerning General Edwin A. Walker's intention to sue the Press ('The boys of the Press should have expected that the General, being from Texas, would hit back!').

The third category of books sold by Britons – Finance and Monetary Reform – is obviously related to its general books on the Jews. To all anti-Semites, Jews and Finance go hand-in-hand and are most commonly described in terms of 'the money powers', 'the financial cabals', 'the swindle of the internationalists', and 'the cult of gold'. All are imprecise terms and are all predicated on the belief that a Jew and his money are behind every conspiracy in the world which they (the anti-Semites) oppose. Few of the books on Finance and Monetary Reform attain the academic level of analysing the subjects simply as parts of a country's or the world's economic life; in most cases, the books give the impression of probing a hostile and mysterious unknown which is full of Jews, money-lenders, Shylocks, Capitalists and Communists.

Some of the publications by Britons on this subject are: *The Rothschilds Rise to Rule* (7/6), by Arnold Leese; *The Web of Gold* (25/–), which claims to show 'how the Money-Power, like small-pox and other dread diseases is a scourge to modern society'; *God and the Goldsmiths* (28/–); *Money Manipulation and Social Order* (6/6);

The Truth about the Slump (18/–); and *I Can't Understand Finance* (3d), by the late Duke of Bedford.

The final classification of books – Soil, Health, and Organic Farming – perhaps forms the basis for one of the strongest thought-streams within the Fascist and neo-Nazi groups. Their deep love for Nature, for the Sun, the soil, and the purity of their blood, acts as a philosophical cement which binds together all their attitudes on democracy, Communism, the Jews, finance, and race into a logical whole. The Fascists and neo-Nazis take their feelings to the point where the love of these items becomes a religion. For many years, this preoccupation with nature has been known as the 'Muck and Mysticism' school of political thought.

According to these people, democracy, Communism, the Jews and Freemasons have perverted the higher qualities in man. The continual industrialization of the country (fostered by all these 'alien' elements) has turned the cities black, has polluted the streams, has fluoridized the water, has corrupted the soil with fertilizer, and has killed God's Nature with insecticides. According to them, these poisons have spread to their own blood not only through the poisoned foods they eat but through the introduction of race-mixing and integration.

Since the Jews, Communists, Capitalists, money-lenders, etc. are held responsible, it explains in part why the Fascists and neo-Nazis attack these people with such vehemence. It is not a question of having cast about among ten or fifteen potential scapegoats and by chance having picked these in particular, but it is because those that they have picked represent everything foreign to them. These elements appear to the Fascists and neo-Nazis as the groups who deny them the Elysium which they seek, and they hate them bitterly for it.

In place of this 'alien-dominated society' in which they believe they live, they attempt to re-create a 'clean' society, free of the evils which they are convinced are degrading their country. What is clean to them is the Sun (witness their reverence for the swastika, the sun-wheel, and the Fylfott), the soil, the air, and in particular Nordic history where life was simpler, apparently more moral, and undoubtedly (to them) cleaner. Their love of the soil is by no means abstract: they want to be near it, smell it, and rub it all over themselves; and they express their love of it with such phrases as 'the fertility of our soil', 'Wholesome community based on blood and soil', and 'the soil as our most precious asset'. The Fascists and neo-Nazis have elevated these terms to the level of a liturgy.

They draw on the history of their ancestors – the Norsemen – in order to re-create the society which they seek. According to them, life was simpler in ancient Nordic times, free of Jews, insecticides, usury, pollution, and black men. It was a life full of clean rivers, beautiful country, fair-haired females, blue-eyed long-faced Norsemen, and Heroic Chieftains who had the qualities they feel are so urgently needed in the world today. They talk of 'the Folk State', 'Britain's yeomanry', and 'the purity of Aryan blood' – phrases that conjure up a heaven on Earth which, to them, *should* still exist but somehow has slipped away. It explains, in part, why these groups reject democracy, for it has been this 'anarchy' that has, over the centuries, lulled the British people into a stupor, thus allowing their 'beautiful Northland' to be sullied by foreigners.

The Britons Publishing Society itself no longer publishes any noteworthy books on the subject of Soil, Health, and organic Farming but they do distribute other publishers' books, particularly the current best-seller in the field, *Silent Spring* (26/–), by Rachel Carson. BPS has also sold in the past, and continues to do so today on order, such books as *The Drama of Fluorine* (15/–), *The Truth about Herbs* (6d), *The Living Soil* (18/–), *Fertility from Town Wastes* (25/–), *The Earth's Green Carpet* (8/6), and *The Rape of the Earth* (32/6).

The current Fascist and neo-Nazis, however, have never developed their 'Muck and Mysticism' concepts as far as did the English Mistery and the Social Credit Party, two organizations which flourished in the 1920s, 1930s, and 1940s but which, for all practical purposes, no longer exist in Great Britain today. In order to appreciate the lengths to which these concepts can be taken, it is necessary at this point to digress slightly from the theme of this chapter and give a brief sketch of these two parties.

The English Mistery (from the word 'mister' which 'implies a servant') was the inspiration of one man: William Sanderson. His two books, *That Which Was Lost – A Treatise on Freemasonry and the English Mistery*[1] and *Statecraft – A Treatise on the Concerns of Our Sovereign Lord the King* ('Gleaned from the Wisdom of the Dead by William Sanderson with the help and guidance of a Latterday Prince')[2], formed the basis for most of the Mistery's policies. The primary objective of the Mistery was service, not only to the King but to an intangible Thing:

> This thing, or spirit of the corps, has been known simply as The Thing. In Nordic Society it was the Thing or All-Thing. In Rome it was the Res Publica. In Norman English it was the Real Thing, or realm – and in later English, the Body Politic. This is the source of culture and all good.[3]

Equally important was its belief that the government's primary duty was:

> Jealously to guard the culture, national characteristics and local

> patriotism of every nation within the imperium. Unless the barriers between breeds are preserved imperialism cannot be distinguished from internationalism. Decay must be the consequence of breaking down the barriers. The Sephardic Jew stands before us as an example and the American nation is a solemn warning.[4]

The proper breeding of Britons, therefore, became a cornerstone of this sect's beliefs and was extended to include hatred of anything foreign, particularly the Jews*. Yet Sanderson saw no solution to the problem of Jewry. 'It would be of little use', he wrote, 'to expel Jews today, for we have all become Jews.'[5] Unlike other anti-Semitic groups, the Mistery accepted Freemasonry as fundamentally important to the preservation of Britain because 'it accepts the importance of good breeding'. Members of the Mistery also were desirous of preserving 'memories' since they were considered necessary to the proper development of traditions. In addition, they believed that the 'priestcraft should not uphold suffering as a virtue but rather as an indication of mental, moral, and physical inferiority'.

The theories of Social Credit were also the product of one man's inspiration. During the First World War, Clifford Hugh Douglas, while working at the Royal Aircraft Factory at Farnborough, developed the 'A + B Theorem,' a method of analysing costs which showed that 'in peacetime there is a "gap" between the total buying power of individuals and the total prices of goods ready for sale'.[6] He deduced that the total of all wages, salaries, and dividends paid out in all industries was insufficient to buy the whole produce. Douglas felt that the issue of goods had to be balanced by equivalent purchasing power by the people. In order to achieve this, he believed that manufacturers should sell their wares below cost, the difference being made up by grants of credit through the issue of paper money as needed.

From these ideas evolved the three Social Credit demands: '(1) Open the National Credit Office, (2) Issue the National Dividend to all, and (3) Apply the Scientific Price Adjustment at the retail end.'[7] These demands were never accepted by Englishmen to the extent they were by some Canadians. They were rejected not only because of their unfamiliar nature but because Britain's Social Credit Party, from the moment it was founded, was subjected to a split. On one side, with virtually no supporters, was the Party's principal philosopher, C. H. Douglas, and on the other side stood the 'activist', John Gordon Hargrave, the man who was to take the Party into the

* A small break-away of the Mistery, called the English Array, felt even more strongly about the importance of breeding. Only Englishmen 'of pure English descent' were permitted to join. The Array was also supposed to have been involved in a plot to poison many prominent Jews.

realm of political mysticism. Hargrave admired Douglas' philosophical abilities but otherwise felt he was 'adrift in a sea of human impulses'.

John Hargrave, before he assumed the title of 'Founder-Leader' of the Social Credit Party, was 'Head Man' and primary inspiration behind the formation in 1920 of an organization known as the Kindred of the Kibbo Kift, in its early years a combination educational-cultural-youth movement. By 1925, Douglas' Social Credit ideas had taken root within the organization and, from that moment on, the KKK (not to be confused with the Ku Klux Klan) downgraded its educational-cultural-youth activities in favour of political ones.

In his book, *Confessions of the Kibbo Kift*[8], Hargrave attempted to recreate in print the atmosphere he created in the Kibbo Kift itself. For instance, the Kift had three major policies, the first of which was to act as a watchdog over Government fiscal policies. 'The Kindred,' he wrote, 'cannot be "shoo'ed" off the financial Chicken-run. It intends to examine this hen that does not lay Enough Golden Eggs.' Its second policy was the Noah's Ark Policy, which was a plan to save all KKK members from 'the flood of a disintegrating period of human association'. Its third policy, – called the Phasmid, or Stick-Insect Policy – was a plan in which he and his followers, in times of crisis, could merge into the political background with 'protective colouring' so that the organization's structure would remain intact.

The Kindred was fascinated by the letter *K* and the word 'kin'. Both were incorporated into its lore: banquets were 'kinfeasts', legal problems were solved under 'kinlaw', the minutes of its meetings were transcribed into the 'kinlog', and members themselves were known as 'kinsmen'. Hargrave perhaps most accurately reflected his and his followers' sentiments to the letter *K* when he wrote:

> The slightly devitalized, shocked by the stark and splended vitality of physical well-being, react to the vibration *K*, sounding sharply on the side of the Positive Living Thing.
>
> Keen, keep, ken, kin, kind, kindle, king, kiss – all vital words. In them the *K* -sound is a sinister reminder to the atonic of having let go the material world.

In 1932, the Kindred associated itself with an organization known as the Greenshirts which was once a part of another organization called 'The League of the Unemployed'. By combining all the ideas of the Kindred with the Social Credit theories of Douglas, Hargrave formed the Greenshirts for Social Credit. Three years later, in 1935, he changed its name to the Social Credit Party. To its detractors, it has always been known as the 'Funny Money Party'.

As a political party, the SCP rejected both the Left, the Right, and what Hargrave called 'the muddled middle' of the political spectrum for a position which he called 'The Third Resolvent'. What he meant by this was never clear but, from time to time, hints to its meaning would emerge. For instance, Hargrave was, first of all, adamantly opposed to financiers, whom he referred to as 'the MOST UNSCRUPULOUS ENEMY . . . the money-power, the hidden power of finance'. He claimed as well to be both anti-Communist and anti-Fascist (which he would lump together under the terms 'Commu-Nazi' or 'Commu-Fascist'); he was also anti-Socialist (Lord Attlee and Sir Stafford Cripps were known respectively as 'Att Lee' and 'Cripes'); and his hatred of Sir William Beveridge, in particular, was well known ('. . . The long, flat-topped skull, the eyes sunken back and lost in their sockets as though instinctively retracted from the blinding light of day, the gigantic bulb-like nose overpowering every other feature – the overgrown pumpkin nose of a gnome . . .'). Although purportedly anti-Fascist, he did tolerate, particularly after the Second World War, many ex-Fascists under his political wings: there was Sir Alliott Verdon-Roe, the aircraft manufacturer; Henry Williamson, the novelist; and Major-General J. F. C. Fuller, the military commentator (who Hargrave claimed could see with the inward eye – 'the eye of Osiris'). All of them were ex-members of Mosley's BUF.

Hargrave's vehicles to political power were many and varied. One of them was his Greenshirts, a body of perhaps a thousand idealistic votaries. They campaigned for Social Credit under a 'Banner of the Sunburst' which was supposed to be as 'powerful as a fairy flag'. They also made use of a mobile propaganda van known as the 'eVANgel'. Before the Public Order Act of 1936 curbed the wearing of uniforms, Hargrave clad his troops from head to foot in green: green beret, green tunic, green belt, and green trousers. After 1936, the Greenshirts had to abandon their uniform for 'an invisible green shirt that [could not] be stripped from [their] backs by anyone'. He had, moreover, a decoration called the Green Oak Leaf which was to be awarded to intrepid Greenshirts for sacrifices above and beyond the call of duty. One was reported to have been awarded to a lady Greenshirt known only as Blue Falcon because she stood up in the Public Gallery of the House of Commons in 1938 and shouted '*Social Credit the only remedy!*'

Hargrave insisted that his Greenshirts obey his 'Twelve Masterwords' which read like a rather elaborate Scout pledge. To quote from it in part, his 'Men in Green' as he called them '. . . must be neat, clean, smart in appearance . . . must be, or must become, wise and strong, or both . . . must listen to the inner voice, and see with the inward eye . . .'

Another vehicle to power was the ballot box. Although no one was ever elected to the House of Commons under the SCP banner, one man – H. Norman Smith, the Labour Party MP for South Nottingham from 1945 to 1955 – embraced Social Credit and was the Party's only vocal supporter in the House. Much of Smith's time was spent either arguing finances with his own party's front-bench ministers or attempting to introduce the SCP-sponsored 'National Credit (Equation of Consumption to Production) Bill' which Hargrave had first drawn up in 1935. Occasionally, Hargrave would attack 'his' MP for not toeing the mark. Referring to a Smith proposal to mix Social Credit policies with Labour Party 'Fabian-Marxism', Hargrave said, 'We feel certain that he does not realize . . . that in doing so he is, in fact, assisting the bankers to shunt Social Credit down the siding . . . God save us from our friends!'

It was, however, Hargrave's weekly news-sheet, *The Message from Hargrave,* which most accurately reflected the positive aspects of his Social Credit policies. The *Message* was first published in 1937 and continued, with a few interruptions, until the early 1950s when it disappeared from the scene. Hargrave believed that the power of Social Credit was closely tied to the power of the Sun. For instance, the 'keysign' of the Party (two vertical white lines cross-hatched at their upper halves with an *X*, all within a rectangular field of green), imprinted at the top of each *Message,* was 'a Life-symbol, alive with meaning and creative force. It is the ancient symbol of the Upright Man'. He went on to describe it as 'not a mere scrawl or scribble, but a valid telesmatic periapt – a dynamic Earth-Sun-hieroglyph that shall be the banner to rally the free, the life-urgent men'. He would often substitute for the date of each *Message* such terms as 'Spring Equinox' and 'Summer Solstice'.

Under the title 'FUNDAMENTALS FIRST – DETAILS AFTERWARDS' in the December 27, 1946 *Message,* Hargrave outlined the order of importance of his organization's 'fundamentals':

GOD
Time-Space-Matter
The Universe
Our Solar System
THE SUN
The Earth
The Soil
Plant Life
Animal Life
Human Life (YOURSELF) as:
Human Spirit
Human Mind

Human Body
in relation to:
(now start all over again)
GOD
Time-Space-Matter . . .

Once these fundamentals had been grasped, said Hargrave, then consideration to details could be given. Details involved tying his Social Credit 'Economic Mechanism' to these physical and spiritual fundamentals. The full extent to which he takes these thoughts can only be grasped by considering some of the many slogans which appear in virtually every *Message*. For instance: 'Social Credit is based upon the Divine Magick of Solar Energy,' he said; 'Social Credit is a Politico-Therapeutic Catalyst'; 'SOCIAL CREDIT IS THE HEAVEN-SENT MECHANISM'; 'Social Credit is *not* a panacea, it is a *Release*'; 'THE WINNER OF THE HUMAN RACE – SOCIAL CREDIT'; 'Social Credit is the Awakener'; and 'THE "IMPOSSIBLE" IS CERTAIN BECAUSE WHATEVER IS IMAGINED IS CERTAIN – AND SOCIAL CREDIT HAS BEEN, AND IS, CERTAIN.'

Having dealt with details, Hargrave carried on into other fields. For example, on politics: 'AWAY WITH THE POLITICIANS! – OVER TO SOCIAL CREDIT!' and 'THE SOCIAL CREDIT PARTY SAYS *TO HELL* WITH BRETTON WOODS!'; on the Scientific Age: 'Social Credit will speed the New Science of the Sun-Power Age'; and occasionally on nothing in particular: 'Bang-on and Crack-O! Logic never won fair lady! Prehistoric Monsters got bogged. Don't get. ARISE AND FIGHT, YE SONS OF LIGHT!'

In addition, he would often boost his own Party's Parliamentary candidates. According to Hargrave, they received 'the wholehearted, warmhearted and clamorous support of the voting public – a mass stampede-vote from an electorate that ISN'T really interested in politics (still less in that 'dismal' subject called 'economics') and is THANKFUL to find a political fellowship that actually 'TAKES THEM OUT OF THEMSELVES' in the midst of this world-wide gloom and . . . gives them a glimpse of gleaming GLAMOUR, dazzle-dusted cross-talk, moon-swooning music, high-tension quizzicalities sequin'd with SOCIAL CREDIT block-busting logic, quick-fire itma-izations, love-lilts, lights and laughter. In a word – ESCAPE! Escape from dreariness and everyday hopelessness.'

In an article entitled: 'ANOTHER SHILLING IN THE SOLAR METER, PLEASE! (clink! thank you! z-w-ooooo-p! – we're off! –)' Hargrave attempted to record the public's reaction to his own creed:

Some people are always hoping to get something for Nothing/ That's silly/Like these Social Credit people. They say Sunlight costs nothing/Costs nothing? They're daft! ... The light from the Sun doesn't COST anything, does it – it's free of charge – the Sun just shines – you don't have to put another shilling in the Solar-meter, do you?/So what?/So, really, EVERYTHING IS FREE OF CHARGE, because everything is Sun-energy ... Oh – you're NUTS!

Even nuts are Sun-energy ... Boy – you're Bats!

And bats are made of wood, and wood comes from trees, and trees are nothing but Sun-energy – and Sun-energy COSTS NOTHING! ...

Certify him under the State Medical Service!
He's bughouse all right!
He's gone Social Credit!
Social Credit? – you've said it!
– take him away – take him away – take him away –

Hargrave's Greenshirt followers never questioned their leader's mental probity, nor did they ever ask what he meant by some of his more obscure slogans. Apparently, they were Hargrave's way of transferring his enthusiasm for Social Credit to his followers. There is no doubt that it was infectious, for seldom has there been a fringe group in Britain more loyal to its leader than the Greenshirts.

Hargrave, however, took his Social Credit Party beyond the worship of the Sun and into the realm of political mysticism, the logical extreme of 'Muck and Mysticism' thought. In 1943, he announced his association with Charles D. Boltwood, a spiritualist and, in his field, an author of some renown. Boltwood's books were not written under his own name but under the name of Charles Kingsley, the Victorian writer, with whose spirit Boltwood claimed to have a clairaudient relationship. Kingsley's thoughts were transmitted to Boltwood (who, in his books, referred to himself as 'Crusader') through a process called 'Trance Mediumship' which provided Boltwood not only with the material for the text but for the Dedication and Foreword as well. In one instance, 'Kingsley' dedicated a book, *Spirit Revelation Unveils the Bible,* to 'Crusader'. All the books were published by 'The Universal Group of Intuitives', of which 'Charles Kingsley' was the founder.

Boltwood's books, like some of Mosley's, are also heavy going. They are full of such phrases as 'The Eternal Christ At-One-Ment', 'True Cosmic Wine of Divine Energy', 'Sunship', 'Godhead', and 'Depolarised from the Divine Umbilical cord of Eternal life'. His translations of messages he claimed to have received from Charles

Kingsley (who died in 1875) may have had something to do with it. For instance, The Lord's Prayer came out this way:

> Our Father-Mother God, Who art Heaven,
> Hallowed is Thy Name,
> Thy Kingdom is the Christ,
> Thy Will is Manifestation,
> Thy food is Truth and Truth is ours today,
> Lead us out of temptation into unfoldment,
> For Thou art Omnipotent, Omnipresent, Omniscient,
> and thus Thou art Glorified.
> AMEN

Boltwood ran a college from his home called the 'Universal Centre of Light and Liberation' where students, for a £20 fee, could earn the UCLL Degree of P.S.Sc. (Practitioner of Spiritual Science[9]). Instructions to his students on the art of spiritual healing were outlined in *Spiritual Science Liberates!* (also by 'Charles Kingsley'). In this book, the author claimed that the secret of curing one's own disease lay in the recitation of an 'affirmation'. This was then to be followed by Boltwood's own particular therapy for the disease. Affirmations were applicable to a host of common illnesses: cancer, diabetes, night sweats, constipation, nocturnal emissions, piles, pneumonia, quinsy, etc. Each affirmation took the form of a prayer; for instance, the one for goitre began:

> O Infinite Leveller, Dispenser of true equilibrium; O Pituitary Organ and Minister of Justice, give unto the Common Carotid System the Iodised-Salt of they substance . . .

Once the affirmation had been made, the actual cure for the disease could begin. The cures took many diverse and unusual forms. Tuberculosis, for instance, could be cured simply by eating air.[10]

Hargrave was an eager student of Boltwood's philosophy. He seems to have earned his P.S.Sc. for, in the April 23, 1948, issue of the *Message,* he related how a Police Sergeant, who had 'ricked' his back, came to him for a cure. 'Gave him 3 minutes hand-radiation at distance of 10 feet away,' he wrote; 'Patient stood up. All pain gone.' Hargrave claimed in the same *Message* that, since his graduation from Boltwood's college, he had been able to cure over 300 cases through the mediums of 'Solar Energy' and 'The Power of Resolute Imagination'.

It is apparent when glancing through the *Messages* that, the older John Hargrave grew, the less he was concerned about the three-fold demands of Social Credit and the more he dwelt on combining his individualistic political views with the deification of the Sun and spiritual faith-healing. Despite the Party developing into little more than a figment of his own imagination, Hargrave was most successful in transferring his philosophy to his faithful followers. The Greenshirts not only seemed to enjoy it but seemed to need it as well. No one within the Movement, save perhaps Douglas himself, ever questioned his wisdom.

Hargrave dropped into the political background in the early 1950s and was seldom heard from again. With him went his loyal supporters. Others attempted to revive the party with a magazine called *The Sun* but it had little success. If the Party still exists today in Britain, it does because no one has bothered officially to disband it.

No one has ever explained adequately how such a party could have existed in England and what the reasons were which gave rise to it. One suggestion is that it developed during pessimistic times and that it drew into its folds those people who were escapists; others suggest that there is a mad streak in most Englishmen that comes to the surface only as a result of the Messianic genius of such men as John Hargrave; and still others claim that the alliance of political thought with spiritual healing and the worship of the Sun was a freak, the three usually developing (at least in Britain) along their own, independent lines. Nevertheless, the current inheritors of the 'Muck and Mysticism' school of thought – Jordan, Bean, Tyndall, and the Northern League in particular – are shadows of John Gordon Hargrave and his Social Credit Party.

On the opposite side of the political spectrum, there are a number of organizations publishing, printing, and selling literature for consumption by their left-wing audiences. Most, if not all, bookstores in Britain carry some literature that is acceptable reading matter to left-wing groups but very few stores consciously make an effort to cater specifically to them. There is Lawrence & Wishert Ltd. which publishes many socialist-orientated books (some of whose Directors are members of the Communist Party of Great Britain); there is also Housmans Bookshop which houses the offices of *Peace News* and which caters primarily to the taste of pacifists; and third, there is Central Books Ltd. which handles Communist Party publications (and on whose Board sit members of the Party as well). But the organization that best mirrors the thought-streams of the entire political Left in Britain is Collet's Bookshop (properly, Collet's Holdings Ltd.), the largest and most diversified organization of them all.

Collet's was established in 1934 by Miss Eva Collet Reckitt whose intention it was at that time to make available to the British public progressive literature, especially that which dealt with the history of the working class. She took over the premises of No. 66 Charing Cross Road which was known at that time (and still today by some old-timers) as 'The Bomb Shop' where anarchists were supposed to have previously fashioned their revolutionary tools-in-trade. For many years after the establishment of the bookstore, the original name of the premises remained unaltered on the lintel over the door.

From these humble beginnings, Collet's has grown into one of the largest chain of bookstores in London. It has been the beneficiary of a 30-year upsurge of interest in radical and 'progressive' (Collet's favourite word) literature. From No. 66, it branched out into a Russian bookshop on Great Russell Street which in turn had to move to larger quarters in 1954 around the corner on Museum Street. In the intervening years, it set up a Multi-lingual Bookshop, an International Bookshop, and Arts and Handicraft Centre, a Chinese Gallery (paintings, jade, porcelain, *objets d'art,* etc.), a record shop (specializing in folk-music and jazz), and a Scientific Bookshop.

In its early years, particularly during the Stalinist era, Collet's toed a very strict Marxist line. Although the British Communist Party in King Street never stooped to the level of dictating policy to the bookstore, the managers nevertheless tended to formulate their policies on the basis of what Moscow (and, *ipso facto,* King Street) were saying and doing at the moment. When Yugoslavia broke with Moscow, for instance, Yugoslavian books were withdrawn from the shelves; *Dr Zhivago,* because it was unacceptable to the Kremlin for many years, was also unacceptable to Collet's. During the height of the Cold War, the most right-wing publication it sold was *The New Statesman.* However, with the death of Stalin and the subsequent easing of East-West tensions, Collet's began to liberalize its policies. In the words of one of its staff, the store went 'polycentric' – free of any direct or indirect pressures from Moscow and King Street. Today, Collet's will sell any literature of a 'progressive' nature, regardless of the prevailing Communist orthodoxy; but it still refuses to sell books by Fascist authors on the grounds that they are not progressive.

The man most responsible for the liberalization, independence, and growth of Collet's is Thomas Russell, a member of the Communist Party, a former manager of the London Philharmonic Orchestra, and currently the Bookshop's Managing Director. He is also a businessman of considerable acumen. Since he took over in 1952, he has pushed the sales of the store's best-seller, the *Russian-*

English Dictionary, over the 10,000 per year mark. He has also been concentrating lately on exporting and importing books between what he calls the 'new democracies' and England. Half Collet's turnover, in fact, is from East-West trade and, according to Russell, it is very profitable indeed.

Of particular interest to the British Outside Left is The Bomb Shop at 66 Charing Cross Road. This one store is the primary outlet for all left-wing propaganda, particularly minority propaganda. Unlike Britons Publishing Society, Collet's make it a policy to stock as many of these groups' literary efforts as possible as part of its over-all desire to promote 'progressive' thought. As a result, No. 66 has developed into the one central point in London where all interested parties can best gauge the pulse of the entire left-wing political spectrum.

There are approximately 150 pieces of left-wing party-political literature being offered for sale at No. 66; there are also many foreign publications of a complimentary nature. Most of this literature is well-thumbed and dog-earred; all shout their imprecations through a thick jacket of either finger grease or dust – or both; and nearly all of them implore the viewer to 'Buy now!' and to 'Pass it on!' All of this literature can be readily segregated into five categories, corresponding roughly to the predominant philosophies found within the Left spectrum: Labour Party, Communist, 'independent' Marxist, Trotskyist, and anarcho-syndicalist.

Labour Party literature, by ordinary standards, is not considered fringe political literature and is mentioned here only because it is required reading among the minor left-wing sects and because it reflects a wide range of left-wing thought. This literature is by no means all sponsored by the Party itself but is interpreted to mean that body of literature which gives greatest aid and comfort to both the Party leadership and its rank-and-file centre. No definite line can be drawn defining the limits of what is or is not acceptable since none of the material is free of controversial points of view. Nevertheless, those publications most acceptable to the Party's centre include the prestigious and widely-circulated (an enviable 90,000 copies per week on average) *New Statesman;* the Fabian Society's *Venture;* the independent but ideologically compatible newspapers *Sun* (formerly *Daily Herald*) and *Tribune;* and the pacifist publications: *Sanity, Peace News,* and *Reconciliation.* Official Party literature itself is quite limited: the monthly *New Advance,* for Young Socialists, is the only newspaper it publishes. However, a wide variety of other pamphlets, under either the Party or Labour Party-affiliated Fabian Society Labels, are available at Collet's. The most noted of them is *Signposts for the Sixties,* the Labour Party platform. Others are *Signposts for Wales,* the *Labour Party Song Sheet** and *Talking Points.*

Communist literature is probably the most numerous of all the publications at No. 66 and can be divided roughly into that which is pro-Moscow and that which is pro-Peking. *The Daily Worker* ('The only daily paper owned by its readers') is the best selling piece of Communist literature in Great Britain with a daily circulation in excess of 61,000. It is only one of approximately sixty pieces of literature (newspapers, pamphlets, quarterlies, weeklies, etc.) that are produced by the British Communist Party and its 'front' groups. Only a small number of these, however, are available at Collet's. In this case, Central Books Ltd. seems to carry the most complete selection of Party literature in Britain. Nevertheless, Collet's still manages to sell the Party's weekly *Comment,* its theoretical journal *Marxism Today* (whose Editor, James Klugmann, is a Director of Lawrence and Wishart Ltd.), the Young Communist League paper *Challenge,* Rajani Palme Dutt's *Labour Monthly, Communism: Your Questions Answered,* by Emile Burns (also a Lawrence and Wishart Director), and the Party's official programme *The British Road to Socialism.* Foreign publications available at the shop with a pro-Moscow bias are *Pravda, Isvestia* (of which approximately 20 copies each are sold per day), the *Soviet Review* (from the USA), and *New Times,* a 'Trud' publication. Some of the above material is printed on the Communist Party's own Farleigh Press Ltd. in Hertfordshire.

Those newspapers and magazines following the Peking line are less numerous. *Vanguard,* the voice of the Committee to Defeat Revisionism for Communist Unity, is the only pro-Peking Communist newspaper in Britain. The Committee, however, sells a few pamphlets with such titles as *Against the Enemy!, Destroy the Old and Build the New!,* and *Truth Will Out Against Modern Revisionism* which outline its differences with the Communist Party proper. Collet's also carries perhaps three-score booklets by oriental Communists all of which are published by the Foreign Language Press, Peking. For instance, there is Liu Shao-Chi's *How to be a Good Communist,* Mao Tse-Tung's *Statement Expressing the Chinese People's firm Support for the Panamanian People's Just, Patriotic Struggle,* and his *Statement Opposing Agression Against Southern Viet-Nam and Slaughter of its People by the U.S. – Ngo Dinh Diem Clique,* as well as Li Fu-Chun's *Raise High the Red Flag of the General Line and*

* Which lists among its numbers such songs as 'The Red Flag' ('The people's flag is deepest red/It shrouded oft our martyred dead/And ere their limbs grew still and cold/Their hearts' blood dyed its ev'ry fold . . .'), 'The International', 'The Song of the AEU', 'The Man that Waters the Workers' Beer', 'Himmo de Riego' (The Spanish Republican Anthem), and 'Dump the Bosses off your Back'.

Continue to March Forward, and Kim Il Sung's *All for the Postwar Rehabilitation and Development of the National Economy.*

All the 'foundation' books, in addition, are available at Collet's: Marx's *Capital,* Marx's and Engels' *The Manifesto of the Communist Party,* Lenin's *The State and Revolution,* as well as selected works by Bakunin, Trotsky, and other Socialist writers.

There are a few newspapers and magazines that are staunchly independent of the Communist Party and the Stalinist-Peking breakaway faction but nevertheless still follow a vague Marxist-Socialist line. The *Socialist Standard,* of the Socialist Party of Great Britain, and the *Socialist Leader,* of the Independent Labour Party, are two of them. The *New Left Review* and the *New Reasoner,* more the voices of two 'spheres of influence' than any particular party, also follow an independent Marxist line; they were, in fact, products of the Hungarian crisis.

Trotskyist literature is well-represented at Collet's. There is the weekly Socialist Labour League *Newsletter**, their quarterly theoretical magazine, *Fourth International, and Keep Left**, an SLL-dominated newspaper circulating among Young Socialists. In addition, there is the well-laid-out and expensively-produced *Red Flag* (complete with blood-red hammer and sickle emblem on the masthead) that is the organ of the Revolutionary Workers' Party; there is *International Socialism* and three monthlies called *Socialist Review, Young Guard,* and *Labour Worker* (the last two of which are newspapers), all of which belong to a 'sphere of influence' known as either the 'Cliffites' or 'Socialist Review Group'; there is *Solidarity,* the mimeographed voice of the anarcho-Marxist 'Socialist Reaffirmed Group'; and there is the sporadically-published 'monthly', *Socialist Current,* the tiny voice of a 'sphere' of the same name.

The only Trotskyist literature not to be found at No. 66 is that of the Revolutionary Socialist League. Most of their English-language literature, for instance, *Fourth International* (not to be confused with the one above) and *World outlook* – are published in Paris. Its newssheet, *Socialist Fight,* has gone through a series of moribund-rejuvination cycles and currently is passing through one of its 'difficult' stages. When it does appear, it is available at Collet's. The Revolutionary Socialist League, however, is not completely unrepresented at No. 66. It is associated with a 'sphere' which is known as either the 'Internationalists' or the 'Nottingham group'. This group publishes *The Week, International Socialist Journal* (not to be confused with the *International Socialist Review,* an American Trotskyist paper), and *Voice of the Unions* (which has its own 'subsidiary' newspapers called *Ford Voice* and *A.E.I. Voice*).

* Proscribed by Labour Party. See Appendix I.

Most anarchist and syndicalist publications are available at Collet's as well; if not, they can be purchased at The Freedom Press (no relation to Martell's Freedom Group) in Fulham. The only anarchist newspaper in Britain is *Freedom.* The anarchists also publish a series of mimeographed monthlies (as is their tradition, they are all published whenever the Editors feel like putting out an issue) called *Anarchist International, Anarchy,* and *Anarchist Youth.* The syndicalist newspaper, *Direct Action,* is also published irregularly; it is supplemented by slim pamplets with such titles as *The Social General Strike, The British General Strike* 1926, *The Bomb, Direct Action and the State,* and the syndicalist Bible, *Workers' Control.* Their most famous pamphlet (published in co-operation with the anarchist, the ILP, *Solidarity,* and the Committee of 100) is an 'exposé' of Regional Seats of Government called, *Resistance Shall Grow.* All are available at Collet's.

Russell acknowledges that the sectarian literature in The Bomb Shop is in a chaotic state but he is at a loss for a solution to the problem. He has no desire to restrict the number of newspapers, magazines and pamphlets of these sects, yet he knows that if the number continues to grow to the point where his shop becomes the indiscriminate repository of all left-wing literature, the situation may become difficult to control. He realizes that if he restricts his shelves to say thirty left-wing newspapers and magazines, he will not only lose some of his best customers, but he will be reneging on his pledge to give all 'progressive' thought a chance to be heard. Russell hinted that he probably will be willing to continue subsidizing all the minority literature indefinitely at a loss on the last point alone: that, no matter how few sales it might generate of iself, such 'progressive' literature deserves a permanent podium. If he choses not to assume the burden, then the left-wing sects will lose one of their best and most respected outlets in England.

1. Constable and Co. (London), 1930.
2. Gresham Cooke (London), 1941.
3. *That Which Was Lost,* p. 35.
4. Ibid. p. 30.
5. Ibid, p. 78.
6. *Social Credit Clearly Explained,* by John G. Hargrave, S.C.P. Publishing Co. (London), 1945.
7. Ibid, Frontispiece.
8. Duckworth (London), 1927.
9. *A Touch of the Sun,* by Tom Driberg, MP. Cornhill Magazine (London), No. 962; May, 1944.
10. Ibid.

7 The Outside Left

'. . . Using our traditional institutions and rights, we can transform Parliament . . .'

THE CPGB'S *British Road to Socialism*

'It must be smashed from without, by force!'

MICHAEL MCCREERY.

'Eventually the organization of the Bolshevik Party will replace the Party itself; the Central Committee will take the place of the organization; and finally, the dictator will supplant the Central Committee . . .'

LEON TROTSKY.

'Socialism can only come about through education . . .'

AN SPGB MEMBER.

'You're all a bunch of bloody dictators!'

ANARCHO-SYNDICALIST CRY.

By my definition, the Outside Left consists of all left-wing groups that are either officially or unofficially outside the Labour Party proper. At the moment, there are twelve recognizable Outside Left groups in Great Britain; and, as pointed out in the previous chapter, they can be readily classified into four major categories: Communist, Trotskyist, independent Marxist, and anarcho-syndicalist.

Within the British Communist camp, there exists a Moscow-Peking split in miniature, between the Communist Party of Great Britain and the Committee to Defeat Revisionism for Communist Unity (otherwise known as either 'the Committee against Revisionism' or 'the McCreery Group'). The argument between these two factions is over the choice of roads to Socialism and who is to lead the way down it. The CPGB, following Moscow's cue as it has done consistently throughout its history, claims that Socialism can be achieved through peaceful co-existence with the West. It has rejected 'Stalinism', the open support of 'colonial' wars, and the need for violent revolution. In Marxist circles, the CPGB has become a conservative organization, more willing to adapt its ideology to British customs and less willing to upset the *status quo*. It demands 'reasonable' solutions; it speaks more in terms of 'flexibility' and 'adaptability'; and it seeks to replace its image as an outcast party with a respectable image. On the other hand, the Committee against Revisionism – the pro-Peking of Stalinist faction – rejects the 'revisionism' of the CPGB, claiming that Socialism, as implicit in Marxism-Leninism, can only be brought about by destroying the capitalist states and the 'Ownership Class'. The Committee reflects all the restlessness of the Chinese Communist Party: its dissatisfaction with the divisions of world power, its truculence and its militancy. It has the same tendencies to invoke the name of Stalin, to support the revolutionaries in Cuba and Viet-Nam, and to resort to name-calling and sloganizing.

Perhaps the one phrase in *The British Road to Socialism*, the CPGB's official programme, which most irritates the Committee is the one which states that, by 'using our traditional institutions and rights, we can transform Parliament into the effective instrument of the people's will, through which the major legislative measures of the change to Socialism will be carried'.[1] To the Committee against Revisionism, this statement is heretical Marxism implying peaceful co-existence, an acceptance of capitalist institutions, and a betrayal of the revolution:

> Marxists have always held that the capitalist state machine cannot be captured and transformed, but must be smashed from without. As Lenin wrote in *State and Revolution* 'It was Marx who taught that the proletariat cannot simply conquer state power in the sense that the old state apparaus passes into new hands . . . As we have seen Marx meant that the working class must smash, break, shatter (sprengung – explosion, the expression used by Engels) the whole state machine'.[2]

The Committee goes on to say that the only way to revive the spirit of Marxism-Leninism within the CPGB is not through reform but by destroying the power of the 'revisionists' in their King Street headquarters:

> We can only build a revolutionary, Marxist Party by *smashing the old party*, by appealing over the heads of the leadership of the CPGB to all honest militants within the working class movement.[3]

The Committee carries its differences with the CPGB into the field of foreign affairs. On the question of peaceful co-existence and nuclear weapons, for example, Arthur H. Evans, a member of the Committee, writes in his pamphlet, *Against the Enemy!:*

> The Chinese leaders assert that Khrushchev's policy of peaceful co-existence is a laying down of arms, an outright betrayal of colonial and semi-colonial peoples now moving into action in Asia, Africa, and Latin America. Khrushchev, state the Chinese, is attempting to frighten people with nuclear statistics, pointing out that in an all-out nuclear war, half the world's population would be destroyed, and much of Western civilization wiped out. The Chinese have replied that even if the worst came to the worst, if such a catastrophe occurred, even then half of the world's population would remain, and that they, on the ruins of the capitalist system, would rebuild and bring into being a flourishing Communist civilization. But the Chinese point out, they don't think this will happen... In the Chinese view, the nuclear weapon is a weapon that can only be used once, retaliation... is swift and certain. Certain people, in my belief, have overlooked the fact that rockets and long-distance missiles need not necessarily have to carry atomic war-heads. A city can be destroyed a little bit slower, but just as effectively by conventional warheads. Particularly when you recall the amount of petrol stored in large cities such as New York City, the height of its buildings and the impossibility of control of major fires under attack.

The McCreery Group indulges in name-calling, much in the manner of the Chinese Communist Party. The CPGB, for instance, is called at various times: 'the cunning King Street gang', 'revisionists' (often thought to mean those people who revise Marxist-Leninist theories; more often, it simply means anyone with whom you disagree), 'tailists' (someone who hangs on to the shirt-tails of the Labour Party), or 'Left-Social Democrats' (those on the extreme left-wing of the Labour Party). The CPGB leaders are also known as 'racialists', 'centrists', 'bureaucrats', and 'opportunists'. Occasionally the Committee against Revisionism will cast doubt on the honesty of CPGB members ('. . . their life work is a *living lie*'); it criticizes the structure of the Party ('In short, democratc-centralism has been replaced by bureaucratic-centralism within the CPGB'), and the Party's very nature ('... a radical appendage to the Labour Party'), Khrushchev himself, while he was Premier, was the subject of sustained and bitter attacks. According to the Committee, his '*entire career* stinks of opportunism', whose 'brain is becoming addled', and who is 'losing whatever self-control he once possessed'.[4]

The CPGB does not let these remarks pass without reply. When it answers these charges, it uses two strategies: it either attacks the Committee against Revisionism directly, for example:

> The McCreery Committee against Revisionism has since made clear its desire – a vain one! – to destroy our Party . . . Our Party has repulsed all previous attempts, whether from the right or the ultra-left to disrupt our unity, discipline, and adherence to Marxism-Leninism and democratic centralism. We shall also repulse the present attack . . .[5]

or, more often, it attacks the Committee indirectly by criticizing the attitudes and activities of the Chinese Communist Party. For example, in reply to the attacks on its nuclear policies, it claims that the pro-Chinese Communists:

> . . . Use a phrase about the 'unprecedented destructive' power of nuclear weapons. But simultaneously they defend the description of the atom bomb as a 'paper tiger', say that the victorious peoples after a nuclear war 'will very quickly create a civilization a thousand times higher on the ruins of destroyed imperialism', and claim they are 'optimistic' because they think that only half, and not the whole of mankind, might perish in a nuclear war . . .
>
> The culmination of their campaign against the Soviet Union is the wild charge that it has the conscious aim of allying with the U.S. imperialists for world domination . . .[6]

The argument between the two groups continues today to follow closely the policies and tactics of their respective 'allies'. When tempers flare in Moscow and Peking, they flare a few days later in King Street and Anson Street (where the Committee against Revisionism has its headquarters); when they cool, so the taunts and polemics between the two British factions lose some of their vehemence.

The Committee to Defeat Revisionism for Communist Unity emerged on to the political scene in November, 1963 in reaction to the revisionist policies of Moscow and, *ipso facto,* the CPGB. Ever since the programme, as outlined in *The British Road to Socialism,* was first adopted by the CPGB in 1952, the Party has been split between those who have accepted the programme and the militants who have opposed it. The McCreery Group – 14-members strong at the time – broke with the Party not only because it rejected this programme but also because it never accepted Khrushchev's 1956 denunciation of both Stalin and the 'cult of the individual'. In fact, Khrushchev's speech sparked the McCreery break. Why it took seven years from the time of Khrushchev's denunciation for the McCreery Group to break away has never been adequately explained. Most of the dissidents will say, however, that it was not apparent until 1963 that Khrushchev actually meant what he said.

When it broke with the CPGB, the Committee published a four-page document, called *An Appeal to all Communists,* in which it accused the CPGB leadership of having 'abandoned revolution, abandoned the struggle for working-class power and socialism, and [having] replaced it with the aim of winning a few crumbs from the table of the monopoly capitalists'. The rebels hoped that their document would appeal to many other smaller rebel factions and so induce them to join in a united struggle to abolish the revisionist policies, to overthrow the Party leadership, and to revert to a policy of 'true Marxism-Leninism'. William Lauchlan, the CPGB National Organizer, told me that McCreery and his few followers were 'unrealistic' and 'opportunists' who were attempting to fractionalize the Party so that they could return to lead it themselves. Other Communists, still loyal to the Party, dismissed the rebellion as the 'work of a few extremist intellectuals'. John Gollan, the Party's General Secretary, referred to the Committee's attempt to unseat him as Party leader as 'a load of nonsense'.[7]

The man who led the revolt is Michael McCreery, a young (mid-thirties) Marxist who joined the CPGB in 1956 after spending two years in the Labour Party. McCreery is an unusual Marxist in that he comes from an upper-class family. His father, General Sir Richard Loudon McCreery, GCB, KCB, CB, KBE, MBE, DSO, MC, was one of Britain's outstanding military leaders during the Second World War. He was Chief of General Staff in the Middle East in 1942, he commanded the Eighth Army in Italy from 1944 to 1945, and after the war he was General Officer C-in-C of British occupation forces in Austria. Michael McCreery himself was educated at Eton and Oxford.

Most of the members of the Committee who surround McCreery, although not of such high caste, consider themselves to be middle-class intellectuals. This is particularly true of his literary companion, Arthur H. Evans, the author of *Against the Enemy!* and *Truth Will Out Against Modern Revisionism,* two of the many documents which outline the Committee's ideological position. Many of his followers – and it is estimated they number no more than fifty – originally came from working-class backgrounds who have elevated themselves to this middle-class status. Few if any of his followers spend their time earning a living on the factory floor.

McCreery spends all his time on Committee activities in a dingy top-floor flat on Anson Street in North London. It is the location from which their newspaper, *Vanguard* is published. With him live a few other bachelors among the squalor of unwashed milk bottles, piles of dirty clothes, unattended dishes in the sink and rumpled beds. McCreery's office in the flat contains a library of perhaps 2,000 books and pamphlets which line the face of one wall. Piles of loose literature are scattered over the floor. In the centre of the room is his desk on which he answers all his correspondence by hand in a neat, almost classic, script.

McCreery is a tall man, quite handsome, with sad eyes, and a mouth that is pulled back into a nervous grin. He was distinctly ill-at-ease with me and answered my questions as if the articulation of his thoughts were a painful process. For instance, in response to why he became a Communist he would only say that, during his many travels throughout the world, he had seen a great deal of suffering and had decided that it was the fault of the capitalist system. He would not elaborate on the point further.

He said that the history of the CPGB was and still continues to be a struggle not for revolutionary action but a struggle to enter the Labour Party. He claimed that the CPGB failed from the start to grasp the essentials of either dialectical materialism or any of the other basic Marxist-Leninist tenets. He felt that the members of the Party were empirical Marxists who had so deviated from 'true Marxism-Leninism' that they were now attempting to become respectable – 'Left-Social Democrats', he called them. Therefore, he believed that they offered no alternative to Labour Party policies.

He is adamant in his belief, and it is evident in all his writings, that capitalism cannot exist side-by-side with a true Socialist state. The necessity to smash capitalism is uppermost in his mind. He is determined to destroy what he considers the biggest evil in the world today. He is convinced that all true militant Marxists will eventually come over to his side and, like the Chinese Communists, is appealing to the 'true Marxist-Leninist' theories. His appeals run to slogans along Chinese lines, examples of which are:

> We say to our Cuban Comrades: NEVER WILL WE FORGET THE INSANE TREACHERY OF KHRUSHCHEV AND HIS GROUP! STAND FIRM AND UNITED! THE FOLLOWERS OF MARXISM-LENINISM WILL ROUT AND DESTROY MODERN REVISIONISM!

> Long live the memory of *Comrade Stalin*! Down with modern revisionism. Long live the struggle for World Socialism!

McCreery claims that, as opposed to the CPGB which, he says, is organized on the electoral level, his Committee's workers are organized on the factory floor. He claims that his followers are in the process of building 'cells' at factory level so that, when the opportunity arises, they will be in a position to strike down, once and for all, the hated capitalist system at its heart.

The notion that McCreery's Committee has any political strength on the factory floor brings horse-laughs from the CPGB and from the militantly anti-Communist sections of the trade union movement.* The CPGB say that McCreery's strength is visionary, adding that few if any of his followers have had any appreciable factory experience. One member of the CPGB told me that McCreery 'probably does not know what the inside of a factory looks like.' The anti-Communists with whom I have talked, in addition to a few ex-Communists, fully agree with these sentiments, saying that they have rarely heard of a McCreery militant at factory level. They claim as well that if he had a growing organization, there certainly would have been a few defectors by now who would have exposed the extent of his influence.

There is some speculation, however, that McCreery might be the beneficiary of the CPGB's long-standing internal split between the

* There are three groups in Great Britain today whose activities are restricted almost exclusively to combating Marxist influence in the trade union movement. They are all independent of the Trades Union Congress and the Labour Party.

The oldest organization is the Economic League, founded in 1919 originally as an anti-Socialism group but which switched its emphasis a few years later to anti-Communism. Today, it concentrates primarily on educating trade unionists and the public at large as well, through the mediums of speeches and literature, on the extent to which Marxist influence has penetrated the unions. It claims to hold over 62,000 meetings of one kind or another every year and to distribute at the same time over 29 million pieces of literature. It operates on a budget of approximately £220,000, most of which it claims is supplied by industrial firms.

The second organization is known as Common Cause which was founded in 1951 by a group of militant anti-Communists, some of whom were trade union leaders. Unlike the Economic League, it places its emphasis in providing background material for trade unionists and a few industrial groups who wish to fight Communist influence at the factory level. Recently, the group has been accused of using McCarthy-like tactics because it published a pamphlet in 1964 which listed 180 people who were associated with Marxist groups, but not all of whom were Marxists.

The third organization is Industrial Research and Information Service ('IRIS') which was founded in 1956 as an 'inside' organization made up of anti-Communist workers. The founders felt that, since Common Cause was an 'outside' organization often accused of 'interfering' in trade union activities, another organization was needed to work secretly among the workers themselves. Many of their best men are ex-Communists. One of IRIS's favourite tactics, when attempting to wean a Communist away from his party, is to suggest the man join a Trotskyist organization. If he does, IRIS knows from experience that within two years the man will be in the political wilderness.

militant trade unionists and the 'revisionist' leadership. Every so often, the CPGB expels a member because its leaders feel the dissident is following a near-Stalinist line. Some of these ex-CPGBers retire from politics while others search around for a new political home. In the past, a few of them have joined the McCreery Group and, undoubtedly, others expelled from the CPGB in the future will continue to do so. Many anti-Communists claim that some members of the CPGB – those with real influence in the trade unions – are ready to bolt to McCreery's Group *en masse*. McCreery believes that Khrushchev's removal from office may speed up the exodus. This feeling is not shared, on the other hand, by many Marxists themselves; they consider the probability of them joining in substantial numbers to be remote because the Committee has no political strength to offer them as bait. If they did join, it is believed that they would elbow McCreery and his few close associates out of the organization and take over the Committee for their own purposes.

McCreery, however, is confident that no such thing will happen and that the true militants will eventually flock to his cause. He claims he is not as powerless as he might seem, pointing as proof to the recognition he says he has received from Albania (but not Communist China). The CPGB claims as well that he is extensively financed from unnamed sources.[8] With such apparent resources at his fingertips, and secure in the knowledge that he alone treads the 'true Marxist-Leninist' path, McCreery is confident of being successful – so confident, in fact, that he predicted to me that, with the inevitable collapse of capitalism, his Committee alone will lead the Socialist revolution.*

The Trotskyist movement first appeared on the British political scene in tangible form in 1932 when three Trotsky sympathizers – Henry Sara, Reginald Groves, and Harry Wicks – were expelled from the CPGB. Trotskyist influences had existed previously within the CPGB as far back as the early 1920s, but 1932 was the first point in time the group appeared as a separate entity in Great Britain. For the first six years of their existence, from 1932 to 1938, the British Trotskyists numbered no more than perhaps a dozen men. Although they had broken with the CPGB over Party policies, they spent most of their time not attacking the Party but arguing among themselves. One of their most noted differences was the question of what to call the USSR (was it a 'degenerated workers' state' or a 'bureaucratic

* McCreery died suddenly on April 10, 1965, from cancer. Who will succeed him as leader of the Committee is not known at the moment. The above passages were written four months before his death and remain unaltered.

collectivist state', etc.). They also argued over the possibilities of reforming the Third International. Perhaps the most important question to divide them was from what source were they to grow as a party. Was it best to work within the CPGB? Would it be wiser to enter the Labour Party and the Independent Labour Party; or was it better to set up an open party of their own? The first and last arguments have never been resolved within the British Trotskyist movement.

During these early years of the Movement, this small handful of Trotskyists began their tradition of splitting and re-splitting which has become one of the most noted of their characteristics. Whenever the questions of terminology or tactics arose, there would be a split, mostly one- or two-man affairs. Some of the splinter groups would rejoin the CPGB, some would 'enter'* the Labour Party, and still others would break away to set up a miniscule party on their own.

By 1938, a number of Trotskyist groups had solidified sufficiently to be recognizable. In their entirety, the total membership of all groups still numbered no more than a few score men, all of whom were ex-members of the CPGB. Among the major groups were: the Marxist League (formerly the Marxist Group), led by C. L. R. James, which published a newspaper called *Worker's Fight;* the Militant Group, led by Starkey Jackson, which published *The Militant;* the Worker's International League (the result of a split within the Militant Group), led by Jock Haston and Gerry Healy; and a small group that centred on Sara and Wicks. Groves had since moved on to the Labour Party.

In preparation for the Fourth International Foundation Conference in Paris of that year, the American Trotskyist, J. P. M. Cannon, of the Socialist Workers' Party came to Britain, apparently at Trotsky's behest, to unite these many factions. He succeeded in drawing all of them together with the exception of the Worker's International League which felt that the fusion was at best a temporary one. Nevertheless, the newly-united Trotskyists went to the Conference under the name of Revolutionary Socialist League and proceeded to denounce the uncooperative WIL as 'factionalist'. After the implications of Trotsky's *Death Agony of Capitalism and the Tasks of the Fourth International* had been thoroughly discussed by the delegates, the RSL returned to Great Britain and, as predicted by the WIL, promptly fragmented into their old warring factions. Within months, all the groups became inactive, with the exception of the WIL. The Con-

* In this context, to 'enter' means joining the Labour Party as a secret Trotskyist. The practise of entering was and still is known as either 'enterism' or 'entryism'. Those who have a compulsive desire to enter are said to be suffering from 'enteritis'.

ference seemed to have sapped the last bit of revolutionary strength from the Revolutionary Socialist League and for all practical purposes it ceased to function.

From 1939 to 1944, the WIL carried on alone. It was at this time that the Trotskyists first began to draw their recruits from outside the CPGB proper. The League's influence, therefore, tended to spread throughout the country rather than to remain centred exclusively in London. By 1944, the WIL claimed 200 members; it felt it had enough strength to bring all the inactive splinter groups together into an 'open' party. Its efforts were successful and the Revolutionary Communist Party was thus duly inaugurated with Jock Haston as General Secretary and Gerry Healy as one of the Party's leading organizers. The WIL went out of existence and most of its members joined the new organization. The five-year life of the RCP, from 1944 to 1949, was the only time in British Trotskyist history that virtually all Trotskyists in the country were united.

By their own standards, the Revolutionary Communist Party grew substantially. It was, for instance, the only organization in Britain besides the Independent Labour Party that advocated strike actions during the war. The CPGB and the trade unions had come to an agreement with Churchill's Coalition Government whereby they agreed not to encourage strikes. Trotskyists, therefore, received a certain amount of support from those groups which were dissatisfied with this arrangement. By the end of the war, the RCP had increased its strength approximately to 500 members – in their eyes, a huge figure.

From 1946 onwards, however, the RCP went into decline because the CPGB and trade unions resumed their support for strike actions. This cut the ground from under the Trotskyist policies and left them in a weak third position. In addition, their demand to 'Break the Coalition, Labour to Power' – a development that Trotskyists thought would not take place and one that the CPGB did not want to see take place – actually came about. Furthermore, Troskyist demands for nationalization, to their incredulity, were actually being implemented by the Labour Party. Finally, the RCP went into decline because the economic slump and revolution that Trotsky had predicted would take place within a year or so after the war did not materialize. According to Jock Haston, it was considered heretical for Trotskyists to suggest that there might be a post-war boom. They had so conditioned themselves to Trotsky's predictions that when it became evident that he had erred, many members quit in disillusionment.

By 1949, the RCP membership had been reduced to the pre-war level of a handful. Bickering broke out again, this time on such questions as: what was the proper terminology for the Soviet satellites ('Because Russia was a workers' state, were the satellites workers' states or deformed capitalist states?'); what was the maximum ceiling above which capitalist expansion could not rise (It was periodically revised upwards amidst assertions that such-and-such a limit was *the absolute* limit); whether India was *actually* a free country or whether British imperialism had simply assumed another disguise; and whether or not the RCP itself should drop its open status and pursue a course of entryism. Haston became, as he says, 'fed up' with the fighting and resigned; he joined the Labour Party where he has remained to this day. Those who were left decided to dissolve the RCP so that all the warring factions could do as each saw fit.

Although Trotsky had since died, he nevertheless contributed to the collapse of the RCP. He had always placed great emphasis on the need to develop revolutionary leaders; the need for theoriticians was not considered to be as great. After his death, therefore, an intellectual vacuum developed within the movement because all the potential theoriticians who joined felt obliged, as the expression was, 'to go down the mines' to develop those leadership qualities. This attitude, which still exists within all the Trotskyist sects, has always prevented a successor to Trotsky from stepping forward. Even today, Trotskyists are forced to interpret all history according to Trotsky; since many of his theses have proved inaccurate, it has left his followers in a state of intellectual chaos.

Moreover, the Trotskyists were hurt after the war because Stalin, for all the faults that they ascribed to him, was actually moving Socialism ahead and not just talking about it. In fact, those British Trotskyists with a sense of reality realized that every Troskyist group in the world was doing nothing but talking – talking so much and acting so infrequently that no Trotskyist group was recognized by any government throughout the world as anything more than a joke. As Russia went from strength to strength, it seemed to many Trotskyists that their own efforts were little more than an exercise in frustration and futility.

Although the dissolution of the RCP in 1949 had fragmented the Trotskyists into many sects (most of which were nameless), most of them remained loyal to their world headquarters in Paris, known as the International Secretariat of the Fourth International. This body was the 'home office' of the Trotskyist movement where information could be obtained, plans coordinated, and policies clarified. The first major break between British Trotskyists and the International Secretariat took place in 1953 and forms the basis for all the present alignment of loyalties among British Trotskyists. On one side stood the Secretariat's leader, Michael Raptis. Raptis has been a life-long Marxist and, although a Greek, he is currently a minor minister in Ben Bella's Algerian Government. In Trotskyist circles, Raptis is more commonly known by his alias, Michel Pablo. In opposition to Pablo stood a British faction under the control of Gerry Healy.

Thomas Gerard Healy, now in his early fifties, has been in politics since 1928 when he joined the Communist Party at the age of thirteen. In 1936, he was expelled (The CPGB, according to Healy, is all in favour of revolution 'just as long as it comes during office hours.') and joined the Militant Group which, at that time, was within the Labour Party. When the Group split in 1938, he moved into the WIL with Jock Haston and subsequently into the RCP in 1944. In 1945, the re-organized Secretariat (it did not function during the War) recognized the RCP as its British section. Healy, however, controlled a faction within the RCP which was given special autonomy to operate in secret while the bulk of the RCP was to present a 'harmless' face to the public. When the RCP was dissoved in 1949, Healy (so he claims) was designated the official British section of the IS. The same year, he and a fellow Trotskyist named John Lawrence organized the Socialist Fellowship. Both this group and its newspaper, *Socialist Outlook,* operated on the extreme left-wing edge of the Labour Party. However, because of its extremism, the Labour Party proscribed it in 1951.

The argument between the Pablo and the Healy-Lawrence factions revolved around a thesis called *The Rise and Fall of Stalinism* in which Pablo argued that a section of the Soviet bureaucracy was moving left and was thus capable of fulfilling the role of a revolutionary party in Russia. Healy and Lawrence maintained the old Trotskyist position that, since the Communist Party of the Soviet Union was degenerate, a new party had to be built on the outside. The argument was, in other words: was the old Trotskyist position correct, or should all Trotskyist groups disband because part of the Soviet bureaucracy could do the job?

To build support for his ideas, Pablo tried to organize a faction within the American SWP, known as the 'Cochranites', but J. P. M. Cannon heard of the plan and expelled them. This drew Cannon to Healy's and Lawrence's side in the argument. (The SWP was always considered a vital ally because Cannon had, at one time, been close to Trotsky. The Voorhis Act prevented the American Trotskyists from actively contributing their time or money to the 'foreign' parties; nevertheless, their moral support was always eagerly cultivated by British Trotskyists.) Lawrence, to complicate matters, then deserted Healy to re-ally himself with Pablo which produced a crisis within the Fellowship for control. Pablo told Healy to turn over control of it to Lawrence which he refused to do so he was expelled. Healy then fought Lawrence for control of *Socialist Outlook,* of which Lawrence was still Editor. Healy won control but the victory was pyrrhic since the Labour Party had recently proscribed it. One of the reasons it was proscribed was because it supported North Korea in the Korean War and thus lost the sympathy of the Labour Party. In addition, the newspaper was driven into bankruptcy by a successful libel action initiated by the Godfrey Phillips Tobacco Company.

At this juncture of Trotskyist history, there were now two definite Trotskyist groups in Great Britain: Healy's group, which from 1953 to 1959 was known as 'The Group' and worked within the Labour Party, and the 'Pabloites' which emerged later under the old RSL title (Lawrence did not lead it because, by this time, he had switched sides again and had returned to the CPGB.). The latter group has since split again between the 'Paris' faction loyal to Pablo and the 'Montevideo' faction loyal to a group of Latin Americans. The British section of the latter is known as the Revolutionary Workers' Party. All three groups claim to be the 'true' heirs to the old Secretariat.

Healy's 'Group' had perhaps 200 followers, mostly within the local Labour Parties of Streatham and Norwood. According to Gerry Healy, from 1953 to 1957, he and his followers spent most of their time 'organizing' within the Labour Party and the trade unions, assisting strikers, building strength at factory level, and toughening themselves for the day they were to take power. His first break came at the end of 1956 following both Khrushchev's Twentieth Congress Speech and the Hungarian revolution. Members of the CPGB were resigning in droves and Healy turned his attention away from recruiting within the Labour Party to recruiting these dissident ex-Communists. In a few months he had doubled his strength to approximately 400 members. He was able to draw into his sphere such ex-CPGB intellectuals as Brian Behan (a brother of Brendan Behan), Peter Cadogan, Chris Pallis (alias Martin Grainger), Peter Kerrigan, and Peter Fryer.

Flushed with his success, Healy began to publish *The Newsletter* with Peter Fryer, the ex-*Daily Worker* correspondent in Hungary, as Editor. He began to step up his industrial strike activities as well – particularly on the docks, among London Transport workers, and at the Shell-Mex South Bank Building site. In 1959, Healy was so confident of his strength that he and Brian Behan founded the Socialist Labour League whose objectives were outlined at their Whitsun conference of that year:

> The Socialist Labour League is an organization of Marxists within the Labour and trade union movement dedicated to fighting

> for Socialist policies in place of the present policies of class betrayal.
>
> As distinct from others, who call themselves Socialists, Marxists do not believe that it is possible to reform capitalism out of existence or to change it into Socialism by peaceful means...
>
> One of the chief tasks of the Socialist Labour League is to help trade unionists and members of the Labour Party, Communist Party and other working-class organizations... to build a new leadership firmly rooted in the working class and devoted to Socialist principles.[9]

In addition, the League's policies included a 'vigorous' fight against unemployment under the slogan 'Not a single worker on the street. Share the available work with no loss of pay', and the nationalization of basic industries under Workers' Control with no compensation to the ex-owners. The SLL also called for an end to the construction of rocket bases as well as the end to the manufacturing of H-bombs and germ-warfare materials.

Healy then applied for affiliation to the Labour Party 'on the same basis as the Fabian Society.' The Party's response was swift and unequivocal: it proscribed both *The Newsletter* and the SLL. In addition, it disbanded the Trotskyist-dominated Labour Parties in Streatham and Norwood.

The Labour Party's attitude towards Trotskyists within its ranks has always been that, as long as they are a loose grouping within the Party, it is more trouble than it is worth to expel them; but once the loose grouping solidifies into some recognizable shape, then the Labour Party moves quickly to eliminate it. When the SLL solidified and was thus proscribed, a wave of resignations and expulsions took place within the League. Fryer resigned as Editor of *The Newsletter;* Cadogan, Behan*, and Pallis were expelled and, by the end of 1959, most of the new recruits had vanished.

With the exit of the ex-Communists, Healy turned once more to the Labour Party for new recruits. Since 1959, he has concentrated on its youth, particularly among the Young Socialists. All British Trotskyists since the war have been attracted to the country's youth because they are more naïve, more active, and more rebellious than their older Party comrades. It has never been difficult for Healy to exert considerable influence over them. The young members of the Labour Party, unlike the older members, ask for political education and Healy does not miss the opportunity to press his views upon

* After leaving the SLL, Behan helped launch two organizations, the Workers' Party and the National Rank and File Movement, neither of which had any success. He is now reported to have retired from politics.

them. Moreover, the young are not interested in the more mundane activities of ordinary Labour Party meetings such as discussing local rates and selling raffle tickets; they are more interested in the 'important' questions of the day. Therefore, they tend to join such organizations as the Young Socialists where the 'important' questions are discussed. In addition, Healy has the advantage of not being faced with the union bloc vote in the Young Socialists as he would be at Labour Party conferences which makes his control over a large segment of its members almost certain.

The nature of Healy's organization, since it is the largest Trotskyist group in Great Britain today, and the only one that might have experienced considerable growth, perhaps best explains why it failed to take advantage of the CPGB schisms and has been reduced to working with politically impotent youth. In the first place, the SLL was founded in 1959 on the premise that revolution was 'just around the corner'. Ever since the war, Healy has been predicting increasing economic difficulties for the capitalists that would eventually be resolved by a Trotskyist revolution. In 1959, Healy apparently felt that the revolution was at hand and he predicted a wave of new strikes and wage restraints leading up to it. Many raw youths were attracted by the prospect of taking part in a revolution, particularly if they did not have to wait too long for it. But as the weeks, then months, and finally years passed with no hint of a revolution, Healy was reluctantly forced to postpone the date of the crisis on the basis of the 'temporary economic stabilization' of capitalism. Many of the rank-and-file became disillusioned at the prospect of having to wait indefinitely for the catastrophe and resigned. In fact, the average length of membership was less than twelve months per man.

However, the primary reason the SLL has not grown has been due to the bureaucratic nature of the organization itself. Healy, as General Secretary, runs a very militant organization with himself as absolute leader and with the assistance of perhaps a dozen trusted aides – a ratio of officials to members that one ex-member estimated, if applied to the Labour Party, would produce 10,000 officials. Two of the closest men to Healy are the Banda Brothers, Mike and Tony, who are wealthy Ceylonese of Dutch extraction. Their proper surname is Vander Poorten. Mike Banda is the current Editor of *The Newsletter* as well as a Director and shareholder (350 shares at time of incorporation) of Plough Press. Healy has no official connection with the Press although he works very closely with those who have, since *The Newsletter* and most of his other literature are printed on its presses. Tony Banda's duties are more obscure but his job is primarily to act as the League's political organizer. Other men closely tied to this leadership clique include Cliff Slaughter, a lecturer at

Leeds University and co-Editor of the SLL quarterly, *Fourth International;* Thomas Dicks, an AEU engineer; and Charles Van Gelderen, a South African journalist.

In an organization of such small size and of such militancy, the presence of this leadership clique looms large. Since most of the rank-and-file members are naïve, they tend to accept more readily the need for secrecy and the changing of rules in the interests of 'security'. As a result, an unusual amount of power rests in the hands of the leaders. They dominate the organization completely with Healy the most dominant of all. The inflexibility of their rule is taken to the extent that they will not tolerate the slightest deviation from either Marxism-Leninism (their version) or the edicts which they issue on occasion concerning group policies and activities. For instance, the expulsions of Behan, Cadogan, and Pallis were the results of each man's inability to develop healthy discussions of theory or policy within the League, their inability to receive any redress for their grievances, and the reluctance of the clique to give them any responsibilities. Peter Fryer, in a long open letter to the Members of the League, written shortly after he resigned in 1959, said:

> The denial of democracy to members of the organization is summed up by the general secretary himself in two phrases he has employed recently: 'I am the party' and – in answer to the question 'How do you see Socialism?' – 'I don't care what happens after we take power. All I'm interested in is the Movement.'

That a split exists between the rank-and-file and the leadership is apparent; the leaders do not accept the ordinary members as equals and the members themselves are baffled by the restrictions placed on their participation in the organization. Such a split suggests that the greater the rigidity of the clique, the greater the twists and turns of policy, which in turn leads to the suppression of any discussion that might question the decisions of the leaders.

Because he does not encourage any communication between his few followers and the leadership clique, there is no effective machinery for the redress of grievances. This works both ways: the rank-and-file are not encouraged to appeal to the higher authorities and the members of the clique, if they feel one of Healy's policies is inadequate, cannot appeal to the ordinary members for support if they wish to retain their privileged position in the clique. Therefore, enough wrong decisions relentlessly carried out, with little or no consideration being given either to the desires and needs of the rank-and-file or to changing conditions, can have a debilitating effect on the organization. In a short period of time all activities are undertaken in a spirit of cynicism. There is some indication that the policy is a deliberate one in order that the leadership remain intact and unthreatened by a rank-and-file that perhaps might have a few of their own ideas to contribute.

Most members who leave the SLL are embittered by both Healy and his methods. Martin Grainger, in another letter to the organization dated June 10th, 1960, explains perhaps why:

> My submission is that the present political conceptions of the leadership of the SLL are unmarxist to the core and an obstacle to the building of a revolutionary movement. Their petty organizational intrigues flow from the needs of politically bankrupt people to preserve their positions by organizational methods. This explains the small secret meetings of committees within committees (justifiable perhaps on the eve of the seizure of power . . . but surely a trifle ludicrous in an organization not 300 strong . . .). It explains their dissolution of branches, their 'moving' of political dissidents, their repeated intimidations of comrades, their obsessional fear of even mildly unorthodox views – or of simple questions for which readily prepared answers are not available – their bureaucratic suspicion of anything diverging from the line they have been faithfully repeating for over 20 years – despite ever-accumulating evidence of its inadequacy to explain the world of today – their ready expenditure of Party funds for long journeys to 'straighten out' comrades diverging even a few degrees from the prevailing orthodoxy, their reduction of all real intellectual life within the organization to the level of a religious service . . . their whistling in the dark in relation to sales of the paper or to membership, their need for a strong man to hide their own intellectual poverty, and finally their almost gleeful use of the disciplinary clauses of the constitution as some modern kind of guillotine. All these denote a profound ideological decomposition and a complete abandonment of scientific methods of thought. In the Transitional Programme, Trotsky speaks of the promises for the proletarian revolution being not only ripe, but rotten ripe. I would suggest that the rot, political and organizational, has now gained a deep foothold in the ideas and parties of his followers.

Healy has been able to maintain a rank-and-file organization only because of the 'romanticism' he has built around the League and because of the pace at which he drives his troops. He promises an immediate revolution, a split within the Labour Party, a wave of social unrest and economic setbacks, and a host of other 'romantic' catastrophes. He encourages clandestine attitudes such as secrecy and militancy, some of which are taken to unusual lengths. For instance, it was reported that at one SLL conference, the speakers did not introduce themselves by name but by number. And, in addition, he has been wooing his rank-and-file since 1950 with the promises of a daily newspaper.

His demands upon his followers are heavy: he requires that they spend *all* their spare time working on SLL activities. He keeps them jumping from project to project with such frequency that they have little time for intra-party intrigue. One week he will conduct an anti-Fascist campaign, the next week he will concentrate on recruiting ex-Communists, the week after that on recruiting 'unemployed youth' (as one ex-member told me, 'The only question for which unemployed youth are prepared to fight is for better recreation facilities'), and the week after that on organizational work among the Young Socialists. With all of 200 men he even ran a campaign to topple the Government over the Profumo scandal. Among other Trotskyists, these short and intense campaigns are known as 'smash-and-grabs', a phrase of which Healy is not particularly fond.

This unending activity creates the illusion of importance, a sense of accomplishment, and a feeling of revolutionary fervour. However, it does not last. As soon as it becomes apparent that the revolution is not around the corner and that very little is in fact being accomplished, the disillusioned members soon quit. Those youths who leave – bitter, harassed, frustrated, and cynical – are old men before they come of age.

The many activities of his followers, however, has a self-generating effect on the membership. Because the new members – raw, eager, and idealistic as they are – work hard, they stir up enough dust to attract new members at approximately the same rate as the losses the organization incurs from the disenchanted. The membership, therefore, remains constant in number which, at the moment, hovers somewhere below the 200 mark. However, Britain does not have an inexhaustible supply of rebellious youths, particularly those who would be attracted to Trotskyism, and there is some indication that Healy has run through all the available reserves. An indication of the lengths he has had to go in order to maintain his membership at its current level was his recent appeal for new members among the 'Mods' and 'Rockers'.

Healy claims that he still has the backing of most of Britain's left-wing youth and that he has considerable strength as well within Transport House itself. He added that his support is larger than most people believe and that it would be foolish for anyone to under-estimate his potential. How true these claims are is difficult to ascertain but most if not all members of the Labour Party with whom I talked discount them. Trade unionists, particularly those who have had some contact with the League, also feel that Healy is somewhat overstating his case.

There is no doubt that Healy has a well-deserved reputation as an organizer of exceptional ability. Whether he uses this talent to build the SLL into a larger, more potentially disruptive force is unknown, but most people, those who are familiar with Healy personally, doubt that he will. They claim that he missed his chance to grow when he could not retain the loyalty of the ex-Communists who left the CPGB during and after the Hungarian revolution. They claim as well that behind the façade of a revolutionary party, Healy is more interested in being Number One in the organization and that it makes little difference to him how few there are to be led.

In spite of these criticisms, there are still a small group of followers who stick by him through all the alarms, crises, campaigns and purges. They are ardent, cynical, and dedicated Marxists who will follow him wherever he leads them, confident that the revolution he has been predicting for 20 years will one day come about.

When Healy split with the Fourth International in 1953, another organization loyal to Pablo was formed in Great Britain which was promptly designated the 'official' British Section of the Secretariat. It was called the Revolutionary Socialist League, the same name that was used by the short-lived amalgam of pre-war British Trotskyists. Since 1953, the League has been under the control of two long-time Trotskyists, Jimmy Dean, a member of the Chemical Worker's Union and Ted Grant, a Post Office employee. During the 12 years of its life, the League has never had more than 50 members, most if not all of whom are industrial workers. Until recently, the organization published a journal called *Socialist Fight* which has led a rather precarious life. It has not been published since late 1963 and there is some speculation that it has seen its last issue.

The RSL is an entryist group first and foremost. It believes that the Trotskyist revolution will be brought about through the Labour Party. It therefore concentrates all its efforts on influencing Party members. The League has particular strength in the East Islington Labour Party and the Stoke Newington & Hackney North Labour Party. The RSL is, in addition, the most clandestine of all the British Trotskyist sects: it publishes no literature, it has no official headquarters, and it does not discuss its problems in public. Recently, it has come to the conclusion that the organization does not need a public face and it has dropped the RSL title in favour of no name at all. It is for this reason that many people feel that *Socialist Fight* may not be revived. The members of the League believe their organization can grow by word-of-mouth and by clandestine work within the Labour Party.

The League does concede, however, the need to sell some literature. For this purpose, it runs a London bookstore call W.I.R. Publications which offers for sale both British and foreign Trotskyist material.

The RSL is linked with a group of Nottingham Trotskyists known as either the 'Internationalists' or the 'Nottingham Group'. It was formed in late 1963 and its only mark of any distinction is its desire to co-operate with Continental Trotskyists. The headquarters of this sect is Jordan's Bookshop in Nottingham which is run by Pat Jordan, an ex-Communist. Its major spokesman, however, is Ken Coates, also an ex-Communist, who was once a member of Healy's SLL. Coates is co-Editor of the Group's publication, *The Week,* which is pro-Algerian and anti-American. Articles with such titles as 'Gangsters in Business' and 'Paunch Corps' are not uncommon.

Another of its major publications is the bi-monthly *International Socialist Journal* which accepts articles from 'Socialists' from all over the world. Its editorial offices are in Italy but its British branch is in Nottingham. The editorial board and list of sponsors for ISJ are not limited, as in the case of *The Week,* to Britons but carry the names of Belgians, Italians, and Frenchmen as well. The *Journal* carries such articles as: 'The XX Congress of the Swedish Communist Party', and 'Trade Unionism on the Attack' ('Oppression of the workers does not begin in the factory. It starts at school . . .'). It also carries advertisements for *Peace News*.

According to Coates, the purpose of the two publications is to offer a constructive point of view to Labour Party thinking rather than a factional point of view. He feels that the evolution of the Common Market, for instance, has posed problems for the labour movement in Europe that the British labour movement has not considered. He would like to see a body of literature brought together, particularly within the *Journal,* so that the issues at stake can be properly focused. He claims that his 'sphere of influence' is intellectually tempered by many factors: all those who support his magazines, he says, are Socialists but they draw their own individual political beliefs from a variety of sources, some of which are Marxist, others of which he claims are not. He told me that a 'Marxist dialogue' is maintained that includes some Trotskyist ideas but he does not think that that makes him or his organization Trotskyist.

The Revolutionary Workers' Party (Trotskyist), British Section of the IV International, to give it its full title, is another British

Trotskyist group of perhaps 20 individuals. This faction split off from the RSL in 1962 and claims that the 'official' Secretariat is now located in Montevideo under the leadership of an Argentinian named J. Posadas. The British section is run by three men: Theo Melville, an ex-member of both the Internationalists and the RSL; John Fairhead, an ex-member of the 'Cliffites'; and John Davis, the Editor of the RWP's newspaper, *Red Flag,* and an ex-member of the Labour Party, CND, Committee of 100, and the Internationalists. Before he became a Trotskyist, Davis spent six years as an employee at the Foulness Island Atomic Weapons Research Establishment. Davis' flat serves as the Party's headquarters and is located in Kensington, near Harrods.

The members of the RWP follow such a revolutionary line that among Marxists they have earned the sobriquet of 'ultra left adventurist maniacs'. The description is due to the RWP's belief that atomic war is inevitable – one of the points on which it broke with the Pabloists. It is the most important point of the RWP policy. Davis, Melville and Fairhead see Britain's and America's atomic bombs as symbols necessary to maintain each country's authority in the world. They believe that both countries will be forced one day to use their bombs on the colonial and/or Socialist nations in order to maintain that authority. They therefore feel that Russia should start a nuclear war with a pre-emptive strike against the capitalist states before the West turns on the Socialist states. Their belief in the inevitability of nuclear war has an hysterical quality about it that is uncommon in British Marxist circles today. For instance, their worldwide leader, J. Posadas, reflected the nature of the hysteria when he said in a 1962 speech:

> . . . With all the historical strength and the decision of our conscience, of our confidence and understanding, we repeat, we dwell upon, we stress, the atomic war is inevitable. It might destroy half of mankind, it is going to destroy all the human wealth. It might – most of it is going to be destroyed, most of it. It is going to destroy and it is going to be a real earthly Hell, but that is not going to hinder Communism . . . All the material possessions that exist might be destroyed, but while there exist ten men who have understood what Communism is, there will be thousands, millions, who will understand and they will conduct the history to come . . .
>
> We are not fighting to get Socialism now. We fight for a biological, physiological need. We feel the intellectual need for fighting. When Trotsky said when he was dying: 'I think I am sure the Fourth International will triumph, go on!', it was because he felt he was going to live thousands and thousands of years.[10]

The ancillary policies of the RWP are, in its own words, 'transitional' and are not to be confused with its policies once in power. These transitional policies demand: a 40-hour week in all industries (in preparation for a 35-hour week); an immediate 20 per cent increase in everyone's wages; 'the profits of automation to go to the workers'; the expropriation of royal palaces, luxury properties and unoccupied dwellings to meet the housing shortage; the expropriation of large farms; the nationalization of all key industries without compensation; workers' control of all industry; the establishment of industrial unions on a militant anti-capitalist programme; state monopoly of foreign trade; the withdrawal of Britain from all 'imperialist alliances'; and the initiation of a 'struggle against imperialism and the defence of the colonial revolution by every means including strike, boycott and sabotage, and the dispatch of arms to colonial workers'.[11]

The RWP supports most of the conclusions of China's 'twenty-five points'[12] and finds that much of its sympathies lie with their oriental comrades. It supports Cuba, Albania, and Algeria; it supports the need for an 'open' revolutionary Party (not a 'league' or a 'group') dedicated to smashing capitalism; it supports the 'Workers' Bomb' (because the 'workers' are not imperialists); and it supports the colonial revolution.

Melville and Davis, the only two of the three leaders with whom I had a chance to talk, expressed nothing but scorn for most of the other political parties in Great Britain. Their hatred of the Conservative Party is total; the Labour Party, they feel, has sold its soul to capitalism; the CPGB has abandoned Marxism for 'peaceful co-existence'; the RSL is useless because it believes in entryism; the SLL does not believe in the inevitability of war and is a 'dictatorship'; and so on. They do not go so far, however, as to consider themselves as the only ones capable of leading the revolution; they are willing to fuse their organization to any other that agree with their policies. So far, Melville and David have found only one faction within another British party who sympathize with them: a small group of dissidents within McCreery's Committee against Revisionism. There is some indication that this faction and the RWP recently have explored the possibility of an alliance. Both organizations are the only two political parties in Great Britain whose views are similar to the Chinese Communist views. Such a link-up is considered feasible by many Marxists. The rebels within McCreery's group (who they are and how large are their numbers are unknown) apparently do not like the anti-Stalinist attitudes of the RWP, nor does the RWP relish Chinese attacks on the Trotskyists. (Melville claims the attacks are only a ploy to attract the old-line Stalinists into the Chinese camp.)

Whether there will be a union between these two groups is not known at the moment, but it is felt by many that, if the two can shield their eyes to the anomalies of a Trotskyist-Stalinist fusion, they might find themselves at least playing mutually complementary roles.

There has been no evidence that the RWP has made any appreciable impact upon either the Labour Party or trade unions. Every member, however, is a worker, some of whom are skilled; most of them belong to a local Labour Party. If they all have the zeal and fanaticism of Melville, Fairhead, Davis, and Posadas, then they could be a minor source of irritation to the anti-Communist sectors of the Labour Party and the unions. Despite their advocacy of sabotage, there have been no indications that they have as yet planned any such acts.

Their newspaper, *Red Flag,* is the most expensively produced piece of fringe literature in Britain. Only four pages long, it is laid out in a professional manner on high-quality paper, and is printed in two colours – red and black. Most of the articles are quite long and they have the same hysterical ring as Posadas's speech. Sample headlines include: 'Out With Imperialism', 'Centralize Anti-Capitalist Offensive', and 'Why the Pentagon Killed Kennedy'. The masthead features a large-type 'Red Flag' which is followed by a red hammer-and-sickle emblem. Above it is the slogan 'Workers of the World, Unite!' and a quotation by Trotsky: 'Without the Party we are nothing. With the Party we are everything.'

Melville and Davis claim to print and sell 1,000 copies of *Red Flag* per month on a budget of £60. Most of this money comes from their Secretariat in Montevideo and explains how such a small group can have such an elaborate newspaper. The break-down of sales is, in rough figures: 20 to RWP members; a few hundred local sales to outsiders; a few hundred to foreign customers; perhaps a dozen to anti-Communist organizations such as the Economic League and Common Cause; and a few to libraries and collectors. The remainder go unsold.

The three smallest Trotskyist groups in Great Britain are less political parties and more 'speres of influence' revolving around their own individual literary efforts. In their own words, they carry on a 'Marxist dialogue', presenting new twists to old theories, re-interpreting Socialist needs in light of present developments, and fending off those theses which they deem as no longer suitable. Each one of these groups is small and has virtually no influence in the trade unions or Labour Party. Each group, however, operates as an extreme left-wing faction within the Labour Party.

The most intellectual of the three is an organization that is known as either the 'Socialist Review Group', the 'International Socialism Group', or the 'Cliffites'. This organization originated in 1951 with the publication of *Socialist Review* which is now defunct. Its Editor was Michael Kidron, now the Editor of the current organization's major publication, *International Socialism*. In addition to this magazine, Kidron and his associates are allied with both *Young Guard*, a newspaper that circulates among the Young Socialists, and *Labour Worker*, edited in Glasgow by Harry McShane. McShane was one of the founders of, but is no longer associated with, the Socialist Worker's Federation, a small political group that advocates the federalization of all factions seeking workers' control in industry.

In addition to Kidron and McShane, the leading members of this organization include Tony Cliff (whose real name is Ygail Gluckstein and who is married to Kidron's sister), the man who provided the initial impetus for the formation of this 'sphere' with the publication of his book *Russia, A Marxist Analysis;* and Alasdair MacIntyre, a lecturer in Philosophy at Leeds University. At one time or another, other Marxists of note have been associated with the group. For example: Martin Grainger, an ex-member of the SLL and the current leader of the Solidarists; Peter Cadogan, also an ex-member of the SLL and currently a teacher in Cambridge; and John Fairhead, now with the RWP.

Kidron says that the primary purpose of his group is to analyse the course of Socialism not only in Britain but throughout the world as well. He claims that his group is not Trotskyist but Trotskyist-derived, pointing out that Socialism is his first concern and that his conclusions may only incidentally incorporate the thoughts and theses of Trotsky. He adds that he welcomes all Socialist thought – from Marx, Lenin, E. V. Debs, or anyone else – if it can be of assistance to him. His and his associates' major preoccupations at the moment are analysing the causes for economic stabilization in the capitalist states and re-appraising Communism and Russia ('State Capitalism') as objectively as possible. Kidron feels that capitalism has stabilized itself on the basis of its expenditure on arms by exporting inflation which, he claims, has minimized the fluctuations of ordinary business cycles. He believes that this stabilization will become increasngly more viable in the 1970s when Russia reaches the point of military strength equal to that of the West. This may lead, he adds, to a nuclear war which could only be averted by workers' control of the state and industry. His solution is based, he says, on a re-examination of Trotsky's analysis that private ownership is a fundamental characteristic of capitalism. Kidron claims that, on the contrary, capitalism is only the unplanned accumulation of wealth and that Trotsky's stress on nationalization as a means to material abundance must be replaced by stress on workers' control as a means to human freedom.

This group concerns itself with additional problems as well, the most noted of which are: the significance of the 'spontaneous imperialist withdrawal' from the colonies (as opposed to the more prevalent Marxist attitude that the 'imperialists' are being forced out by pressure from the Socialist states); the possibilities of transmuting the arms competition into something else; a re-appraisal of the Sino-Soviet split; and a re-appraisal of Castro's Cuba ('Yanqui No! Castro No! Cuba Si!').

Most of the articles in *International Socialism* are beyond the ken of other Marxists. The Cliffites are criticized on the grounds that they live in an ivory tower and do not understand the 'real' problems of the day. Contrary to this claim, Kidron and his associates descend into the political arena to compete for the political allegiance of the Young Socialists. They, like Healy, have their own faction within the Young Socialists which vies yearly with the other left-wing groups for the empty privilege of controlling the YS Executive Council. To date, the Young Socialists are still controlled by individuals faithful to the Labour Party but their margin of control is slim. Healy and his militant janissaries are pressing this leadership to its limits; Kidron's group is running a poor third. With the exception of their activities among these youths, however, Kidron and his followers stay out of the political hustings to dispense analyses on whatever subjects they deem worthy of their efforts.

Another Marxist group with a Trotskyist bias is the 'Socialism Reaffirmed Group', otherwise known as the 'Solidarists', which was founded in 1961 by Martin Grainger (i.e. Chris Pallis), an ex-member of the SLL. Its offices are located above the ILP's on Kings Cross Road. Leading figures in this group besides Grainger include: Bob Potter, an Australian and ex-member of both the CPGB and the SLL; and Ken Weller, an ex-member of the Young Communist League who is also presently associated with the Committee of 100.

The Solidarists are known by other Marxists as 'anarcho-Marxists' because they combine their Socialism with the theories of the anarcho-syndicalists. They seem to be sufficiently anti-Marx, anti-Lenin, anti-Trotsky, and anti-bureaucracy to permit them to fuse their brand of Socialism with the anarcho-syndicalist concepts of spontaneity and Workers' Control. They publish a pamphlet called *Solidarity* ('For Workers' Power') which the Communist Party considers to be 'violent [and] peppered with bad language to show how "proletarian" they are . . .' Grainger and his associates were responsible, in part, for the publication of the pamphlet on the Regional Seats of Government called *Resistance Shall Grow*, which states:

> You can be Tory or Labour, Communist or Empire Loyalist, Christian or Atheist, genius of moron, tear-arse or layabout, capitalist or worker, prostitute or Duchess of Argyll, pimp, bastard, or bugger-boy, copper's nark or pacifist fruit-juicer, it doesn't matter who or what. Your future is to be equally radioactive and you are all to be equally dead. The only survivors will be a few Top Bureaucrats, with of course one month's supply of uncontaminated food and water at their disposal. We need a Kafka to write a novel about the last days in the Bunkers for Bureaucrats.

The solidarists, like the anarcho-syndicalists, concentrate on disruptive (their own word) activities, particularly among the trade unions; to date, their efforts have been negligible. Their basic aims are Workers' Control and a Socialist society free of bureaucracy. Their hatred of bureaucracies – both capitalist and Socialist – has become an obsession with them. They feel justified, for instance, in associating themselves with any other organization if that organization is anti-bureaucrat. Whenever a new campaign against this 'Evil' is about to be launched, say by the Committee of 100, the Solidarists are the first to join. Membership in their own organization, therefore, is at best a casual affair.

The smallest definable Trotskyist group in Great Britain is a sect which revolves around a magazine called *Socialist Current*. This organization split from the RSL in 1957 over the question of entryism (it believes in 'deep' entry into the Labour Party) and over the question of party leadership (it claims that great leaders are not necessary to do the job of the working classes). Like all other Trotskyist groups, its members claim that they alone hold the 'classical Trotskyist position'. They say that the SLL is 'Stalinist', that Pablo and the RSL are 'capitulationists', and that the 'maniacs' in the RWP are living in a 'dream world'. They believe that the present period of history is not a period of imperialism but of 'état-ism' where the state intervenes in all disputes. They do not believe in the Bomb – capitalist, 'workers' or otherwise – and they are convinced that the only way capitalism can be overthrown in Britain is by converting the Labour Party to its cause.

At the time of its split from the Revolutionary Socialist League in 1957, the Socialist Current group consisted of three members. It has since grown to nine, which led one of them to say to me: 'We grow by one member per year.' Its leaders are Sam Levy, the Editor of *Socialist Current;* Frank Rowe and Morry Sollof – their intellectuals; and Ted Bunker, the magazine's Business Manager. Five members remain as rank-and-file which probably makes this 'sphere' the most highly bureaucratic of all left-wing groups.

On the whole, the Trotskyists seem to be in a political limbo, neither growing nor dying. Their failure to grow is due to many factors, the most noted of which, as previously pointed out, was Trotsky himself. His theories have not stood the test of time and his emphasis on leadership has choked off the development of a new generation of theoreticians. Worst still, most if not all of Trotsky's premises were pessimistic: it has taken nearly a quarter of a century following his death for some Trotskyists to realize that most Britons are no longer the pessimists they were in the 1930s. With rising wages, better living and working conditions, the growth of colonial independence, a wider scope of opportunity for their children, the moves to limit the use of nuclear weapons, etc., the working classes – those 'down-trodden masses' whom Trotsky believed would one day throw off the yoke of capitalism – are not only optimistic but far more self-confident than they have ever been. They have no intention of throwing away their hard-earned good-fortune on an organization that advertises itself as an instrument of governmental destruction. Troskyists are a small group of pessimists in a sea of optimists.

Why then do they still exist? Certainly one reason would be the desire of some of them to escape from reality. There are very few Trotskyists who spend much of their time discussing relevant subjects. Their primary interests still seem to be arguing over terminology and the merits of entryism, as well as justifying their own claims as Trotsky's only heir. These questions provoke the inevitable response of 'Who cares?' from their opponents and tends to frighten off all potential converts except the most dedicated escapists.

Another reason why the Trotskyists have not faded from the scene is that they can still flourish within the Labour Party. Since it is impossible to weed out every last Trotskyist, those individuals and their ill-defined groups who have not been expelled or proscribed, find the Labour Party a vast field, full of opportunities for them. It is difficult for Trotskyists to maintain morale in an organization of say 50 individuals who do not belong to the Labour Party. The resolutions they pass and the activities they undertake give no impression of being relevant which, in fact, they are not. But those same 50 Trotskyists within the Labour Party can exert some influence, particularly over a small local Labour Party. If they are not even capable of that, their activities at least give them the impression that they are fighting a real and live enemy – the Party's right wing. In addition, if these 50 people succeed in passing a resolution in some local Labour Party, it creates the impression that they are accomplishing something. They have little competition from left-wing ginger groups within the Party – the 'Bevanites', 'Tribunites', and 'Victory for Socialism' group – because, as 'Left-Social Democrats', these are more democratic, more disorganized and less cohesive than the militant Trotskyists. Furthermore, Trotskyists are often defended by these same ginger groups because they are a convenient fulcrum which can be used to prod the Labour Party leadership faster down the road to Socialism.

In spite of these reasons why the Trotskyists have neither grown nor died, there is one overriding reason why they have never received any support from the British people. British Trotskyists, since their emergence on to the political scene in 1932, have always been experts on Russia and the Russian revolution but, in contrast, they have never understood Britain or the British revolution.

In addition to the Marxists of the Stalinist, 'revisionist', and Trotskyist traditions, there exist two British parties that can only be classified as 'independent' Marxist. They are known respectively as the Independent Labour Party and the Socialist Party of Great Britain, two of the oldest left-wing parties in existence in the country today.

The Independent Labour Party has been involved in a slow struggle with death ever since its disaffiliation from the Labour Party in 1932. From its inception in 1893 until 1932, the ILP prospered with the growth of the Labour Party for, indeed, it was a part of it. It was the seed-bed for many prominent Labour Party figures, from J. Keir Hardie to Fenner Brockway. The Party reached its greatest peak of strength in the 1929 General Election when it could count 37 MPs as its own. In 1932, however, the ILP broke with the Labour Party over many long-standing differences, the most noted of which were: that the Labour Party should not try to administer capitalism during an economic decline; that the Labour Party refused to accept its programme called 'Socialism in Our Time'; and that, under the circumstances, its own members could not accept the Labour Party whip. Since that time, the fortunes of the ILP have been in decline;

both the CPGB and Trotskyists have attempted take-overs; it long ago (1947) saw the last of its representatives in Parliament; and its membership and electoral strength have ebbed away in the same proportion. By 1959, for instance, two ILP Parliamentary candidates standing in the General Election could corner no more than 923 votes between them.

It is generally felt that the prospects of an ILP renaissance are slight. One of the reasons is the nature of its policies. Certainly the most outstanding feature is their bland nature – boring Socialism that gives no hint of ever having undergone a re-appraisal. Its members talk in terms of 'class struggle', 'a classless society', 'capitalist oppression' and 'public ownership of the means of production', phrases for which they have no definitions. In an age when many Marxists are sophisticated intellectuals – questioning the old dogmas, searching for new answers – these policies seem to many left-wingers to be dull and out-dated. Critics point out that there are at least half a dozen Socialist groups in Britain of one hue or another that not only incorporate basic ILP policies within their own, but also analyse their policies better, sell them (relatively) more effectively, and act more vigorously upon them.

Emrys Thomas, ILP Chairman, claims that his Party has assets which his critics do not possess. The ILP, he said, is strongly anti-Apartheid, anti-Spain and anti-conscription; it is, he continued, enthusiastically pro-Marxist, pro-Workers' Control and pro-industrial (as opposed to craft) unions. He added that the Party's greatest asset is its altruism.

If its policies do not excite the imagination of left-wing groups neither does its organization. Membership is down to an estimated 250 and its industrial activities are practically non-existent. Those members who remain seem less interested in Marx than complaining in general about the society in which they live. Much like the Solidarists (who operate from the floors above), the ILP members skip from group to group in search of an injustice – the Committee of 100, the anarcho-syndicalists, and the CND, for instance – and their catholic tastes are perhaps unconsciously reflected in their newspaper *Socialist Leader* ('Founded by Keir Hardie'). In it are articles and advertisements concerning the anarchists, *Peace News*, and the CND, for example; virtually nothing can be found on the goals of the ILP. They even have articles in Esperanto.

The primary reason the ILP does not die is that it is probably the wealthiest political organization per member in Great Britain. Its wealth stems from two sources: the land and buildings it owns (or has sold) and its printing presses. In its early years, the ILP found it difficult as a left-wing group to rent premises and to have its own propaganda printed. It therefore made it its policy, whenever possible, to own its own land and presses. This policy has paid off financially: as the membership shrank so the land values have increased; the Bristol branch, for instance, is thought to have £6,000 in the bank, the Armley (Leeds) branch approximately £5,000 and the Glasgow branch about £4,000. Its presses, National Labour Press Ltd. in London which incorporates Blackfriars Press Ltd. of Leicester, have branched out into a successful commercial printing firm with an estimated turnover of £250,000 per year.[13]

From a financial point of view the future holds promise for the Party, but from a political point of view the future is clouded. The members are still remarkably resistent to take-overs by more ambitious groups, but there does not seem to be the slightest intellectual or physical ferment emanating from their Kings Cross headquarters. As the *Sunday Times* once put it, they probably will die intestate.

The members of the Socialist Party of Great Britain do not feel their Marxism to be bland or simplified but to be the purest form of Marxism advocated in Great Britain today. They disclaim all prophets – Lenin, Engels, Bakunin, Stalin, Trotsky, etc. – except Karl Marx and, at that, do not subscribe wholeheartedly to all his theses.

As with the ILP, the SPGB pre-dates the formation of the Labour Party by a few years yet, unlike the ILP, it has never played a leading role in British politics. No great leaders have emerged from the SPGB ranks; its electoral efforts have been and continue to be disastrous (they have been reduced to the stage of asking voters to deface their ballots with the word 'Socialism'); and there are no signs that it is any closer to its goals than it was 60 years ago. In the eyes of the SPGB, the Labour Party, the CPGB, the Trotskyists, and any other group calling itself 'Socialist' have betrayed the tenets of Marxism, either by compromising their ideals or allying themselves with capitalism. Only the SPGB, its members say, have resisted the temptations of expediency. As a result, they claim they have been forced to live in the political wilderness.

The SPGB holds that 'society as it is presently constituted is based upon the ownership of the means of living by the capitalist or master class' and that, therefore, there is an antagonism of interests, manifesting itself as a class struggle between those who possess and do not produce and those who produce but do not possess. This antagonism, it asserts, must be abolished by the emancipation of the working class who, in order to ensure its freedom, must control the means of production and the machinery of government. Once this stage has been reached, it believes that Marxist theories will then come to full flower. The State will wither away, each man will produce according to his abilities and each will receive according to his needs.

Joe MacGinnis, a long-time member of the Party – it has no leaders in keeping with the belief that, with the withering away of the State, leaders become unnecessary – and a musician by trade, explained to me that the current 'governing of men' would be replaced by 'the administration of things'. There would be no pricing system, he said; no buying or selling, no need for locks and keys (since personal property would cease to exist), and no laws 'restricting the activities of the masses'. Because there would be no vehicle for the personal accumulation of wealth, he added, there would be no possibility for personal domination. He said that whatever one person needed would be given to him free of charge. He gave as an example a man going to the water tap and drinking as much as he pleased, leaving it when he was finished for anyone else who wanted to use it. He added, 'No one thinks of owning the pigeons in Trafalgar Square; they belong to everyone'.

In addition, he said that members of the SPGB are 'materialists' and are not religiously oriented*. They do not associate themselves with any group such as the Labour Party or the CPGB because they claim those groups retain the symbols and tools of the old order: religion, the wage system, capital, class, and so forth. MacGinnis stated that the SPGB does not think in terms of success but rather in terms of a 'process based on urgency in the face of overwhelming odds and failure'.

Throughout the left-wing, the SPGB is known facetiously as the 'Small Party of Good Boys'. In one sense, the description is apt for the party does not feel that the revolution – the overthrow of capitalism – need be violent. It believes, on the contrary, that only through the education of the working classes will pure Marxist Socialism be achieved. It does not imply that capitalism and the parliamentary system can be reformed. Capitalism must be destroyed, it believes, but only when the working classes have 'a conscious understanding and desire for Socialism'. At that time, capitalism will peacefully disappear and Socialism will take its place.

To this end, the Party carries on a number of educational activities: its members are indefatigable street-corner speakers – at Marble Arch, Lincoln's Inn, and Charing Cross – who are cruelly heckled by the

* Religion is still a delicate subject among all British Marxist groups since many Marxists retain vestiges of their early religious upbringing. Whenever the subject is raised, particularly the question 'What is your religion?', it is usually answered with 'I am a Presbyterian Atheist', 'I am a Church of England Atheist', 'I am a Catholic Atheist', etc.

less idealistic Marxists in the crowd. In spite of the abuse they receive, the speakers tour the country, talking to whoever wants to listen, debating with Communists, anarchists, and capitalists alike. All SPGB meetings are open to the public and, in this respect, it is the least clandestine and most friendly of the Marxist groups. Very few aspects of the party are secret except their membership figures which are not made public, in all probability to hide the fact that they are so small a group. Their literature – *Socialist Standard, The Western Socialist* (the organ of the World Socialist Party of the United States, an SPGB ally), *Questions of the Day,* and *The SPGB, its Principles and Aims* – is pressed upon visitors with unusual zeal, despite the fact that it is yellowing with age.

They are not a confident group but they are sincere and convinced Marxists who believe that some day, in the distant future, their views will come to the fore. In the interim, they keep struggling on, without funds, without friends and without rancour, secure in the belief that when their brand of Socialism arrives they will have properly educated the working classes not only to accept its arrival but to welcome it as well.

On the extreme end of the left-wing spectrum sit the anarchists and the syndicalists. Their philosophies represent a distinctly separate stream of thought from Marxism, Socialism, and capitalism. They consider themselves to be so far left, in fact, that they insist *all* other philosophies are right-wing.

The largest of the two groups are the anarchists; they number no more than 400 to 500 people. They are, in turn, scattered among groups which belong to the Anarchist Federation in Britain: the Freedom Press Group, the London Anarchists, Glasgow Anarchists, Edinburgh Anarchists, Dundee Anarchists, Bristol Anarchists, and half a dozen university anarchist groups.

Anarchism, developed primarily from the philosophies and writings of Pierre Joseph Proudhon, Mikhail Bakunin, David Henry Thoreau, Count Leo Tolstoi, and Prince Peter Kropotkin, represents the extreme expression of individualism. Anarchists believe that all governments, laws, and bureaucracies are unjust and unreasonable and exist only to maintain the power and privileges of the State. They believe that all authoritarian governments – capitalist, Communist or otherwise – should be abolished along with the manifestations of that authority, such as voting,* conscription, taxation,

* British anarchists, like the SPGB, advocate the defacing of ballot papers with the slogan 'Politics means war!' as a means of registering a protest against authority.

police forces, the military services, and the peerage. This authoritarianism, they say, should be replaced by a 'libertarian' society of free people where responsibilities would lie with each individual who would work in voluntary co-operation with others. Anarchists want to encourage this co-operation through the creation of social organizations in which the people themselves can control their own destinies. In most cases, these organizations are known as 'workers' committees' since anarchists believe that the primary path to freedom lies in controlling the means of production.

As implicit in their name, anarchists have no leaders, no hierarchy, no formal organizations, no official membership, and no clear-cut political structure. Among British anarchists there exists practically as many different philosophical interpretations of the word anarchy as there are members in any one group of them. According to one anarchist there are at least nine distinct groupings in Britain. The first consists of the individualistic anarchists. They are split, in turn, between the individualists of the Thoreau school and the 'Sternerites' – the most extreme expression of individualism. Sternerites take their individualism to the point where they refuse to join an anarchist group and in some cases even refuse to call themselves anarchists. They are very difficult people to interview. The second group consists of the anarcho-syndicalists – the vast majority of all British anarchists – who combine their anarchistic beliefs with syndicalism but who tend to emphasize the anarchic traditions. The third group consists of the anarcho-Communists (Communist in the old sense of the word) who believe that the community is the centre of society and not the individual. The fourth group consists of the pacifist anarchists, the individuals who played a leading role in the CND and the Committee of 100. Most British anarchists are pacifists, but these anarchists simply feel more strongly on the point than others. The fifth group consists of the revolutionary anarchists who believe in 'the propaganda of the deed' which means throwing bombs and shouting from the visitors' gallery in the House of Commons. There are virtually no revolutionary anarchists in Great Britain although one, Stuart Christie, was sentenced in 1964 by a military court in Madrid to 20 years in gaol for smuggling explosives into Spain. Most revolutionary anarchists consider themselves more syndicalist than anarchist. The sixth group consists of the anarcho-Marxists, an apparent contradiction in terms, who have fused some of Marx's theories with anarchist theories. As pointed out, they are usually found among the Solidarists, the ILP, and the Committee of 100. The seventh group consists of the Catholic anarchists, very few of whom are Britons, who believe that their church should replace the state. The eighth group consists of individuals called 'permanent protesters'. They believe that anarchy is impossible to achieve and that their job, therefore, is to protest permanently against the ills of society in hopes of somehow ameliorating them. The last definable group consists of the anti-industrial anarchists, a group of modern Luddites who believe that machines have only a quantative value (not a qualitative value) and therefore represent the basis of all evil. They also believe that the leisure achieved by freeing man from the bondage of the machine is not necessarily the answer to his needs.

Because they are so diverse a group of people, anarchists find themselves in many other organizations: the CND, Committee of 100, Direct Action Committee (when it existed), North and East London Anti-Fascist Committee, INDEC, and 'Spies for Peace' are some of the better known ones. Anarchic exclusiveness is frowned upon on the grounds that it would be authoritarian, so they join other organizations – in a form of anarchist entryism – each to promote his own personal brand of anarchy.

Since they have no particular leaders, few of their activities are coordinated. Whatever coordination there is comes from their propaganda organs *Freedom, Anarchy, Anarchist Youth* and *Anarchist International.* All plead for participation in a variety of activities ('ANARCHISTS! Get active in the current anti-election campaign NOW!') but seldom are any details given. How the activities are to be carried out is for each individual anarchist to decide.

If there are no official leaders, there are informal leaders, both theoretical and practical. The practical leaders include Jack Robinson, the Editor of *Freedom* and the major spokesman for the Freedom Press Group, who looks exactly like Trotsky without the eyeglasses; Brian Hart, a young, ebullient ex-seaman with a red beard and gold ear-ring who currently works in the sewers of London (With a laugh, he told me, 'Whenever anyone asks my anarchist friends who will do the dirty work when anarchy is achieved, they all say "Brian Hart!"'); his blonde and sultry wife Margaret who edits *Anarchist International;* and Wynford Hicks, an Oxford graduate who, in the course of a few years, has drifted ideologically from the Socialism of the Labour Party, through the CND, then the Committee of 100, to his present resting place of anarchism. He does not feel he can go much farther left. The current theoretical leaders include Rudolph Rocker, Laurens Otter, Alex Comfort, Vernon Richards, and Sir Herbert Read (whose knighthood is a source of embarrassment to some anarchists).

Brian Hart and Hicks, although they subscribe to some of Marx's views, show nothing but scorn for Marxists who want to capture the State; anarchists, they say, want to abolish it, 'by far the best solution'.

Marx's theory of the withering away of the State, they add, has been abandoned in the desire to create a one-party dictatorship. The only thing that ever withered away in Russia, said Hart, 'was Stalin's arm'. No matter what form Marxism takes, both agree that it is 'the same sweet wrapped in a different shade of pink paper'. They reserve almost as much scorn for the Labour Party which they claim is just tinkering with capitalism. Capitalism itself, of course, is considered such an unspeakable vice that they often found difficulty in describing its short-comings at all.

Like all anarchists, Hart and Hicks vehemently deny that the popular image of an anarchist – as a bomb-thrower, 'bearded weirdy', and bohemian idealist – is the proper one. They claim they no longer plan coup d'états, no longer throw bombs (because 'the State is better at it'), and no longer plan revolutions because it would mean replacing one dictatorship with another. Stuart Christie's activities are considered isolated events not in keeping with the true picture as it exists today. They assert that these old-fashioned activities have been replaced by an emphasis on education – promoted through their newspapers and their alliance with sympathetic groups – which they believe will eventually bring the public around to the point where they will place greater emphasis on the values they choose for themselves rather than on values established for them by authoritarian governments. However, the most effective weapon they could use – satire – is not used at all. Most anarchists that I met (the Harts and Hicks are notable exceptions) take themselves far too seriously; they also think that satire is decadent.

Some time ago, a research psychologist named Tony Gibson conducted a survey of the anarchist personality using methods that were based on Eysenck's 'The Psychology of Politics.' His findings were published in *Freedom* and showed that the typical anarchist was an unusually intelligent man with considerable neurotic drive, and possessing a good deal more idealism than he would care to admit. Gibson also found that anarchists had an almost unlimited faith in the possibilities of human reason – at least as defined by themselves – which produced men who would willingly and cheerfully take on hopeless tasks.

The syndicalists are a shadow of the anarchists in both size and substance for they limit their activities almost exclusively to industrial action. They draw their philosophy primarily from George Sorel's *Reflections on Violence* (1908) which argued that the wage system is unjust and helps to maintain an 'immoral' capitalist system.

Syndicalists, like Marxists, maintain that the communal ownership of the means of production – they call it 'Workers' Control' – is the only means through which workers can obtain their freedom. Like the anarchists, they advocate the establishment of 'syndicates' (from the French *syndicat,* meaning trade union) on a local industrial level that would work in voluntary cooperation with other syndicates for the mutual benefit of everyone. Unlike the anarchists, syndicalists speak only in terms of freedom for the worker and not freedom for man. They believe that this freedom can only be achieved through a 'Social General Strike' which, in turn, would be encouraged by boycotts, revolution and sabotage.

There are no more than 150 avowed syndicalists in Great Britain today, 50 of whom belong to the Syndicalist Workers' Federation and perhaps 100 of whom associate themselves with the Confederacion National del Trabajo, a group of ageing and fairly respectable Spanish anarcho-syndicalists living in exile in Britain. Most of the members of the SWF have been recruited in the last five years. None of these individuals have any influence in the trade unions or Labour Party, despite the Economic League's belief that they are a danger[14] They spend most of their time arguing with the tourists at Marble Arch or demonstrating in trade union parades. Occasionally they will jump into the middle of an industrial dispute and claim credit for promoting it. However, there is no evidence that they have ever been responsible for any strikes, boycotts or acts of sabotage.

The man who closest resembles a leader of the SWF is Ken Hawkes, a reporter on the *Sunday Citizen.* He writes copiously for the syndicalist newspaper *Direct Action.* He speaks vaguely in terms of 'working-class solidarity', the need for a social general strike, and the necessity to transfer 'power to the workers', but he gives only the briefest outline of what he means. Somehow, controlling the machinery will set the workers free. How the gap between what exists today and what is wanted tomorrow is to be bridged is never explained.

Most British syndicalists seem bored with planning their own steps to success and, as a result, spend practically all of their time talking about the near misses of syndicalism, particularly the one in Spain. The syndicalism which developed for such a brief period during the Spanish Civil War is discussed with both resentment and wistfulness. In fact, they are so thoroughly rooted to this point in history that everything Spanish has become a fixation with them. General Franco, quite naturally, is hated with uncommon fervour because he crushed the one good opportunity of syndicalism taking root in the world. But this hatred is so intense that it distorts every other aspect of Spanish life. If Franco gaols a political prisoner, for instance, the 'martyr' automatically becomes a syndicalist. In Stuart

Christie's case, there is some truth to the claim that he is a syndicalist but in most others there is not. Asturian miners, for instance, because they dare strike, are all syndicalists at heart. And with a zeal that borders on self-flagellation, British syndicalists describe the horrors of garrotting, crucifixion and torture to which only 'Spanish syndicalist heroes' seem to be subjected. Their preoccupation with Spain is fed by the CNT in exile, the informal leader of which is Augustin Roa, whose public pronouncements are almost exclusively devoted to attacks upon the Franco Government. British syndicalists follow the CNT's lead with enthusiasm but in the process obscure their own objectives in Britain. As a result, the few people who have ever heard of the word syndicalism tend to think of it as something foreign, obscure and irrelevant. Because of their single-minded hatred of Franco and his Government, British syndicalists have ensured that that image has not been altered.

1. *The British Road to Socialism,* Programme of the Communist Party, (1958) p. 10.
2. *An Appeal to all Communists,* The Committee to Defeat Revisionism for Communist Unity, November 11, 1963.
3. *Destroy the Old and Build the New!* Michael McCreery, November, 1963, p. 10.
4. *Vanguard,* Vol. 1, No. 4, May 1964, p. 7.
5. *Comment* supplement, May 16, 1964, pp. III and IV.
6. *Comment* supplement, May 2, 1964, p. IV.
7. *The Times,* November 11, 1963, p. 6.
8. *Comment* supplement, May 16, 1964, p. III.
9. *Labour Review,* July-Aug. 1959, p. 43.
10. Publication of the Latin Bureau of Fourth International, No. 29, April, 1962.
11. *Red Flag,* Vol. 1, No. 3, November – December, 1963, p. 4.
12. A Proposal concerning the General Line of the International Communist Movement, Foreign Language Press, (Peking,) 1953.
13. *Sunday Times,* May 3, 1964.
14. *The Agitators,* the Economic League, 1964, p. 33 ff.

8 The Campaign for Nuclear Disarmament

'It is nonsense to pretend that national safety can be secured by nuclear weapons. The pursuit of safety through armaments is now, more than ever before, the pursuit of an illusion.'

BERTRAND RUSSELL

There is a body of opinion in Britain that believes that the Campaign for Nuclear Disarmament should not be considered a part of Britain's political fringe because it was a genuine mass movement that dwarfed all other fringe groups in comparison. There is another body of opinion, however, that feels the CND is nothing more than just another left-wing Group within the Outside Left. I have included it as part of the political fringe because, in fact, both opinions are correct; there is no doubt that, at one time during its brief history, the CND had the support of a significant number of Britons (far exceeding what other fringe groups claim they have) and it is just as true that the Campaign has been reduced today to the equivalent significance of one of the many Outside Left factions.

Organised pacifist activities began in Britain during the First World War when the passage of the Military Service Act introduced universal conscription into the country for the first time in its history. For as long as anyone could remember, the ranks of the British Army had always been filled in times of conflict with volunteers. The pacifists in the country, previously under no legal obligation to serve, were left free to opt out of the struggle for reasons of conscience. But with the demands of Total War, this was no longer possible. All able-bodied citizens were subject to the draft regardless of personal convictions. The most influential body at that time prepared to take up radical action on behalf of its beliefs was the Society of Friends. Pacifism has always been a fundamental tenet of the Quakers, and the passage of the Military Service Act was a gross affront to all its members. Reaction to the Act was so strong among pacifists that it led some of them to form the No Conscription Fellowship. This organization vowed that it would refuse to bear arms for its country and that it would oppose the implementation of compulsory military service in Britain. The Government, not accustomed to this manner of dissent, used every means at its disposal to break the organization. Five of the leaders (one of whom was 26-year-old Fenner Brockway) were sentenced to a year's imprisonment and fined a total of £800. By the end of the year, over 6,000 pacifists, Quaker or otherwise, were jailed for refusing to obey the Military Service Act.

Between the Wars, pacifist activities were scattered and unorganized. The Quaker-led NCF was re-christened the No More War Movement. A 'Hands off Russia' movement was formed to keep Western armaments from being delivered to the anti-Bolshevik forces operating freely within Russia immediately after the Revolution. There was also a small, independent group of pacifists in Wales revolving around the nationalists in Plaid Cymru. Fenner Brockway was again active, laying down the foundations for the War Resisters International. There were, in addition to these groups, many other even smaller pacifist organizations, all pursuing their own individual objectives.

The largest pre-war organization of its kind was the Peace Pledge Union, which was founded in 1936. Its membership was drawn primarily from the No More War Movement, and to a lesser extent, from the War Resisters International. By 1939, the PPU could claim that over 130,000 Englishmen had pledged themselves unwilling to support a war on Britain's behalf. Over 51,000 of these people had declared themselves to be Conscientious Objectors who, for reasons of conviction, would not fight anyone at any time.

Founded at the same time in 1936 was a weekly newspaper called *Peace News* which was officially linked to the Peace Pledge Union. Its early years were difficult ones, not so much financially (its leaders still claim that they have never been concerned about losing money), as emotionally. In its desire for peace, particularly as the war clouds began to gather over Europe, it often appeared to the public as a spokesman for appeasement. 'Peace at all costs' was its theme. Such a sentiment, even though it undoubtedly reflected the feeling of British pacifists, did not sit well with a large segment of the population. When war broke out, the paper's cries of peace turned more and more towards despair and unconsciously reflected the anguish in the hearts of most British pacifists. Headlines taken at random from the paper best reflect their feelings at that time:

'PEACE CAN ONLY COME THROUGH NEGOTIATION' – August 11, 1939.
'PEACE TALKS NOW!' – October 13, 1939.
'WOMEN CALL: END THE WAR, NEGOTIATE PEACE NOW' – February 16, 1940.

'HATRED OF WAR IS NOT ENOUGH' – *May 3, 1940.*
'I AM A PATRIOT – SO I WANT PEACE TALKS NOW' – *January 24, 1941.*
'ABOLISH NIGHT BOMBING' – *May 16, 1941.*
'WE MUST REVIVE THE PASSION FOR TOTAL PEACE' – *April 10, 1942.*
'PACIFISM AND PESSIMISM' – *January 22, 1943.*

The emotional stability of *Peace News* was further complicated at that time by allegations that it was not only a voice of appeasement but that it was also pro-Hitler. Some if its journalists, in their desire to avert war, had joined pro-Nazi organizations such as the Link and the British Council for Christian Settlement in Europe. On the whole, these people were politically naïve and unaware that such organizations were anything more than peace groups. They had joined more out of a genuine desire to avert war than out of sympathy for Hitler and his régime, although in retrospect it is difficult to see how they could have ~~been~~ so blind.

The leading writers for the paper also contributed to pacifist anguish, for none of them spoke with any unanimity. They were a mixed bag, including among others: J. Middleton Murry, the paper's war-time Editor; Sir Richard Acland, of the Common Wealth Party*; M. K. Gandhi, Salvador de Madariaga, Laurence Housman, Bertrand Russell, Aldous Huxley, H. G. Wells, and the late Duke of Bedford.

The newspaper survived the war and immediately switched its attention away from the horrors of war itself to other crusades – the 'Save Europe Now Campaign', opposition to the re-arming of Germany, the 'sham of Civil Defence', etc. – none of which, in its own words, made much of an impact on the public. However, with the increase of pacifist activities, *Peace News* was to prosper to the point where it has become the most pervasive voice of pacifism in Great Britain today. In 1961, it severed its connections with the Peace Pledge Union in order to serve all the broad-based peace groups in the country such as the CND, the National Peace Council, the War

* Common Wealth was founded in 1942 by Sir Richard Acland as a radical left-wing opposition party to the war-time Coalition Government. It put up candidates in a number of Parliamentary by-elections and actually won a few seats. The Party was Socialist oriented and concentrated particularly on demanding the common ownership of all wealth. In addition, it allied itself closely to the nationalist parties in the belief that nationalism was not the problem of Wales, Scotland and Ireland, but the problem of England. When the two-party system was restored in 1945, Common Wealth lost its main *raison d'être* and faded into the background. It never has had the energy to die and it still exists today as a rump under Trotskyist influence.

Resistor's International (of which the PPU is the British Section), and the Fellowship of Reconciliation. Although each of these groups has its own individual publication, *Peace News* has gained the reputation of being the general spokesman for them all.

Complementing the left-wing sentiments of its readers, the post-war *Peace News* has laced its pacifism with a stiff dose of both Socialism and general social protest. The paper is no longer solely concerned with peace although this theme underlies all its other interests. When peace is not news, it concentrates on such topics as Apartheid, neutralism, OXFAM, the Bomb, nationalization, religion, police reform, and morals.

The activities of pacifist groups were disorganized and scattered after the Second World War. By 1950, however, these groups had fused together four closely related precepts which were to become the spiritual foundations on which the CND was built eight years later. First of all, there was the strong Quaker influence which has always held that war is contrary to the spirit of the Gospel; second, there was the influence of Gandhi's non-violent resistance philosophy which was so successful in India; third, there was a sympathy among pacifists for acts of civil disobedience (similar to those actions taken by the Conscientious Objectors in both World Wars) if, in their own minds, there were ample moral justification for them; and fourth, there was a general Christian spirit guiding the pacifists that was not confined to the Quakers alone. All these moral and physical guidelines were very closely tied together, one being very difficult to separate from another. They were all to be inherited by the CND.

From 1950 to 1958, pacifist activities increased perceptively. The Peace Pledge Union formed a Non-Violence Commission, out of which grew Operation Gandhi (the name was later changed to The Non-Violent Resistance Group). Its objectives included: the cessation of the manufacture of atomic weapons, the withdrawal of American forces from England, the withdrawal of Britain from NATO, and the disbanding of all British forces. It backed up its convictions with demonstrations at the War Office in January 1951, a sit-down at the Aldermaston Atomic Energy Research Establishment in February of the next year, and similar protests at Mildenhall Air Base and the Microbiological Research Centre at Porton.

This group believed that any form of protest, whether or not it took the form of civil disobedience, had to be carried out openly, with the authorities in full knowledge of its plans beforehand. Its attitude was that it had nothing to hide and was simply bearing witness to a moral wrong by demonstrating. The group had an idealistic zeal that bordered on self-righteousness; it saw no need to co-ordinate its activities with other groups; it did not care how effective were its demonstrations just as long as a protest was being made; nor was it willing to soften its views to broaden the base of its operations. As a result, the group was always small and ineffectual. It was scorned by many pacifists who felt that it was mis-using the opportunities it had to demonstrate effectively. By 1954, the organization had disappeared from the scene but it was to pass on its philosophy to the Direct Action Committee (known briefly by the unwieldy title of the Emergency Committee for Direct Action against Nuclear War) which took up where the Non-Violent Resistance Group left off. This new organization was also convinced of its own infallibility and did not feel the need to compromise. It remained aloof from other pacifist organizations and seldom bothered to help them. This thread of self-righteousness can be traced all the way through the history of the CND. It was picked up by the Direct Action Committee from the Non-Violent Resistance Group and its predecessors, then it passed into the body of the CND for a few years and finally emerged as a small faction within the Committee of 100. This strain of pacifism was to be one of the weakest and, ultimately, one of the most destructive forces within the CND movement.

There were some people, however, who felt that effective opposition to warfare – in particular nuclear warfare – had to be established in a broad-based organization that would encourage all the small and ineffectual pacifist groups to band together in a mass movement. Only in this way, they felt, would anyone in the centres of power pay any attention to them. They felt that the international political situation had been deteriorating ever since the end of the Second World War and that very little was being done by the Government to remedy the situation. The only way to combat this slide towards ruin, they felt, was to have one single organization which would stand in united opposition to this drift.

Accordingly, Canon L. John Collins held a meeting in his house on January 16, 1958 to sound out the possibilities of organizing such a movement. Among those included in the meeting were Bertrand Russell, Ritchie Calder, Kingsley Martin, J. B. Priestley, Michael Foot, Vicky, the Bishop of Chichester, Miles Malleson, Gerald Gardiner QC, Doris Lessing, Peggy Duff, and Reginald Sorensen. They agreed that such a movement was more than justified given the unsettled state of world affairs at that time. A broad policy was outlined to which all present subscribed. The organizational machinery, with Canon Collins in charge as Chairman, was set in motion, and in less than two weeks the Campaign for Nuclear Disarmament was born.

The CND, however, did not become a mass movement because a few pacifist intellectuals willed it so. It appeared on the scene as the result of many very complicated factors. First of all, the development of nuclear bombs was, without a doubt, the reason why pacifist activity grew so quickly in such a relatively short time. Whereas conventional warfare has always been considered the curse of Mankind, the development of the Atomic Bombs (and later the Hydrogen Bomb) brought a new dimension to the problem. The incredible destructive power of nuclear weapons was more than an instrument of warfare, it was a device that had the power to destroy civilization itself.

As a result of this development, a new breed of pacifists had suddenly appeared on the scene: the *nuclear* pacifists who, although they generally supported the possession of conventional arms, were adamantly opposed to any weapon with such frightening capabilities.

Their apprehensions were shared by the general public. For 13 years there had been no appreciable lessening of world tensions. In fact, to many people they seemed to be getting worse. The public could look back on the Berlin Airlift, the Korean War, Suez, Hungary and similar confrontations. They realized that if any of these conflicts had broken out into a nuclear war, it would have been the end of civilization. They also began to sense that nuclear war was a possibility, however remote it might be. They realized that both Russia and America were producing larger armies and larger nuclear arsenals and that parts of both were stationed on foreign territory (such as England). They knew that if these two giants ever went to war, the conflict would spill over into these other areas as well.

Another factor which led many Britons to support the CND was the suspicion that Great Britain wanted her own nuclear force. Although Great Britain had been working on the Bomb for a number of years, the need for a British nuclear force became apparent only after the failure at Suez. Britons were no longer convinced that America, her traditional ally, would always be at her side in time of trouble. In order to mount a successful military venture in the future, they realized that Britain would need a nuclear force of her own. Those who were cognizant of the realities of power politics knew that Britain was not going to abdicate her pre-eminent position in the world without a struggle. With a Bomb of her own, this would mean that Britain would possibly become a primary instead of a secondary target in the event of a nuclear war. It also led many people to the conclusion that other countries would want their own atomic arsenal as well; to many Britons this was a particularly disturbing thought.

Another factor which led to mass support for the CND was the effects the testing of nuclear weapons had on the world's atmosphere. New words such as Strontium 90, radio-active iodine, and fall-out were appearing in the Press. No one knew very much about these words but they had a disturbing ring about them. It was claimed by some that the Strontium 90 covering the world's surface – which was picked up by cows eating the contaminated grass, and eventually transferred to humans via milk – would do irreparable harm to the human foetus, as well as damage to living humans in the form of loss of hair, decay of teeth, and failing eyesight.

There was also speculation that accidental warfare was a statistical possibility. Imperfect radar, a human failing, the malfunctioning of the bomb's safety devices, etc., all seemed like reasonable causes for accidents. Although the public knew very little on this subject for years, the Mershon Report[1], published in 1960, gave credence to the fear that accidents were a real possibility. Furthermore, the public was led to believe that the Government, because it issued very little information on the subject was not as concerned as it should have been about the problem.

The rise in CND support* was not due only to external factors weighing on the public's mind, but was immeasurably assisted by personal factors as well. The original impetus to support the Movement unquestionably came from moral indignation that such destructive weapons were being used in the pursuit of peace. Not only was this indignation drawn from the Christian and pacifist consciousness of the past, but it was drawn from general moral principles as well. No nation, they felt, was so right that it could feel justified in using nuclear weapons to redress what they considered to be a wrong. Nuclear warfare would not only be folly of the first order, they said; it would also be immoral.

This indignation, however, had no effective outlet until the advent of the CND. Many people, particularly the idealistic youth who had lived their entire lives in a period of acute world tension, were attracted to the cause because it was an organization through which their indignation and apprehension could be focused. The CND seemed to have a relevance to the problem that the individual alone did not have.

The CND grew because of other factors as well. There has always been a strong iconoclastic element in British society, found particularly among the left-wing and radical sections of the political spectrum. Many people joined the movement because it promised to attack all the shibboleths of the day to which they were opposed. They came from iconoclastic backgrounds: from the anarchists, syndicalists, Marxists, Victory for Socialism, and similar groups from the radical left.

Left-wing factions within the Labour Party itself were drawn to

* The CND never has had any membership as such. As long as one was in sympathy with its aims, or wore the CND badge (the semaphore signals of N and D – also interpreted as a broken cross in the Circle of Life), he or she was considered a member.

the CND because they were dissatisfied with their own Party's leadership. The struggle for Party control between the left-wing and right-wing groups was heavily weighed in favour of the more conservative trade unions with their massive bloc votes. Hugh Gaitskell, the Labour Party leader at the time, was a conservative Socialist who did nothing in the eyes of the left wing to formulate a coherent Socialist alternative to Conservative Party policies. The 1951, 1955, and later the 1959 electoral defeats only increased the left-wing's bitterness towards its own Party's leaders. They felt that their Party had been reduced to sniping feebly at the Government's more obvious failures. Under these conditons, it was natural that militant Socialists such as Michael Foot MP, Barbara Castle MP, and Sydney Silverman MP, were drawn to this Movement. They realized that there had been no electoral mandate on the nuclear question in the first place and that, if enough people were opposed to Britain possessing an atomic arsenal, they could conceivably bring down the Government. In addition, they knew that the CND could be turned into an instrument which they could use to influence the future course of their own Party. In this, they had some measure of success, but it was fleeting.

Besides the moralists, iconoclasts, pacifists, and members of left-wing ginger groups, there were many supporters who joined because they were bored with conventional politics. There were revolutionaries, the incipient demagogues, the undesirables who thrive on trouble, and idealistic students – perhaps the largest general group within the CND. Every one of these groups, ideologies, and emotions were thrown together under one banner, in a kind of 'Fervour Stew' initially in pursuit of one common objective: banning the Bomb.

Part of the reason that all these divergent groups were willing to associate themselves with the CND was the nature of the Campaign's policy. At its first mass meeting in Central Hall, Westminster, on February 17, 1958, the CND Executive demanded a British initiative to reduce the nuclear peril and stop the armaments race, if need be by unilateral action by Great Britain. As a first step towards disarmament, the Campaign demanded that the British government press for negotiations at top level on the following issues:

1. The stopping of all further tests of nuclear weapons.
2. The stopping of the establishment of new missile bases.
3. The securing of the establishment of neutral and nuclear free zones.
4. The securing of the abolition of the manufacture and stock-piling of nuclear weapons.
5. Prevention of the acquisition of nuclear weapons by other nations.

In order that Britain show her sincerity, the CND suggested that she could, pending negotiations:

1. Suspend patrol flights of aeroplanes equipped with nuclear weapons.
2. Make no further tests of Hydrogen Bombs.
3. Not proceed with the establishment of missile bases on her territory.
4. Not provide nuclear weapons to any country.

In essence, this was the full policy of the CND until well into 1961 when the success of the movement demanded that more positive and specific policies be put forth. It is not known whether the framers of this policy – those distinguished personalities who met at Canon Collins' house a month earlier – were consciously aware at the time that the policy should be as broad as possible, with no emphasis being placed on specifics. Hind-sight by many of the leaders, particularly Canon Collins, says that it was. In any event, by not being too precise about what it meant by unilateralism, by not defining how the Bomb would be controlled, or by not saying what should take its place, the movement was able to take in under its wings the scores of splinter groups who advocated banning the Bomb. Policy was so loosely defined that pacifists, left-wing Socialists, anarchists, Communists*, and visionaries could all flock to the cause with no twinge of conscience. This, more than anything else, was the reason why the CND turned into a mass movement. The moment the Campaign began to define policy and lay down rules of behaviour, as it tried to do from 1961 onwards, all the various factions under CND's umbrella began to bicker and argue about what exactly was 'the true course'.

The propaganda issued by the CND has always been pitched towards the heart rather than to the head. It can be seen most clearly in the Campaign's newspaper, *Sanity*. Most of the articles play on all the fears that everyone has about their own personal safety. For instance, some of them deal with the horrors of genetic permutation; and others deal with the visible side-effects of radiation. There is also a large body of CND literature that describes, in rather frightening detail, the stories of Hiroshima and Nagasaki. There is also a section of CND propaganda that is concerned with the manner in which the Bomb is handled, either by the Government itself or by the US Air Force stationed in Great Britain. Much of this literature also explores either the probability of accidents or the operational procedures of nameless button-pushers.

Very little of CND's literature, even today, is pitched towards the

* The CPGB was at first anti-unilateralist but switched later when the CND was having so much success among the young.

intellect. There has never been a body of writing that has realistically analysed the problems accompanying the possession and use of the Bomb. Many of the intellectuals, of course, have been concerned about alternatives, but whatever they wrote on the subject never reached the public in any appreciable quantity.

Most of the initial adherents to the CND policy did not want intellectual arguments. They were content with slogans and simple formulas. The question of nuclear armaments was an emotional one for them and they were content to keep it that way. Their attitude was: 'First things first – get rid of the Bomb, then we'll think about future policies!'. When confronted with the accusation that such a policy was negative, their answer has always been that all pressure groups start out being negative and that only by raising one's voice in protest does something positive follow. In CND's case, however, its members always thought they knew precisely what was *not* right, but they were never sure what *was* right.

The history of the CND itself can be divided clearly into three phases. The first phase was the Campaign's period of growth from 1958 to September, 1960. Its growth developed primarily as a result of two factors: increasing public participation and sympathy, and general recognition by the Press. The Aldermaston marches, over the Easter week-ends of 1958, 1959 and 1960, were the cause for both gains. Over 2,000 people participated in the first one, and by 1960, the turn-out had swelled to approximately 20,000. Thousands of spectators turned out along the march route to watch the procession go by, some in sympathy, others in curiosity. From all accounts, the singing or otherwise silent protestors had a profoundly eerie effect on the crowds. The Press, although it initially ridiculed the CND, soon turned sympathetic because the Movement appeared to represent very deeply held convictions.

But from the outset, the CND was beset with troubles. Although there were hundreds of varying factions within the Movement submerged beneath the common opposition to the Bomb, two discernible but never clearly defined attitudes emerged. On the one hand were those people who generally followed the philosophy of the CND Chairman, Canon Collins. Collins believed that constitutional methods were the most effective means by which CND objectives would be achieved. This meant parading in protest, signing petitions, pressuring MPs, and building grass-roots support among the people, particularly within the Labour Party. He felt that all these methods had to be carried out strictly within the Law. The Campaign's strength, he said, would lie in the mass of popular support behind it.

On the other hand, there was a radical faction supported by the CND President, Bertrand Russell. His attitude towards nuclear disarmament was more militant and uncompromising. Most of his supporters were scattered among the anarchist, Marxist, and DAC groups. Russell and his followers felt that constitutional methods were acceptable only so long as they accomplished the job. They also believed that more militant and more hostile actions should be undertaken when necessary to bring home to both the people and the Government the perils of possessing such weapons. They were more prepared to step outside the law if necessary to make their point. Whereas Collins was more concerned with a slightly broader aspect of the nuclear question (bases, stockpiles, alliances, etc.), these radicals were obsessed with the question of getting rid of the Bomb. They felt strongly enough about it to feel fully justified in using extreme actions.

The tactical arguments between the Collins and Russell factions finally came to a boil during the summer of 1960. The radical sections of the CND had come to the conclusion that Collins' constitutional methods were not sufficiently effective to move public opinion and the legislative gears at the speed at which they felt the perilous state of the world warranted. They felt that something had to be done to make the whole Movement more relevant. The CND seemed to be operating in a vacuum that had little effect on changing the public's or Parliament's attitude. They were confident that everyone would eventually swing over to their point of view but, because of the urgency they placed on controlling nuclear weapons, that was too long a time to wait. The Russell radicals wanted to confront the Government with massed opposition to the Bomb, hoping perhaps they could stare the authorities down quickly, or at least show up the folly of their nuclear policies by forcing them to jail thousands of people who were opposed to those policies.

It was Ralph Schoenman, a young American graduate student at the London School of Economics, who suggested in a letter to Bertrand Russell in the summer of 1960 that a new organization be established that advocated *mass civil disobedience*, as opposed to the scattered activities of the DAC. What was needed, he said, was an organization, backed by prominent people in the arts, who would take collective responsibility for whatever act of civil law was broken by the mass of demonstrators. He felt that the Government would think twice before arresting so many prominent people. It would also put the CND case before the Government in a quick, incisive, and bold manner. Schoenman also felt that, in any demonstration, the secret to success was *mass* action. Any demonstration planned by the group, he declared, would guarantee a certain minimum number of demonstrators showing up – not 40 or 50 as was the practice of the DAC, but two or three thousand, according to the type of demonstration. This would do two things: it would present the Government with the problem of gaoling every demonstrator – something they were unlikely to do – and it allowed the man with a job and a family to take part in the demonstration with a minimum of risk to his future. This protection was vital because the nature of the demonstration would change. Whereas before, if a demonstrator was fined, it was for no more than trespassing, obstruction, or breach of the peace. Schoenman's idea of mass civil disobedience, however, subjected the leaders, and other participants as well, to charges of conspiracy; a much more serious offence. A man with family responsibilities could not consider risking his future, by going to gaol for a year or so, without such protection.

Russell was in favour of the idea, having never been fully in agreement with Collins' views. Accordingly, the Committee of 100 was established in October, 1960, with more than 100 prominent people from the arts pledging their support to it. The names of the supporters were impressive by any standard: Bertrand Russell, Augustus John, Henry Moore, Benjamin Britten, Phillip Toynbee, the Rev. Michael Scott, John Osborne, Shelagh Delaney, Lindsay Anderson and Doris Lessing, to name only a few.

The second phase of CND's history, from September 1960 to September of the next year, was the period when CND reached the height of its influence and power. A public opinion poll showed that, during this period, 31 per cent of the British population was in open sympathy with the Campaign and that at least 57 per cent were opposed to the possession of nuclear weapons.

Despite this apparent success, the Movement was still plagued by internal schisms. Since Collins would not accept the proposal by Russell that the CND adopt a policy of civil disobedience, the Committee of 100 was forced to organize itself on its own, outside the CND. For two months, in the autumn of 1960, Collins and Russell were engaged in an acrimonious argument over their differences. Russell had planned the formation of the Committee in semi-secrecy, asking the support of the artists by confidential letter. One of the letters, however, was mis-sent to an anti-CND journalist with the same name as a prospective backer. As a result, the story broke prematurely in the Press late in September. Collins was upset by this; first, because Russell had promised not to make his plans public until after the Labour Party Conference in Scarborough (where there was a good chance that a unilateralist policy would be adopted); and second, because the premature leak, unintentional as it was, looked as if it were a doublecross. The argument became so bitter that many of the original artists on the Committee came to the conclusion that the character of the whole operation was unsavoury. In less than two months after they had agreed to support the Committee, over 30 of the original subscribers had resigned.

To the public, it looked as if Collins and Russell were splitting hairs, since they (the public) were not aware of the fundamental differences of attitude within the organization. When it became obvious that neither Collins nor Russell would compromise their position, Russell resigned as President of the CND.

The argument died down in the Press but was carried on privately well into 1961 where it was partially resolved at the CND Conference in the spring. At that meeting, Collins declared that the CND would continue its protests along constitutional lines, but that individual members of the CND – as their consciences dictated – could work with the Committee of 100. He was, in effect, accepting a reality. The split itself, between Collins and Russell, was basically a top-level one. The bulk of the rank-and-file were never too concerned about the differences. If they took sides, they did so with less conviction than the leaders of the constitutionalist and militant factions. In fact, most of the rank-and-file had always divided its time as it saw fit between constitutional and civil disobedience activities. Collins was simply acknowledging publicly a split that had existed within the Campaign almost from its inception.

The first major victory realized by the CND was at the 1960 Labour Party Conference at Scarborough. Despite the fears of Collins, the Conference passed a resolution in favour of unilateralism. This victory was made possible by the support of four unions: The Transport and General Workers Union, the Amalgamated Engineering Union, the National Union of Railwaymen, and the Union of Shop, Distributive and Allied Workers. The bloc votes of these four unions combined with the scattered unilateralist strength among the remaining delegates was sufficient to pass the resolution by a narrow majority.

The victory caught most of the CND supporters by surprise. Since 1957, a few ginger groups within the Labour Party had been trying without success to persuade their Party to adopt a unilateralist position. By 1960, after three years of effort, the members of these ginger groups came to the conclusion that the initiative for organizing an anti-nuclear position had passed out of the hands of both the Labour and Conservative parties and into the hands of outside organizations such as the CND. This is one of the primary reasons why the militant anti-nuclear Socialists so warmly encouraged the formation of the CND in 1958. During the first two years of its life, therefore, the CND concentrated on changing public opinion in general, feeling that any specific effort within the Labour Party would be a waste of time. When the Conference passed the resolution, the members of the CND found themselves unprepared to handle such a situation.

Their reaction was one of elation, although they themselves had not engineered the passage of the resolution. Many CND supporters were convinced that the victory was irrevocable. With the trade unions apparently swinging over to a policy of unilateralism, it seemed as if the right wing of the Party had been defeated. They felt that this victory was the turning point in their history – the beginning of a public-opinion landslide in their favour. The Campaign was bursting with confidence – in fact, over-confidence.

As they were to learn all too quickly, the right wing of the Party was not defeated, just disorganized. Immediately after the Conference, an organization called the Campaign for Democratic Socialism was formed to help the Party leader, Hugh Gaitskell, 'bring back sanity and honesty' to the Party by working for the reversal of the unilateralist position. Two men, W. T. Rodgers and Denis Howell, both of whom were later to become MPs, were the original leaders and they were supported by the more conservative Labour MPs and trade unionists. The following year, at the 1961 Labour Party Conference in Blackpool, the work of the CDS and its allies bore fruit: the 1960 resolution on unilateralism was decisively defeated.

This defeat had many repercussions within the CND. Most of the young followers of the Campaign had always been sceptical of the traditional political parties in Great Britain. Both the Socialists and the Conservatives were viewed with a certain amount of suspicion which bordered on disgust. The parties seemed corrupt, petty and selfish – incapable of bringing about a lasting peace on earth. When the Campaign failed to convert the Labour Party to its cause, it only hardened this attitude. There was no doubt in their minds then that those parties were evil – something with which no decent citizen would be associated. The idealistic members of the Campaign were not prepared to accept the Party leader's thesis that nuclear disarmament had to be considered in the light of other problems as well. They thought this was a cynical indication of how ordinary politics worked, and they never forgot it. Even today, the bitterness towards the two-party system is very much in evidence. Many of the younger people in the CND, for instance, never worked within the ordinary two-party framework; they had come out of school or the universities straight into the CND. The apparently cynical attitude of the Labour Party towards unilateralism only convinced them that their initial decision to work within the CND was the correct one.

Back in September 1960, the militant sections of the CND began agitating for more activity by the movement. They wanted to press on at every opportunity to follow up their Labour Party Conference victory. All the various factions had their own ideas how this was to be done, and they all began to strike out on their own with no overall planning or co-ordination. The shouts of the militants were beginning to silence the voice of moderation within the CND. No one person or group was able to control the Movement at this moment. Its cohesiveness, maintained by Canon Collins and his deputies for over two years, was beginning to break down the moment there was a scent of victory. Every little faction now believed that it had the only key to success.

If there had always been repressed differences within the CND, they now began to come to the surface. For the first time, the fundamental differences between the idealists, realists, intellectuals, activists, pacifists, anarchists, syndicalists, Socialists, and Communists, were clearly evident. With the appearance of the Committee of 100, the process of disintegration increased considerably. Within the Committee of 100 (the DAC merged with them in 1961) were two main factions: the 'Gandhians' – representing the left-overs from the DAC who still believed in civil disobedience of an open character ('Tell the police first, then go and do it . . .'), and the 'secret' group who were more clandestine. This group represented the bulk of the people associated with the Committee and were those most responsible for its formation. They believed in Schoenman's philosophy that *mass civil disobedience* was the key to success, and they were prepared to be clandestine to ensure its effectiveness. There were many other factions within the committee as well; those whose interests began to stray from the problems of the Bomb to such subjects as police brutality, 'political' prisoners in Greece, Apartheid, and the general functions of democratic government. The situation became even more complicated because the many factions within both CND and the Committee of 100 freely intermixed with each other. It was not only difficult to say who belonged to what group but it was equally as difficult to say who was leading whom.

From September 1960 to the spring of 1961, demonstrations by both the CND and the Committee of 100 were generally peaceful in character. The fourth Aldermaston march over the Easter weekend of 1961 took place without incident and was considered by many to have been the most successful of all of the Campaign's demonstrations. The Committee of 100 staged a sit-down in front of the Ministry of Defence in February 1961 in which over 4,000 people took part. A declaration was pinned to the door demanding that the agreement to base Polaris-carrying submarines in Britain be rescinded. It, too, was an orderly demonstration.

But as the spring and summer wore on, the generally tolerant attitude of the Government began to crack. There were increasing indications that the militant sections of the Committee of 100 – those who were willing to confront the Government with the possibility of a revolution – were gaining the upper hand. There were signs that the Movement was taking a more conspiratorial attitude towards the Government's nuclear policy. There were also indications that the organization was more willing to risk charges of conspiracy and sedition to bring the Government to its knees. More and more of their demonstrations were becoming invitations to riot.

During July and August 1961, the Committee began planning another large demonstration to take place in Trafalgar Square on September 17th. It was also the time of the Berlin crisis, and the time when both Russia and America resumed their nuclear tests. Emotions, as a result, were running unusually high in the Movement. The Home Office authorities, considering both the tense international situation and the disruptive attitudes of the Committee, denied it permission to use the Square. Nevertheless the momentum of the Movement and the increasing domination of the militants within the Committee brought the authorities to the conclusion that the demonstration was going to take place whether permission was granted or not. Accordingly, on September 7th, the authorities struck. They arrested four members of the Committee, including Bertrand Russell himself and sentenced them all to two months in prison for conspiracy to incite to riot. Russell's sentence was reduced to seven days in consideration of his age (89).

The demonstration was held in Trafalgar Square on September 17th as planned despite the ban and the arrest of the Committee's leaders. Over 6,000 demonstrators infiltrated into the Square. As the police began to clear the area, a riot broke out. By midnight, over 1,300 people had been arrested, including Canon Collins himself – the man who believed in constitutional protest.

Public sympathy for the Campaign swelled enormously at this moment. To many people, Russell's arrest was a callous move by the Government. The authorities' reaction to the illegal demonstration was considered to be repressive and unwarranted. The allegations of police brutality, moreover, did little to enhance their position. The members of the CND and the Committee of 100 were elated by this surge of sympathy and were convinced that the Government, at last, was on the defensive. They felt it would be only a matter of time before it capitulated to their demands. This was the second instance when the Movement became over-confident, and this time its attitude proved fatal.

From this moment on, the third phase of the CND's history began: the period of decline that has lasted up to the present day.

At first, it was not apparent that the Campaign and the Committee had reached their high-water marks. There was every indication that both groups were riding on the crest of a wave of public sympathy. However, this elation lasted less than two weeks. The first blow came at Blackpool, where the Labour Party, after a year's diligent work by the Campaign for Democratic Socialism, reversed its position on unilateralism. The second and crucial blow came two months later.

After the September 17th demonstration, whatever moderation remained in the CND was lost to the militants and the DAC factions within the Committee of 100. They were fully in control of the impetus of the entire movement. The influence Canon Collins ever had was now largely lost. Every splinter group which was so disposed went off on its own tangent and organized protests in fits and starts – in almost perfect imitation of the previously ineffectual DAC activities. As a result, they dissipated the great backing they had from the public through poorly organized demonstrations. The secret of their past successes lay in the proper use of *mass protests,* and they had failed to learn the lesson.

No one was there to lead them and indeed to a great extent they did not want any leadership. They became self-righteous when the Press, police, and public began to criticise their activities. At times, their attitude bordered on arrogance. As one member told me, 'No one was going to tell *us* what to do!'

It was the demonstrations of December 9th, 1961, however, that actually broke the back of the Movement. The militants in the Committee of 100 planned simultaneous civil disobedience demonstrations at eight locations, some of which involved American and British nuclear air bases. Among other things, they planned to occupy these air bases physically 'for peaceful purposes'. They sent out leaflets asking for 50,000 volunteers; the language was arrogant, the preparations were slight, and there was a minimum of co-ordination between the groups. Fewer than 6,000 people responded to the appeal.

Here the Committee of 100 made a major tactical error. To demonstrate *en masse* in Trafalgar Square was one thing – the Government will even tolerate, under some circumstances, minor conspiratorial acivities such as organizing peaceful civil disobedience demonstrations – but it was another thing blatantly to advertise that they planned to invade nuclear air bases and take them over. This involved conspiracy, sedition and other major crimes falling under the heading of 'actions prejudicial to the security of the State'. This form of demonstration was wholly different in kind to previous ones, and the Government was not amused. When the Government realized the serious nature of these eight 'raids', the velvet glove was removed and the demonstrations were quickly broken up by the efficient work of the military and civilian police.

Six of the ring-leaders were tried in February 1962 under the

Official Secrets Act of 1911. Five were sent to prison for 18 months; one, a woman, received a 12-month sentence. (Shortly after her release, she committed suicide.) CND protestations to the contrary, the trial was carried out under the strictest letter of the law. The Judge would not allow the defendants an opportunity to expand on the Government's nuclear policy, nor did he allow them to discuss the aspects of the case which required the airing of secret information, for they were charged only with conspiring together to enter a prohibited place and inciting others to do the same thing. Bertrand Russell was called to the stand to testify that it was he who was responsible for the whole thing – hoping presumably to be indicted himself. His appeal for martyrdom was ignored.

The history of both the CND and the Committee of 100, for all practical purposes, ends at this moment. Since February 1962, the Movement has been in steady decline. It has lost most of the sympathy accorded it in the past by the public. Most of the people who were ready to lend the Movement their spiritual and financial support during its period of growth and glory have silently drifted away. What is left of the CND today bears little resemblance to the organization as it was known in 1961.

The CND is now visibly split into 'Old Guard', 'New Guard', 'INDEC' (Independent Nuclear Disarmament Election Committee)*, Carthusian Street (CND headquarters) Group, *Sanity* (the newspaper) faction, and so on, until it becomes difficult to tell which groups actually still constitute a part of the organization, and which consider themselves independent. Canon Collins** sees little hope that the CND, as presently constituted, will ever regain the strength it once had. There are too many groups, he says, that are not willing to accept any outside leadership, even leadership in the mildest sense – someone who would co-ordinate and assist, rather than direct. He feels that the CND will probably end up as a small left-wing pressure group, perhaps emerging years later under a new banner for another cause.

The CND is still an 'umbrella' movement, accepting anyone who wishes to join. This has proved to be increasingly embarrassing to the Campaign since more and more groups are joining for reasons that have little to do with the Bomb. Canon Collins has been urging the organization to abandon this policy in order that the less desirable groups be purged. 'How long can we go on being an 'umbrella' movement', he said, 'giving our protection to all kinds of fringe movements like the Communists and Trotskyists? This battle is now going on and unless I and those who think like me win, I would not expect to

* Proscribed by the Labour Party. See Appendix I.

** In conversation with the author, 1964.

be a member of the CND much longer.'[2] Failure – or rather relative failure – to reach the objectives the CND set for itself brought his leadership qualities under fire. Not even the rank-and-file was willing to listen to him. Collins finally resigned as Chairman early in 1964.

The Committee of 100, the faction most responsible for the Movement's fall from grace, no longer even remotely resembles the original Committee. Most, if not all, of the 100 prominent personalities from the arts have resigned quietly in disgust. Lord Russell himself resigned in 1962 when he realized that the developments taking place within the Committee were contrary even to his philosophy. Since February 1962, the Committee has developed a quasi-outlaw character, defiantly challenging the authorities on a wide range of subjects, few of which have anything to do with the Bomb. It has set itself up as a critic of all things governmental, attracting to its cause anti-Government groups such as the anarchists, syndicalists, Trotskyists and Communists. As a symbolic indication of its present character, the traditional black background of the CND badge has, for some of the factions, been changed to red. Furthermore, its major propaganda organ is known as *Resistance* which stands in opposition to practically every British political institution and policy of the day (if not everything British).

Its activities since 1962 have become increasingly more extreme. Its members have attempted 'take-overs' at Marham and Ruislip Air Force bases; they have booed the Queen in public; and they have rioted over the State visit of Queen Frederika of Greece in 1963. Each time they venture into public, they only increase the scorn which has been heaped upon them since 1962.

They have encouraged all revolutionary activities that might undermine the security of the State. The most notable instance of this was in 1963 when 'Spies for Peace' stole the plans of a Regional Seat of Government. As one critic put it, the Committee's attitude in this case seems to have been: 'Spying can be fun'.

These activities of the Committee of 100 have spilled over to cloud the reputation of the CND – one of the original fears of Collins when he split with Russell. Much of the good work of the Campaign has been lost in the publicity given to these revolutionaries who dominate the Committee. An example of how the Committee has hurt the reputation of the CND was during the 1963 Aldermaston march. It turned it into a farce; a splinter group broke off from the line of march to parade past an RSG; others argued with the parade marshal over which route should be taken; and at the end of the trek, Collins had a sack of flour dumped on his head. It was a sad ending to what was originally a great crusade.

* * *

It can be argued that the CND was doomed from the start because of the vagueness of its policies. The dilemma of either having to choose a broad policy to attract mass support or having to choose specific intellectual goals which would have kept the Movement small and less effective was never resolved. Only recently has the CND tried to solve this problem which has taken the form of a compromise. It has recognized that the factions within the Movement will never again give their undivided allegiance to one leader. The moderate leaders of CND are now trying to give their organization a sense of direction, pointing out to other factions the general objectives which they themselves seek. They are then saying to the splinter groups: 'These are our aims; we will support all your activities which tend to complement our goals, we will not, however, support those activities of yours that are not complementary'.

There has been no noticeable success of this policy for two reasons: first, because the CND is bargaining from a position of weakness. None of the splinter groups feel that it is a particular asset to have the co-operation of the Campaign. Second, partial assistance is, in a way, full assistance since the full reputation of the CND is behind their partial support. Invariably, those activities of the factions, which are not supported by the CND, reflect poorly upon the Campaign itself. The CND suffers from guilt by association, which does little to help its public image.

It would be fair to say as well that the CND was reluctant to do any grass-roots work; that its members were over-confident, arrogant, and self-righteous; that they were impatient with democratic procedures; and that the Campaign was a negative effort that never changed its mood.

But by far the most serious failure of the Campaign was that, from its inception, it failed to do the hard thinking necessary to give the Movement a firm intellectual foundation. Throughout its entire history, the philosophy of the CND never went much deeper than the slogans on its posters. This was as much a fault of the intellectual Left as it was anyone else's. Of all the great radical leaders who associated themselves with the CND, very few of them gave the Campaign the full measure of their intellectual assets. They squeezed all the emotion and publicity they could from the Movement and left very little in the way of an intellectual legacy on which it could build in the future. They took full advantage of the idealism and enthusiasm of the young who flocked to the cause, content only to fan the flames of protest for their own personal reasons. They never bothered to outline a broad policy in which the CND could operate efficiently and effectively; they never defined the limits of the Movement; they never made any real effort to find a way in which the

Movement could be effectively controlled from within; indeed, they never seriously tried to work together with Canon Collins – despite the antagonisms he aroused – in order to ensure the Movement's success.

Few of these men bothered to define a step-by-step approach to success; few bothered to define and explain the methods through which success might be achieved; and few felt it necessary to define the terms they used, such as unilateralism and nuclear disarmament. Only Bertrand Russell felt the need to outline to his followers what he meant by civil disobedience.

The Socialist intellectuals had the equipment to provide the Movement with the fundamental precepts it needed to carry on with confidence, yet they never deigned it worthy of their efforts to donate their full skills and knowledge to the cause. They simply milked the CND for all it was worth and when the cow went dry they quietly left for other crusades, apparently without the slightest trace of remorse.

Few of the radical intellectuals feel responsible today for the present chaotic state of the Campaign. They do not feel they are accountable for the lack of policy, lack of philosophy, and lack of cohesiveness that still plagues it to this day. Nor do they feel that the current seditious activities of the Committee of 100 are any fault of their own. The intellectuals deny that it was they who allowed the activities of the Committee to get out of hand. To quote one ex-member: 'Somehow, things just turned out that way.'

Worst of all, few of the intellectuals feel responsible for the residue of bitterness that pervades the CND at present. They feel no guilt for turning many of the members into hardened opponents of the democratic process. Many politicians with whom I talked said, in substance, 'If they are cynical, perhaps it is just as well'. Those people who reneged in their responsibilities towards the Campaign seem to have forgotten that most of the people who originally joined the CND had much to offer, not only to the Movement itself, but hopefully to the nation as a whole in the future. These people were not an irresponsible rabble, but for the most part were university-educated youths with an enthusiasm for politics who – although tinged with idealism – are still considered to be vital to the proper functioning of a democratic society. A significant section of Britain's educated youth have become sufficiently embittered, disillusioned, and cynical about democratic institutions and methods that it opens to question their future usefulness to their country.

1. *The Mershon Report,* Accidental War, Ohio State University, 1960.
2. *Daily Express,* July 5, 1963.

9 *Plaid Cymru & Mebyon Kernow*

'Mae hen wlad fy nhadau yn annwyl i mi . . .'[1]

'Nyns yu Marow Myghtern Arthur'[2]

The pacifist tradition of the Campaign for Nuclear Disarmament is also found in many of the Celtic nationalist groups. According to those who are familiar with the activities of the Welsh, Cornish, Irish, and Scottish nationalists*, the degree of pacifism found in any one of these groups varies in the same proportion as the generally recognized relevancy of its demands and complaints. That is to say, the Welsh and Cornish nationalists, the most docile of the groups, tend to concentrate on the more pertinent problems of their areas while the Irish nationalists, the most pugnacious of the nationalist sects, seem to spend most of their time arguing the merits of outdated questions. Somewhere in between these two extremes are scattered the Scottish nationalists who, because of their diversity, have a capacity not only for pacifism and pugnaciousness but for pragmatism and irrelevance as well.

This rule, however, it not absolute. The Welsh nationalists, although predominately pacifist by conviction, are still capable of violence and, conversely, the Irish nationalists upon occasion can articulate a few reasoned thoughts. Furthermore, every British nationalist sect has its blind spots, its phobias, its idiosyncracies, and its ideological convolutions; but, as a general rule of thumb, the point still applies: that the more relevant and legitimate the claims of a nationalist party, the more pacifist it is.

Contemporary Welsh nationalism was born in 1886 with the establishment of an organization called the Cymru Fydd (the Welsh

* There once was a fifth nationalist group of sorts. Willian Brownrigg, a farmer from Kirkbampton, stood as an independent candidate for Penrith and the Border in the 1951 and 1955 General Elections. He campaigned under a banner of 'Home Rule for Cumberland'. He also advocated the return of land confiscated from Jacobites to their descendants, the increase of mole-catchers' salaries, restrictions on the docking of Clydesdale horses' tails, and legalized cock-fighting during the month of December. He received very little support for his views in either election.

Federation), one of whose founding members was David Lloyd George. The Federation had two aims: the disestablishment of the Church in Wales (which was eventually realized in 1920) and the securing of Home Rule for their country. Coming at a time when the Irish Question was beginning to dominate the political conscience of Britons, these Welsh nationalists hoped to benefit from any concessions granted to Ireland. However, their efforts were fruitless and they made no impact on the Government in Westminster. In 1895, the Cymru Fydd was superseded by the Cynghrair Cenedlaethol Cymru Fydd (the Welsh National Federation) which attempted to bind together all the local nationalist groups into one organization. However, at the inception of this new organization, a split took place between the 'nationalists', represented by the rural Welsh who favoured a clean break with England much in the manner of the Irish, and the 'cosmopolitans', represented by the urban Welsh who wanted to tie their nationalism to English Liberalism. This split destroyed whatever momentum the Movement had and for nearly a quarter of a century, from 1900 to 1924, the Welsh nationalist cause fell by default to the Liberal and Labour Party candidates in Wales who used Home Rule as a means to win the bitter electoral contests in which they were engaged.

During this period, the Welsh nationalists were plagued by a vagueness of attitude towards Home Rule. It was best exemplified in their favourite slogan of the day: 'Codi'r hen wlad yn ei hol' (To raise the old country to its pristine glory). No one ever bothered to define precisely what was to be restored nor did anyone ever clarify what was meant by 'Home Rule' or 'nationalism'. These terms were usually expressed as a jumble of Liberal, jingoistic, and sentimental thoughts that seldom went deeper than a self-righteous demand for independence.

All this changed, however, in 1925 when Plaid Cymru (the Welsh National Party) was established. Its founders realized that no one would ever take their demands seriously unless they organized themselves into a responsible and broad-based political party whose sole interest was the welfare of Wales. They recognized the impossibility of imitating the Irish (who had received their freedom in 1921), because, unlike Ireland, Wales was not an island where rebellion could be carried on under favourable conditions. They also knew that they could not be as intransigent as their Irish cousins and that the only way to success lay through political and economic pressure, reasoned arguments, and electoral activities – all of which they hoped would be backed by a subtle *threat* of violence.

The paramount goal of Plaid Cymru (pronounced Plide *Cum*-ree) has always been Home Rule which its members define today as complete independence from England. The desire for Home Rule is based on many real or imagined ills. First and foremost, these nationalists believe that all their country's wealth – its coal, iron ore, steel, tin plate, and water – is being removed to England by the English for the benefit of England with no apparent compensation to the Welsh. This, they say, has had many disastrous effects on their country; it has turned many of their valleys black with soot; it has disfigured the topography of the land; it has maintained an unempolyment rate that, for over a century, has usually been double the English rate; it has, they claim, debased Welsh traditions; and it has forced over three-quarters of a million Welshmen to emigrate since the First World War. They claim that the only remedy for this situation is to put Welshmen in charge of their own affairs. A distant and impersonal bureaucracy in Whitehall and Westminster, they believe, is unfit to govern Wales properly, particularly since those bureaucrats are predominately Englishmen, with English ideas, English plans, and English goals.

In addition, the Welsh nationalists claim that the English tradition of primogeniture, which guarantees that wealth remains in the hands of the few, is alien to the Welsh tradition of 'perchenthyaeth' which roughly translated means the owning of one's home, and infers a co-operative society where everything is owned either by the family or the community. They assert as well that Wales has a tradition of pacifism – based, they claim, on religious beliefs rather than on any inherent Welsh characteristics – which is similarly foreign to the 'nuclear-imperialism' that has been imposed upon them by the English.

Because it does not like this situation, Plaid Cymru has drawn up on paper – as far as is feasibly possible – a complete plan for an independent Wales. Home Rule is no longer a vague ethos that revolves around the mumbo-jumbo of 'pristine glories' but involves the establishment of a political, economic, and social system which these nationalists feel is indigenous to Wales. If they ever came to power, they would set up a parliamentary government in Cardiff (their capital city) whose authority would be decentralized among the communities. This phobia for decentralization stems from a reaction to the apparently 'All-Wise London Government' and also from what seems to be a genuine belief that no amount of centralized cleverness is an adequate substitute for local participation. As a reaction against London's apparent indifference to the safeguarding of Welsh assets, Plaid Cymru would set up a National Industrial Board, a Welsh TUC, a National Development Authority, a Land Board, a Land Bank, a Marketing Board, a Forestry Board, and a Water Board to ensure the proper use of their country's wealth. In addition, the nationalists would revive the co-operative spirit where all assets would be owned by 'the people'; they would print their own money, fly their own flag, join the UN, issue their own passports, resign from NATO, reorganize the tax structure, and alleviate many other 'inequities' too numerous to name here.

A surprisingly small amount of space is reserved in their policy for that one subject that all outsiders are convinced is the dominant driving force behind all Welsh nationalist activities: the preservation of the Cymraeg language. Nationalists want to preserve it because it is a part of their heritage like their Eisteddfodau, theatres, and art. They do not believe that it should be scrapped just because so few people speak it. Even to these nationalists, the English language would be vital to an independent Wales just as it is vital to Japan, Sweden, and Germany; but they complain that the English, in their desire to discredit Welsh nationalism, play up their desire to preserve their own language as the only policy they have. Nationalists point out that there is no harm in having a multi-language society such as is found in Belgium and Switzerland (which has four) if it does not divide the people and at the same time can preserve some of the country's heritage.

I asked Emrys Roberts, Plaid Cymru's young and dynamic General Secretary, whether a free Wales could afford its independence. He replied that there was no doubt that it could. He pointed out that, between 1948 and 1956, over £40,000,000 more was paid in taxes by Wales to the Exchequer than was returned to Wales in the form of expenditures.[3] Whether or not this figure is actually a true reflection of the situation is difficult to prove but there is no doubt in the minds of the Welsh nationalists that the Exchequer is taking more out than it is putting back. The English critics of these claims point out that Wales receives many services from England that cannot be measured in terms of taxes versus expenditures such as defence, preferential prices, economic protection, freedom of mobility between the two areas, and so forth. To Roberts, this is an absolutely valid argument but it does not outweigh the feeling that Wales could do better on her own. Roberts added that, if independent, Wales would not be saddled with the heavy expenses of defence which burden England as a nuclear power. A free Wales, under Plaid Cymru leadership, would have no army, navy, or air force to support; only an internal police force. The savings from this would, to the nationalists, far outweigh the losses incurred by cutting themselves off from England.

Much of Plaid Cymru's electoral support comes from Welshmen whose view of Wales is as pessimistic as that of the Party. The nationalists have taken advantage of these feelings and their success in exploiting them has been reflected in the steady growth of support for them at the polls. The Party fought one seat in Caernarvonshire in 1929 and ended up at the bottom of the poll with 609 votes. In 1931, it fought two seats, doubling its vote in Caernarvonshire and winning 30 per cent of the vote for the university seat at Aberystwyth. By 1945, it could claim 6.5 per cent of the vote in the six constituencies in which its candidates stood. By 1959, the Party was confident enough to fight 20 seats (out of 36 in Wales) and it was able to secure 77,571 votes or 5.2 per cent of the *total* Welsh vote. This total was more than double the Communist Party vote in the entire country for the same election. In 1964, Plaid Cymru fought 23 seats. This time their vote shrank to 69,507, or 4.8 per cent of all Welsh votes cast. However, Plaid officials blame this decline on the high Liberal Party poll. This, they claim, took away whatever gains their party might otherwise have expected and that it represents only a temporary set-back.

The Party's electoral strength is found primarily among the rural Welsh voters. Those people living within a general sweep of land stretching from Anglesey in the north and moving south along the western reaches of Wales to Carmarthen will give nationalist candidates approximately 12 to 21 per cent of their votes. The three rural counties of Pembroke, Radnor, and Brecknock, however, are so thoroughly Anglicized that they will give Plaid Cymru candidates only about 5 per cent of their votes. The same percentage applies to the two populous and industrialized counties of Glamorgan and Monmouth (a county that Welshmen claim as their own but which Englishmen claim is neither English nor Welsh). Over half the population of Wales lives in these two southern counties and, with few exceptions, return Labour Party candidates to Parliament with huge majorities. It is in these two counties that Plaid Cymru realizes that it must make a significant break-through if it ever hopes to establish itself as a potent political force in Wales. It claims it is making some inroads on the Labour vote in this area but, so far, the rush to the nationalists there has been imperceptible.

At this moment, there are approximately 15,000 members of Plaid Cymru and they can be divided roughly into three ideological groups: romantics, pragmatists, and revolutionaries. One of the primary reasons why Plaid Cymru has remained the sole nationalist voice in Wales is that these three groups and their derivatives are allowed to remain within the Party. Plaid Cymru does not toe a narrow, dogmatic political line – so prevalent among the Scottish and Irish nationalists – which encourages split after split.

The romantic Welsh nationalists comprise the smallest faction within the Party, which is unusual for a British nationalist party.

These people are the ones who dream of a Wales that never was and seek a Wales that never will be. For the most part, they are either hold-overs from the old 'pristine glory' days or expatriate nationalists living in England. Together they number no more than 10 to 15 per cent of the Party's membership.

The largest single group within the Plaid – perhaps 80 per cent of all members – are the pragmatists, those members who concern themselves with the relevant problems of Wales. The Party's leadership comes from this group. The President, David Gwynfor Samuel Evans, is perhaps the best-known personality in the Party. He is youngish (mid-forties), a pacifist, a market farmer by trade, a trained lawyer, a Congregationalist, and one of the Party's best vote-getters. Every time he comes into contact with the English authorities, he insists on speaking Welsh; he makes a practice of filing his election papers in Welsh and takes the oath of secrecy in his native tongue as well. The President of the Party since 1945, Evans has been the recipient of a personality cult by his loyal followers. For instance, in *Welsh Nation,* Plaid Cymru's English-language newspaper (its Welsh version is called *Y Ddraig Goch – The Red Dragon*), a double-page spread celebrating his return from an American tour contained six photos of him and such quotes as: 'On television he looks wonderful – strong, handsome, dignified, distinguished and reasonable'. The development of the cult stems in part from what one member described as the Party's 'love of polish'.

Another well-known leader of the Party is Huw T. Edwards, a long-time member of the Labour Party who bolted to Plaid Cymru because, he claimed, the Labour Party in Wales is 'useless'. For many years, Edwards has been known as 'the Prime Minister of Wales'. Harri Webb, the Editor of *Welsh Nation,* Dr R. Tudur Jones, the Party's Vice President, and Emrys Roberts, one of Plaid Cymru's chief tacticians, are also part of this pragmatic group.

The thousands of rank-and-file within this group, from all the indications I have seen, are composed primarily of students, schoolteachers, pacifists and those Welshmen with a sense of history. Unlike other nationalists in Britain, they are quite spirited, fairly free of rancour, and not without a sense of humour.

The revolutionaries within the Party are small in number and operate under a variety of names. One group, approximately 120 strong, is known as 'Cymru Ein Gwlad' (Wales Our Country) and believes in direct action. Its informal leader is Raymond Edwards, a bald, plump and seemingly mild man who teaches mathematics to girls. He speaks disparagingly of the 'Gwynforites' – the Evans pragmatists – because he and his few followers do not believe that standard political tactics are effective. Exactly for what acts of violence this faction has been responsible is not clear.

Another revolutionary sect within the Party is 'Mudiad Amddiffyn Cymru' (Movement for the Defence of Wales) which is otherwise known as 'MAC'. A third faction is the 'Welsh Freedom Army'. The last two groups are of unknown size and strength but it is thought that the membership in all three groups is generally one in the same and that they use different organizational names for different operations. For instance, the Welsh Freedom Army was supposed to be responsible only for the destruction of equipment at the Tryweryn damsite in 1963.

The fourth group, although not strictly revolutionary, would include the operators of the 'pirate' radio station that is known as either 'Radio Wales' or 'Radio Free Wales'. It is a bucket-shop operation that jumps from site to site to avoid the authorities. The transmitters themselves – it claims to have at least fifteen – are weak and can reach listeners only within a five-miles radius. In the hills, this distance is sometimes reduced to less than a mile. The broadcasts are usually 20 minutes long and come on at irregular intervals at the end of the evening just before BBC-TV Channel 5 is about to close down. The programme usually starts with 'Do not turn off your sets . . . you are about to hear the Voice of Freedom! . . .' which is followed by a rendition of 'Men of Harlech' and then by recordings of recent speeches by Gwynfor Evans. The programme closes with the Party's own version of the news.

At one time, Plaid Cymru was considering the possibility of informing the police of the location of one of its transmitters so that the radio operators could be arrested. The Party then planned to test through the courts both the monopoly of the BBC and ITV and the ban on Plaid Cymru party political broadcasts. There is some indication that they may not have to bother. The wireless monopolies are already under fire from off-shore 'pirate' radio stations and informed quarters seem to think that the '50 seat Rule' (which denies party political broadcasts to parties contesting less than 50 seats) may be revoked in the near future*.

Emrys Roberts claims that the violent actions of a few do not herald a shift in emphasis away from the traditional course of the Party. 'We have chosen the ballot box', he said. 'Any campaign of violent

* In early 1965, a joint committee from the Labour, Conservative and Liberal Parties allowed Plaid Cymru five minutes per year of party-political TV time in Wales. The three major Parties allocated for themselves one hour, one hour and 35 minutes respectively. The radio time is slightly less for the big three but the same for Plaid Cymru. This break has failed to pacify the nationalists. They say they received seven-tenths of the Liberal vote in the 1964 General Election and should therefore be given the same proportion of time.

action in Wales today would be morally unjustifiable and politically foolish. It would alienate rather than win support.' But, he continued, 'that does not mean that Plaid Cymru must remain a timid party, always keeping within the letter of the law. We cannot be expected automatically to bow the knee in milk and water fashion when the rights and wishes of our nation are trampled under foot. Violent action cannot be justified if it is a case of a minority trying to force its views on the majority in Wales. But when it is undertaken in an attempt to force the Government to respect the wishes of the people of Wales, it has ample justification.'*

He went on to cite the few instances of violence or non-standard political actions in which the Party has been involved. It was, for instance, responsible for the destruction of a bombing station in Llewn, Caernarvonshire in 1936. Three members of the Party, one of whom was Saunders Lewis, a noted Welsh poet, playwright, and the Party's President at the time, went to gaol for nine months as a result. In addition, many Welsh nationalists went to gaol during the Second World War for refusing to fight for Britain. They protested that as pacifists they should not be forced to fight; nor did they feel that England had any right telling them – Welshmen – that they had a duty to serve in a 'foreign' army.

In 1958, the leading members of Plaid Cymru turned down an invitation to a garden party for the Queen in protest over the then Minister for Welsh Affairs', Henry Brooke's, remark in the Commons that Wales was legally a part of England. And on one occasion, a group of Plaid Cymru militants organized what can only be described as a 'law-breaking outing' where they descended on to Aberystwyth and committed petty offences. They then ignored the summonses because they were not printed in Welsh.

The two new dam sites at Tryweryn and Clywedog have also been the targets of provocative acts by the Party. In 1963, two nationalists were convicted of destroying equipment at the Tryweryn site. One was sent to prison for 12 months and the other, because of his age (19), was bound over for a year. (Emotions ran so high among the nationalists during the trial that it moved one elderly gentleman to leap to his feet in the courtroom and shout: 'Cymru Am Byth!' (Wales For Ever!), whereupon he was forcibly bundled out of the room.) Officials of Plaid Cymru hasten to point out, however, that they did not officially sanction the activities of the two convicted men and that their actions were directed only against the English authorities and not against the English people. The destroyed equipment

* Shortly after the 1964 elections, Emrys Roberts resigned as General Secretary and moved to Middlesbrough where he is organizing an industrial Eisteddfod. His successor's name is Elwyn Roberts.

apparently were symbols of Government authority to which they took exception.

At Clywedog, some of the nationalists have bought three acres of land in the area to be drowned by the dam and have subdivided it into 75 lots. Each lot has been sold to four joint owners some of whom live out of the country. All of them have tied up their property in trust or in complicated legal webs so that when the authorities come to negotiate for the purchase of the land they will be dealing with 300 separate owners all of whom are willing to drag their cases through the courts. The Bill which authorized the construction of that dam becomes null and void in December, 1966, and the nationalists are confident that these legal tactics will outlast that date.

Another organization within Plaid Cymru calling itself 'Meibion Glyndwr' (Sons of Glyndwr)) claimed in 1963 that it had secreted a large bottle of poison in the Clywedog area that was potent enough to kill anyone who drank the water. Gwynfor Evans, for one, thinks the story a hoax. 'On the fringe of every movement', he said, 'you get loonies'.

The Cornish nationalists differ from the Welsh and other nationalist parties on two counts: they are a tiny group in comparison and they are the only nationalists in Britain who are demanding anything less than immediate Home Rule.

Mebyon Kernow (Sons of Cornwall), the current Cornish nationalist organization, grew out of a movement called 'Tyr ha Tavas' (Land and Language) which was founded in the early 1920s by a group of Cornish intellectuals whose primary purpose was to promote Cornish culture. Tyr ha Tavas had a slight political bias in that it spent some of its time pressuring MPs and Government authorities to give more consideration to Cornish problems. This group, never larger than 100 members, had little influence in or outside of Cornwall and, until its death during the Second World War, could claim no notable achievement to its credit.

In 1951, the organization was revived under the name Mebyon Kernow and was given a much stronger political bias. Its long-term goal, which most of its members admit will probably not be realized for many years, is self-government in local affairs within a federated United Kingdom. It would like to see Cornwall be given the same status as Northern Ireland and the Isle of Man – complete with its own 'Cuntelles Kernow' (Cornish Assembly). Its claim for control over its own affairs is based on the belief that Cornwall has a Celtic character that makes it distinctly different from the Anglo-Saxon counties to the north. Because it is treated as just another English county, Mebyon Kernow feels that:

> CORNWALL is neglected by the London Government, and will never prosper until Cornish People can control their own domestic affairs. A Regional Government, based on Gloucester or Bristol, will not improve matters for Cornwall.
>
> WE ARE English-speaking in Cornwall, but have a Celtic origin that affects our thoughts and way of life to the present day. We are uniquely placed to maintain our distinctiveness and thereby be led naturally into opposition to outside control. Co-operation in local communities, not class warfare, is what Mebyon Kernow seeks to promote.[4]

Its short-term goals, all of which are incorporated under the slogan 'Cornwall for the Cornish', include 'the retention of things Cornish', particularly its language (dead since the 18th century), its place-names, its historical monuments, and a few other less well defined aspects of the Duchy's 'Celtic flavour'. Its goals do not include, however, the preservation of Celtic blood although some members claim that this has happened despite English incursions into Cornwall. In addition to its cultural interests, MK has a few short-term interests of an economic nature that brings it into the sphere of political activities. One of them, for instance, is rail transport in Cornwall. MK has set up the Cornwall Transportation Committee to oppose Dr Beeching's plan to reduce local railway services. The Committee campaigns under the slogan 'Thousands are slaughtered on our highways; don't let them murder our railways!'

Recently, MK has become embroiled with the local Boundary Commission over the alteration of Cornish political divisions. The bone of contention, however, is not over the threat of gerrymandering by the English but over the possibility that the new divisions will be given either dull or non-Cornish names:

> The Boundary Committee have suggested some of the following: 'East Cornwall', 'North Cornwall', 'Mid Cornwall', 'South East Cornwall', and even Penwith is to be renamed 'West Cornwall'. To say that these ghastly and featureless names are unimaginative would be an understatement. The next logical step is the renaming of the Boroughs as 'Southville' for say Fowey, 'Northton' for Bude, and 'Westville' for Penzance. This no doubt would be followed by carving the Duchy up into exactly equal squares and calling them 'One', 'Two', 'Three', etc. The new proposals suggest that such a mixture between a crossword puzzle and a cocoa factory will be the pattern for the future.[5]

Mebyon Kernow has recently asked all the brewers who have pubs in Cornwall to change their 'Ladies' and 'Gentlemen' signs to 'Myrghes' and 'Gwesyon'. It is asking as well that all 'Welcome to Cornwall' signs be replaced with 'Wolcum dhe Gernow'. Mebyon Kernow is also promoting the establishment of a Cornish University (even though neither the site nor the type of university has yet been decided); it is promoting the introduction of a 3d Cornish stamp and postal frank (which would say 'Kernow'); and it is promoting a debate on the choice of a Cornish national flower ('*Furze,* a dear, bright, persistent right-through-the-year blossom which could be strikingly stylized . . .').

The current membership of Mebyon Kernow numbers no more than 200 individuals; on the whole, they tend to be well-educated and articulate. MK's Chairman is a civil servant named Robert A. Dunstone who runs the organization from his home in Truro. He is a gregarious and pleasant man but he becomes annoyed whenever people fail to take his organization seriously. The Treasurer of MK is George Pawley White, a bank manager in Hayle; its Secretary is Stephen Fuller who is the proprietor of a Padstow shop called 'The Candle House'; and its unofficial London Organizer is Hugh Miners, also a civil servant. Miners teaches the only course on the Cornish language outside of Cornwall and claims to have an average attendance per class of 20 pupils.

These men and their associates have been responsible for the revival of the Cornish Gorseth. Although it was actually revived in 1928, prior to the formation of MK, these men have been the ones most responsible for its growth and are very active today in its affairs. The Cornish Gorseth (Meeting of the Bards) is considered by Cornish nationalists to be the 'daughter' of the Welsh Gorsedd. Unlike the Welsh Gorsedd, which is the central ceremony of the Eisteddfod, the Cornish version is a simple meeting where Cornish songs are sung and prizes are awarded to individuals excelling in cultural exercises. The Gorseth is held on the first Saturday in September at some ancient Celtic shrine or monument and is conducted entirely in the Cornish language, to the incomprehension of most of the dispassionate spectators. The members of both the Cornish Gorseth and the Welsh Gorsedd take their duties very seriously and consider the 'London Druids' at Stonehenge to be 'fakes'.

Mebyon Kernow is a member of two organizations through which it hopes eventually to achieve control over its own affairs. One of them is called the Federal Union of European Nationalities which was founded in the late 1940s to take up the problems of national minority groups. Hugh Miners, who represented MK at the 1964 FUEN Conference in Regensburg, Bavaria, said that, after listening to the problems of such minorities as the South Tyroleans and the Sudeten Germans, he felt 'like a bit of a fraud'. The second organization is the Celtic League of which there are only six member groups: Breton, Cornish, Irish, Manx (Isle of Man), Scottish, and Welsh. The League was founded in 1963 and its main function, according to Miners, is 'to let off steam'.

Mebyon Kernow sees itself primarily as a ginger group which brings pressure to bear on the authorities on subjects of interest to Cornwall. It claims to have one sympathetic MP in the House of Commons, F. H. Hayman, the Labour Party member for Falmouth and Camborne. MK does not plan at the moment to put up candidates in either the General Elections or the local ones since it prefers to work behind the scenes so that the politicians and the bureaucrats can take the credit for any change. It will only consider putting up candidates if it cannot achieve what it wants through the existing channels. The members of MK realize that their organization is not well-known and that many Cornishmen tend to be apathetic towards Cornish problems. But these nationalists claim that they have the latent support of many other Cornish people who, if their sympathy is properly harnessed, may provide them with the backing they need to be successful.

1. 'The Land of My Fathers is Dear to Me . . .', the title line of the Welsh national anthem, by James and Evan James.
2. 'King Arthur is not Dead.', the last line of the song 'Arta Ef A'dhe' (He Will Come Again) which is sung each year at the Cornish Gorseth. Until the 18th century, there was a strong folk tradition in both Cornwall and Wales that King Arthur was not dead and that he would one day return to lead his people.
3. His reference: *The Social Accounts of the Welsh Economy* 1948–1956. Edward Nevin, (University of Wales Press) 1957.
4. *Mebyon Kernow, an introduction to the work of the organization.* Pamphlet (no date).
5. Letter from MK Chairman, R. A. Dunstone, to members; dated August 1963.

10 *The Scottish Nationalists*

'Do with me what you will,
Scotland shall yet be free.'

WILLIAM WALLACE.

The history of Scottish nationalism, unlike Welsh and Cornish nationalism, is the story of the inability of people with similar goals to work together in harmony. From 1885 to 1928, Scottish nationalists were scattered among a variety of organizations such as the Scots National League, the Scottish Party, the Scottish National Convention, the Scottish National Movement, the Scottish Home Rule Council, the Young Scots Society, and the first and second Scottish Home Rule Associations. These groups spent most of their time quarrelling, fighting, splitting, re-grouping and re-splitting among themselves with such frequency that Scottish nationalists gained the reputation – a reputation that is still partially valid today – that each nationalist was more interested in jockeying for personal supremacy in the field than in working together for the freedom of Scotland.

In 1928, the nationalist picture temporarily stabilized itself with the formation of the Scottish National Party, the main trunk from which all the current factions have branched out. For twelve years, from 1928 to 1940, Scottish nationalism spoke with as much of one voice as it has ever known; but it did not prevent the Party from being torn by internal strife. Part of the organization sympathized with Mosley's British Union of Fascists; others were pro-Communist; and still others were dedicated pacifists. There were some factions who were divided over the Party's policy to fight elections (the 15 nationalist candidates in the 1929, 1931, and 1935 elections all performed very poorly), and there were others who wanted to tie their nationalism to Social Credit, the Knights of Columbus, or Esperanto.

This period of the Party's history is known as its 'romantic' or, more accurately, its 'most romantic' era. The SNP was small and isolated, devoid of any realistic approach to politics. Its hallmarks were predominately escapism and lethargy. What little effort it made to convert the public to its cause seldom went beyond demanding that all the vague and imprecise values and customs of Scotland be preserved – a difficult task under the most favourable conditions. It put up candidates for Parliament with no apparent plan of attack and distributed propaganda that seemed more intended to bolster the

Party's own morale than to arouse the moderate Scot to its cause.

In 1940, the first split occurred within the SNP. Douglas Young, a shaggy-bearded intellectual (who was later to go to gaol for refusing to comply with the National Service Act), convinced half the SNP members at their annual conference to embrace 'constitutional pacifism'. In opposition stood Dr John MacCormick – 'King John' to his followers – who, when he could not have his way, walked out with the other half of the members. It was not only a split between the moderates and the radicals (each side accused the other of being the radicals) but a split between two men who, because of a clash of personalities, were not willing to work together.

MacCormick and his followers set up the Scottish Covenant Association. Its history was brief but significant because it represented the last time any Scottish nationalist organization sought anything less than absolute freedom from Britain. The Covenant felt that a Parliament should be established to handle only local matters such as industry, agriculture, housing, education, and broadcasting; it felt that the Westminster Parliament should restrict its activities in Scotland to defence, Crown matters, currency, and foreign affairs. In addition, it wanted both the Scottish and Westminster Parliaments to deal jointly with such matters as taxes, postal and telephone services, and docks and harbours. This plan was modelled, in part, after the relationship between the Ulster Stormont and Westminster and is very similar to the Liberal Party's current policy for Scotland.

In 1949, the Covenant began a drive for signatures to a petition asking Westminster's consideration of its objectives. In less than two years, the Covenant was reported to have over two million names on the petition. However, for a number of reasons, the petition failed to interest Parliament. First of all, the wording was ambiguous and calculated to appeal more to Scottish patriotism and sense of tradition rather than to sober political judgements. Furthermore, no one was certain whether the signatures were those of qualified voters; nor was there any fool-proof way of proving that a signature did not appear more than once. It was rumoured at one point that the petition was hawked around the pubs in order that the two-million mark be attained. By the time that the document reached the Secretary of State for Scotland, it was apparent that it was little more than a joke. The petition had been handled in such an amateur manner that the Secretary had no choice but to ignore it. The Covenant still exists today, but its heart was broken by this disaster; it has never recovered from it. Dr MacCormick himself receded into the background of nationalist politics and was seldom heard from again.

The rump of the Scottish National Party in 1940 was left in the hands of Douglas Young, Roland E. Muirhead, a director of the

Gryfe Tannery in Bridge of Weir (and who is known as the Grand Old Man of Scottish Nationalism), and Dr Robert McIntyre, a chest specialist from Sterlingshire. For a few years, they and their few followers plodded on with little confidence. In 1945, however, they did engineer the one electoral victory ever afforded their party. In a by-election in the Motherwell, Lanark constituency, Dr McIntyre was elected to Parliament by the scant majority of 617 votes over his Labour Party opponent. His victory, however, was short-lived; two months later Prime Minister Churchill called a General Election and McIntyre was decisively defeated by 7,809 votes.

In 1950, the nationalists rocketed to fame when four Glasgow University students stole the Stone of Scone from Westminster Abbey. Most Scots feel that the Stone is a sacred Scottish relic that rightfully should be returned to its native land; therefore, when it was stolen, they were delighted. Wendy Wood, at that time associated with the SNP, intimated that she was involved in the plot. She triumphantly raised the Lion Rampant banner in front of reporters and proclaimed: 'The fact that the English promise and order of its return to its rightful owners has not been carried out during the last 600 years in no way invalidates Scotland's right of possession'.[1]

For four months, the police were unable to track down either the thieves or the Stone. They were accused at one point of employing a clairvoyant to assist them in their task. They were also harassed by being continually reminded that, according to legend, English kings will cease to reign if not crowned on the Stone. Eventually, in April 1951, the Stone was found at Arbroath Abbey, Angus, wrapped in a St Andrew's flag.* The authorities, to deny the nationalists a further excuse to make headlines, refused to prosecute the offenders.

Although the theft marks the point where Scottish nationalists first emerged from obscurity, it also marks the end of their 'most romantic' era and the beginning of their 'less romantic' era which has lasted up to the present. The publicity from the theft brought the nationalists under public scrutiny for the first time and, lest they be laughed to death, many of them realized that their old attitudes and activities had to be tempered in the future with more thought and reason. Scottish nationalism today is by no means free of frivolousness or romanticism, but from 1951 onwards, the first glimmerings of realism were noticeable.

A few months before the theft, McIntyre and Muirhead split, again because of each man's unwillingness to submerge his individualistic

* Wendy Wood claims that the real Stone of Scone is not the one that rests under the Coronation Chair but that it is a piece of black basalt with hieroglyphics on it, buried 'somewheres in the Scottish hills' that will only be unearthed when Scotland is free.

points of view for the good of the cause. McIntyre, in his early thirties, took over the reins of the SNP while Muirhead, then 82 years old, defected with a small band of followers and set up the Scottish National Congress. Muirhead felt that contesting elections was a waste of time and money (he himself had stood as a parliamentary candidate in the 1929, 1931, and 1935 elections, each time losing his deposit); he was convinced that only by swinging Scottish public opinion over to Home Rule would freedom ever be achieved. McIntyre, on the other hand, was content to fight for Scottish independence through the electoral process. This difference in policy has remained basic to each group to this day.

In 1959, the SNP experienced its last major schism when Wendy Wood left to form her Scottish Patriots. Wendy Wood has been active in nationalist politics since the formation of the SNP in 1928 but she was never closely tied to one organization for any length of time. She set up the Scottish Democratic Self-Government Organization in 1932 apparently to bring about Home Rule with the aid of the working man. She was and still is a dedicated anti-Fascist and anti-Communist; she and her few followers were, at that time, the only Scottish nationalists willing to fight in the streets for what they believed. By the 1950s, she had associated herself with the SNP but, nine years later, the friction between her and Dr McIntyre were so intolerable that she resigned. She claims that he was jealous of her and did not like competing with a woman. The SNP, in return, claims she is a radical whose activities gave the whole organization a bad name. Whatever the true reasons were, the split had a familiar ring.

Despite these schisms, the Scottish National Party still remains the major nationalist party in Scotland. It claims to have over 14,000 members and a 'nation-wide' organization of branches. Most of these members are drawn from the middle class: students, shopkeepers, small businessmen, educators, and professional people are the most evident. Very few manual labourers are drawn to the Party.

SNP policies parallel the policies of Plaid Cymru: it seeks full freedom for Scotland and, to strengthen its case, has drawn up what it considers to be a complete economic, fiscal, and political programme for Scotland – from the preservation of the Gaelic language to opposition to nuclear weapons. Its complaints against England are also the same as Plaid Cymru's: that the English dominate her land, that they practice economic discrimination, that they pervert Scottish customs, and that they discriminate against the SNP itself.

According to Ian MacDonald, the SNP's young and energetic National Organizer, 'Government policies are always decided by English conditions and needs'. As examples, he said that a rise in the Bank Rate is always governed by conditions in England and not in

Scotland. Railways are closed, he added, in terms of what good it will do England; factories are built not on the basis of what good they will do Scotland but on the basis of how much wealth they can return to England; and, he said, Prestwick and Renfrew airports are not allowed to expand their operations because they do not fit into the English scheme. MacDonald stressed, after each example, that 'England puts England first and Scotland second – or worse!'

Furthermore, he said, 'Anything for England is of national importance done at Government expense and at great speed while anything done for Scotland is purely of local importance, much of the financing of which has to be done locally.' He claims that the Forth and Tay Bridges, for example, were or are being built with locally-raised money which is to be paid back through the income received from tolls. On the other hand, he added, 'England has miles and miles of toll-free roads, bridges and tunnels, all built by the Government.'

Like Plaid Cymru, the SNP claims that Scotland pays more into the English Exchequer than is returned to her in the way of 'local' expenditures. The argument that certain expenditures such as postal services, national defence and foreign affairs are difficult to break down into the English versus the Scottish share is dismissed by the SNP on the same grounds as Plaid Cymru: that, according to their own calculations, Scotland is getting short shrift from England and that, as a free nation, it could certainly put the money to better use. It dismisses as well the Balfour Commission and Catto Committee Reports as prejudicial in favour of England.* It claims that *all* of

* The Balfour Commission Report (*Royal Commission of Scottish Affairs Report,* HMSO Cmd. 9212; 1954) and the Catto Committee Report (*Report on Scottish Financial and Trade Statistics,* HMSO Cmd. 8609, 1952) attempted to put the economic and fiscal relationship between England and Scotland into proper perspective. The Catto Committee Report concluded that it was not possible in many instances to separate accurately the statistical figures between the two areas. The Balfour Commission, which incorporated the conclusions of the Catto Committee, concluded that, in many instances, Scotland was being subsidized by the Exchequer. The report shows that Scotland, with 11.7 per cent of England's and Wales' population (in 1953), was contributing only 9.69 per cent of the revenue to the Exchequer. She was receiving, in turn, in the form of 'local' expenditures, 51 per cent of the revenue she contributed. England and Wales, on the other hand, contributed 90.31 per cent of the total revenue to the Exchequer (Northern Ireland excluded), and was receiving back only 38.5 per cent of their contributions in the way of 'local' expenditures. Practically all the comparisons between Scotland and England and Wales are similar, showing Scotland receiving a higher percentage return than her southern neighbours.

Whether the two reports accurately reflect the true nature of Scotland's position vis-à-vis England is not known; but these two reports represent the only efforts in recent years by either the English government or Scottish nationalists to explore the problem.

Scotland's contributions to the Exchequer should be returned to Scotland; it sees no reason why Scots have to pay a 'brokerage fee', as they call it, to England for outsiders to run Scottish affairs.

Often the language used by the nationalists in criticizing these reports is quite strong. For instance, quoting from the booklet, *Scotland the Satellite,* by Oliver Brown:

> The Balfour Committee reported:
>
> 'WE HAVE BEEN UNABLE TO FIND ANY EVIDENCE OF FAILURE TO APPRECIATE THE EXCEPTIONAL DIFFICULTIES IN SCOTLAND WHICH DO, IN OUR OPINION, JUSTIFY EXCEPTIONAL TREATMENT.'
>
> The writer claims that this statement is false and is due either to the cuplicity or the culpable ignorance of Lord Balfour and his associates.

The general SNP attitude towards England and/or the Exchequer usually infers that both are a den of thieves, purposely bent on stealing what is Scotland's for their own personal enrichment. For example:

> No one can seriously study the financial accounts issued by our masters without coming to the conclusion that we are governed by confidence tricksters.[2]

> Cynically London maintains she 'GIVES' Scottish Oil a 'Preference' (i.e. She charges YOU less per gallon than the Duty on Imported 'cheap-labour' Oil from the Middle-East . . . the Defence Bill for which goes to the TAXPAYER and NOT to the Oil Companies). SCOTTISH OIL COSTS NOTHING TO DEFEND! . . . Perhaps, also, a *Thief could argue* that if he robbed you of £1,000 and someone else of £2,000, he was really giving you a 'Preference.'[3]

> Clause 16 [of the Act of Union of 1707] declares: '*And a Mint shall be continued in Scotland under the same rules as the Mint in England*'. The generous English closed down the Mint.[4]

MacDonald told me that the SNP has always believed that only by contesting elections will it, or any other Scottish nationalist group, ever be successful in its quest for freedom. The SNP fights elections, according to MacDonald, for two reasons: first, to keep the Party before the public eye so that the electorate builds up a habit of voting for it; and second, to give the impression of strength by fighting the two giant parties. Presumably, what MacDonald means by this is the strength of a David.

The Party's definition of the phrase 'success at the polls' is enlightening for it gives a clue to the psychology which governs its electoral activities. It bears no relationship to anyone else's definition. To give an example: in a strong Labour Party constituency, if the SNP candidate elbows the Unionist candidate into third place, this constitutes a 'success' or even a 'victory', despite the fact that the winning Labour candidate may have received two to three times the vote of the second-place SNP candidate. The SNP's star candidate at the moment, a young and personable businessman named William C. Wolfe, engineered just such a victory when he defeated not only the Unionist but a Liberal and Communist as well in the 1962 by-election in West Lothian. Nevertheless, the winning Labour candidate cornered more than twice Wolfe's vote. Ian MacDonald is another good SNP vote-getter. He came very close to beating the second-place Unionist in the 1961 Glasgow-Bridgeton by-election. But, by and large, most SNP candidates do very poorly at the polls. With the exception of Dr McIntyre's real victory in 1945, no SNP candidate has ever come close to success; only 21 per cent of all SNP candidates have ever received more than 20 per cent of the votes in any one constituency. Most of the SNP candidates lose their deposits.

The SNP operates on the horns of an electoral dilemma. Many Scots sympathize with the general aims of the Party, but the SNP finds it impossible to translate this sympathy into votes. Like the English and Welsh voters, the Scottish electorate tends to renounce the minority parties at the moment of truth and votes for parties capable of forming a government in Westminster. Those who do vote for the SNP do so more as a gesture of protest rather than for any deep conviction of SNP aims. Because the SNP vote is primarily a protest vote, the presence of the Liberal Party – the ordinary Party of protest – stands as an obstacle in the way of the SNP's growth. The Liberals have always been able to siphon off a significant number of votes that otherwise might go to the nationalists. Under those circumstances, it has been felt for a number of years that the two parties have been considering the possibilities of a *détente* whereby neither party would compete with the other in certain constituencies. MacDonald, for one, said that his party could never work with the Liberals because, like the Tories and Socialists, it is an English party that thinks and acts English even though it does claim to support some form of independence for Scotland.

In conjunction with its electoral efforts, the SNP is associated with Radio Free Scotland, a semi-autonomous pirate radio station that is run by a young lawyer named Gordon Wilson. Its broadcasts differ from those of Plaid Cymru (which believes in the theory that irregular broadcasts excite the imagination of the listener and drives home the point that the Government discriminates against the nationalists) in that it broadcasts for a regularly-scheduled 30 minutes every Monday evening on both the ITV and BBC television channels after they close down. The programmes follow no rigid pattern but usually feature strains of 'Scotland the Brave', followed by the news from the nationalist point of view. The radio seems to be run semi-professionally; it does not give its listeners the impression that it is an illegal organization. In fact, the authorities have not interfered with its broadcasts to date because, according to RFS literature, 'the radio, although illegal, is morally justified in its existence and those in authority know this.'

MacDonald claims that his party does not believe in violence; it disclaims any responsibility for any past activities of that nature. The reputation that Scottish nationalists blow up EIIR pillarboxes, throw eggs at the Queen (during the opening of the Forth River Bridge in 1964, for instance), and practice military manoeuvres in the Highlands under the name 'Scottish Liberation Army' is due, he says, to the irresponsible activities of the other nationalist groups which he and all SNP members refer to collectively as 'political incompetents'. With regard to the Scottish Liberation Army and a group called the 'Scottish Nationalists', MacDonald said that they virtually do not exist; at best, he added, they are the figment of a few 'crackpots'' imaginations.

The second major nationalist group in Scotland today is actually a combination of three organizations: the Scottish National Congress, the Scottish Secretariat, and The Scottish Provisional Constituent Assembly, all of which are dominated by Roland E. Muirhead. Muirhead at present (1965) is 97 years old and has been active in nationalist politics for over 75 years. No nationalist activity since the 1890s has been free of his influence. Although physically frail and barely able to walk, his mind is as active as a man's generations younger than he. His voice is clear and firm and there is no question that when he speaks he speaks with a passion and love of Scotland that is barely comprehensible to an outsider. He has the reputation of being single-minded, dedicated, and at times irascible; he says he plans to continue to be until Scotland is free.

The largest of his organizations (approximately 300 members, and declining) is the Scottish National Congress which he set up in 1950 in opposition to the SNP and its electoral policies. The Congress believes that, by needling the English Government when its steps out of bounds and by educating all Scotsmen in their responsibilities and duties, it will hasten the day when all Scots will vote for their own independence. 'We must awaken all Scots,' said Muirhead,* 'to their rights. The Scottish people have not been taking a proper interest

* In conversation with the author, 1964.

in their Government; otherwise they would not have allowed their rights to have been taken away.' He went on to say that 'the English are splendid people; our argument is with their Government, not with the people themselves.' He, like all the Scottish nationalists, believes that England has wilfully broken the Treaty of Union of 1707 time and time again, specifically noting that Scotland has no Mint; that Clause XXI, relating to the 'rights and privileges of the Royall Burroughs' has been broken (but he did not elaborate how); and that Scottish regiments have been amalgamated with English ones. He added that Scotland, moreover, is never consulted on problems which affect them, such as the establishment of the Polaris base at Holy Loch.

The Congress claims that it practices civil disobedience and non-co-operation on the Gandhi model but, in fact, this policy has always been in the nature of wishful thinking since it has never been able to convince many Scots that that is the proper method of protest. In most cases, the Congress is content to snipe at England through its newspaper, *Forward Scotland*. For example:

> It is said when two elephants fight it is the grass that gets damaged. The elephants being Tory and Labour and the grass Scotland.
>
> Young Tories! Young Socialists! Young Liberals! A more fitting name for this lot in Scotland would be Young Traitors – certainly potential young immigrants.
>
> We read – 'The meek shall inherit the earth.' The docile Scot can look forward to this day and if we have faith, our portion should encompass at least half the earth's surface.

Muirhead's second organization, the Scottish Secretariat, is an information centre to which anyone interested in Scottish nationalism may subscribe. All the nationalist groups, even though they do not agree with Muirhead's personal views, freely subscribe to the service.

His third organization, the Scottish Provisional Constituent Assembly, is his newest creation, founded in 1962. This group consists of 104 nationalist delegates from every Scottish shire who were organized for the purpose of drawing up an absolutely new Scottish Constitution. The Assembly is supported by a group called 'Friends of the Constitution' (the membership of which is always quoted as 'thousands') many of whom are members of the other nationalist factions. At the formation of the SPCA (not to be confused with the RSPCA), twelve delegates were picked to carry out the necessary research; they spent two full years at their task. The essence of this Constitution, according to Muirhead, was drawn from both Scottish history and selected foreign methods of government. According to one critic, it is 'surprisingly free of cant'. Muirhead would like to present the Constitution immediately to the Prime Minister but the majority of delegates would prefer that a plebiscite be held so that the nationalist's cause will be strengthened by a vote of confidence. They do not want to repeat the mistakes of the old Covenant Association. However, at this moment, no decision has been taken although one eager group did raise £3,000 towards the estimated £100,000 cost of a plebiscite (over £2,000 of which was used for organizational expenses).

To complete the picture of Scottish nationalism as it exists today, three additional organizations or groups must be mentioned: the Scottish Patriots, the independent nationalists, and the newly-formed Vigilantes.

The last stronghold of romantic nationalism is found among the Scottish Patriots, the leader of whom is the indomitable Wendy Wood. The Patriots believe that the preservation of kilts, ceilidhs and claymores to be only marginally more important than the propagation of Gaelic, grouse, and gorse. It is the party, as one person put it, 'where all the mumbo-jumbo abstractions about Scotland are revered.' It is also the party where all the public's vague and often imprecise images of every Scottish nationalist group come home to roost.

Wendy Wood is the only figure of importance in the Patriots; without her, the organization would cease to exist. At 73, white-haired, pink-cheeked, and cheerful, she is the picture of Mother Scotland in her Ross Tartan – fierce, proud, devoted, charming, and dedicated all at the same time. Her admirers are legion: books are dedicated to her, callers come to listen to her, she is swamped with invitations to speak, and periodically she has to turn down offers of marriage.*

Once started talking, she works her way enthusiastically through story after story – never stopping, always laughing, and for ever demonstrating how this or that happened. She told me that she has been in gaol three times in her life and that she is an expert on them. The first time was before the war in Edinburgh's Saughton prison ('a very good gaol'), the result of an encounter with Mosley and his BUFs ('I heckled Mosley so badly', she said, 'that, in desperation, he offered me the microphone; he didn't think I would take it!'); the second time was in London's Holloway ('an interesting place')

* A proposal of marriage, she said, once gave rise to the rumour (untrue) that she was English and not Scottish. According to her, the late poet and nationalist, Lewis Spence, asked for her hand in marriage some years ago and 'in order to put him off,' she said, 'the only thing I could think of saying was that I was English.' Wendy Wood admits to being born in England but, she added, 'that no more makes me English than a Zulu born in Glasgow is white.'

because, she claims, the police objected to her talking to 'her boys' in Trafalgar Square after an England-Scotland football match; and the third time was in Glasgow's old Duke Street Gaol ('a frightful hole') which she claims she entered in protest over terrible prison conditions.

In her own words, she likes to 'tweak the sensibilities' of the English. She makes a point of harassing Sir Alec Douglas-Home, she has thrown eggs at EIIR signs, and whenever she is in London she organizes what she calls 'visual demonstrations'. After all, she told me, 'I don't want to go all the way to London and do nothing.' For instance, she once slipped a sign under the grille protecting the Coronation Chair in Westminster Abbey that demanded the return to Scotland of '*the* Stone'. She knew that the sign could not be removed until all the mechanical and electrical protective devices had been unlocked or cut off. On another occasion, she asked in a loud voice if she could buy a Bible in the Abbey and, when told that none were sold there, she launched into an impromptu speech about 'the two English Gods of War and Retribution' which ended only when a few harassed clerics demanded that she leave.

She publishes the most colourful newspaper in Scottish nationalist circles, called *The Patriot*, and it is pure Wendy Wood set to words:

> Marples has again refused to see a Scots deputation on railway closures though he did not call them 'b—— Scots' this time.
>
> Sir Alec [Douglas-Home] then proceeded with a more blatant untruth in order to get a laugh, saying that he crossed swords with Miss Wood many years ago. Miss Wood said later that she had never set eyes on him till that meeting! . . . However he stated that he was not a nationalist but a Scottish Patriot, whereupon Miss Wood told him 'I am the leader of the Scottish Patriots and I don't remember your name on the list of members' (which equalized the laughs). His whole talk, as was to be expected, was on foreign policy, and it was obvious that until Scotland is recognized as a foreign country, he will have but little interest in it, except to use it as a convenient clown land for his political treachery.
>
> The English Channel Tunnel which is to cost about £170 million is to be added to things which Scotland is expected to pay for . . . What Scotland most needs is a deep, wide channel across the Border, and no tunnel.
>
> FOR ANY SAKE! Between 'Lovey', 'Dears', and 'Darlings' in shops and buses, and footballers hugging and kissing each other for every point or goal – how sloppy can we get?
>
> One of every ten persons in Britain is mental; we knew where

they seem to congregate most; would a mental hospital not have been of more use than a post office at Westminster?

Her policies are so vague that they can all be reduced to no more than a cry for Scottish independence. She told me how the Treaty of 1707 had been broken; how she hoped to see the return of the Three Estates; how the English Post Office refuses to honour Robert Burns as it has Shakespeare (in retaliation, she sells blocks of hand-printed Burns stamps which she herself perforates on a sewing machine); and how her Patriots are the only people 'actually *doing* anything for Scottish independence – such as taking down road signs that say 'England' when they are actually on Scottish soil – instead of just sitting back and talking about it.'

As I was leaving her house, she gave me a small card that she distributes among her audiences. On it were three words:

GO HOME
ENGLISH

If the previous groups are considered right-wing and reactionary, then the 'independent' Scottish nationalists are the last bastion of left-wing and radical Scottish nationalism. They are a loose grouping of individuals who tend to stay out of the immediate arena of nationalist politics and only descend into it as the spirit moves them: to make speeches, write articles, or occasionally to stand for Parliament. Most of these independents are either academicians, wealthy lairds, or professional men of some prominence. Their political philosophies are not limited to nationalism but vary from Communism to anarchism.

Some of the most noted of these independents include Lord Boyd Orr of Brechin, the Nobel Peace Prize winner in 1949, a member of the left-wing World Peace Council, and a world authority on food; Hugh MacDiarmid, the professional name of Christopher Murray Grieve, who is a Communist (he stood against Sir Alec Douglas-Home in the 1964 General Election*); Sir Compton Mackenzie, the author, who is also Honorary President of the Scottish Patriots (one of his books is dedicated to Wendy Wood); John Rankin, the Labour MP for Glasgow-Govan; Douglas Young, the educator; Thomas Johnson, PC, an ex-Secretary of State for Scotland; Dr

* MacDiarmid was the least successful of the 36 Communist candidates (all of whom lost their deposits). He received 127 votes out of 24,995 cast in the constituency.

Archie Lamont, the geologist; and such titled figures as the Countess of Erroll and Sir Ian Moncreiffe of Moncreiffe.

The Scottish Vigilantes Association is the newest nationalist organization to appear on the Scottish scene. It was founded in 1964 as an amalgam of small anti-English organizations which previously operated under such banners as 'MacPuff' – a group established to fight Dr Beeching's surgery on Scottish railways – and 'MacJet' – a similar group opposed to restrictions being imposed on the activities at Prestwick and Renfrew airports. The association is supra-political and almost wholly free of romanticism; but it is still nationalist to the core. It draws its strength from the economic sections of the community – those people who feel they are being threatened financially by England's apparent disregard for Scottish needs. These men have come to the conclusion that Scotland is always going to be treated as a branch line to England, and that if Scotland is ever to be saved from this fate, it will have to be saved by Scots themselves. It is not a question of losing some vague and ephemeral Scottish-ism but a question of economic survival. Only the nationalists proper can become excited over the decline in Gaelic, but all Scots are concerned about the cut-back in railway and airline services, the closure of mines, the decline of shipbuilding, and the withdrawal of assets to England. The membership in the Vigilantes is unknown at present, due to its recent birth, but it is supposed to be growing rapidly.

Dr Beeching is perhaps the one man who sparked the formation of the Vigilantes because the closure of a rail line is something tangible that can be opposed; it is not a vague and frustrating problem – such as the southward drift of the labour force – which an ordinary citizen would find difficult to combat. Dr Beeching has given the Scots a good opportunity to fight and it may prove to be the biggest break the nationalists have ever had.

The advent of the Vigilantes, however, has not yet snapped the other nationalist groups out of their romantic strait-jackets, but it is helping. Wendy Wood's Patriots still believe that anything English is bad, and the other nationalist groups are not that far removed emotionally from them. For instance, they spent two years drawing up a new Constitution but have not yet considered it worthwhile to spend two years investigating the problems of Scotland's economy; they still present Westminster with so many demands that have so few supporting arguments that the authorities have shied away from giving them any serious consideration; their literature still runs to such phrases as 'There is only *one* solution . . .' and 'We are a people

DESERTED . . .' As if intentionally, they still seem bent on obtaining Scottish independence the easy and/or lazy way instead of the proper way.

The Vigilantes are forcing the other nationalist groups to become more pragmatic; many nationalists now realize that only through proper research, hard work and difficult negotiations will Scotland ever obtain what she wants. If the Vigilantes can avoid the pitfalls of cant and romanticism that have plagued the other groups for so long, they may be able to lead all the Scottish nationalists into a new era.

1. *The Times,* February 6, 1951.
2. *Scotland the Satellite,* Oliver Brown. Scottish Secretariat. (no date). Chap. XIV: 'Financial Trickery'. p. 43.
3. *West Lothian Shale Done to Death,* SNP Election Pamphlet (no date).
4. *The Anglo-Scottish Union of* 1707, *Then and Now,* Oliver Brown. Scots Independent Publication. (no date) p. 13.

11 *The Irish Nationalists*

'Too long our Irish hearts we schooled
In patient hope to bide,
By dreams of English Justice fooled
And English tongues that lied.
That hour of weak delusion's past –
The empty dream has flown;
Our hope and strength, we find at last,
Is in Ourselves Alone.'

BALLAD BY JOHN O'HAGAN

'Not an inch!'

LORD CRAIGAVON

Like their Scottish cousins, the Irish nationalists have never been a homogeneous group of patriots demanding with one voice the withdrawal of an 'alien' government from their land. All Irish nationalists seek the same goal: the reunification of the six 'lost' counties of Ulster with the 26-county mother country of Eire; but the fratricidal strife within the nationalist camp, which has been endemic to their cause for over 45 years, clouds their appeal to the people and ensures at the same time that the reunification of the two areas is no closer than it was in 1920.

The issue which splits the nationalists is tactics. On the one side sit the old Sinn Fein party and its military wing, the Irish Republican Army. These nationalists are considered the extremists within the nationalist camp, for they refuse to brook the slightest compromise with their 'enemy', England. They believe that the 'spirit of Easter Week 1916' – the time when a handful of patriots died as martyrs at the hands of the English in their quest for freedom – is just as valid today as it was almost five decades ago. Their posters in 1964, for example, perhaps best reflect their attitude. A recent one states: 'Easter 1916 . . . Fight the COMMON MARKET tie. Support SINN FEIN'.

Opposed to the extremist attitudes of Sinn Fein is a loose grouping of 'republicans' in Ulster who are known on both sides of the border only as 'the nationalists'. They are considered moderates in so far as they believe that contemporary realities demand contemporary tactics and attitudes to bring about the desired reunification. Although revered in its own context, Easter Week remains a period piece to them, not to be confused with current developments and necessities. Their relative moderation, however, does not preclude the same demand that partition be ended and that the six Northern Ireland counties be reunified with the Dublin Government.

More than ever, the Sinn Fein party of today lives up to its English translation of 'Ourselves Alone'. It is outlawed in Ulster and barely tolerated by Dublin; its military wing, the Irish Republican Army, is outlawed on both sides of the border; it is a party that is rejected by the majority of moderate Roman Catholic Irishmen, despite the fact that, from time to time, it can organize a show of strength and spirit; and it is a demoralized party – defensive, self-pitying, and self-righteous. From the days of Arthur Griffith, Patrick Pearse, James Connolly, Joseph Plunkett, and Eamon De Valera, the party has been reduced to the stage of being led by a waxen-faced, middle-aged Government clerk named Tomas MacGiolla. His party's headquarters, in a run-down building in a lower-class section of Dublin, are airless, unpainted and dusty; and they reek of disinfectant. Scattered throughout the two small offices are old pieces of furniture, ancient maps of Ireland, ragged banners, and stacks of yellowing literature, some of which contain copies of the 1916 Declaration.

MacGiolla told me that Sinn Fein prefers not to be known as a party but as a 'national organization and an integral part of the Republican Movement'. The subtleties of this definition, however, are lost on the vast majority of interested Irishmen and for better or for worse Sinn Fein is still known today as a party.

According to its literature, Sinn Fein's objectives are 'to break the connection with England; to end the entire British Imperial system in Ireland; to end poverty and insecurity; to abolish the existing partition institutions of Government in Ireland and to replace them by a National Government having complete and effective jurisdiction over the entire territory of the Nation.' The crux of its argument revolves around its abject refusal to accept the Partition Act of 1920 or the Treaty of 1921 (known as the 'Treaty of Surrender'). Members of Sinn Fein, otherwise know as Fenians, believe that Ireland is a 32-county country as it was in 1918 and that the partition was only a temporary expedient which no longer has any validity. Their actions for the past four decades, therefore, have been based on the fiction that British Ulster does not exist. They will, for example, contest the twelve 'Imperial' parliamentary seats in Ulster because the Westminster Parliament is recognized by them as existing; but they will not contest Stormont elections because in their eyes the Northern Ireland Parliament does not exist. (Since Sinn Fein was outlawed in Ulster in 1959, its candidates have stood for the 12 Westminster seats under the name of 'Republican'.) If elected to the Imperial Parliament, Fenians refuse to take their seats on the grounds that it would give *de facto* recognition to the permanency of the six-county Ulster Government. Only when the majority of the people in Ulster vote for Sinn Fein candidates – that is to say, when they are given a clear mandate – will they take their seats; not to legislate for reunification in Westminster, however, but to turn the six 'lost' counties over to the legislative jurisdiction of Dublin. How this actually would be done has never been made clear. Their political objectives in Eire are similar: they contest seats for the Dail only because they recognize its existence, but they will not take their seats in Leinster House until it becomes a legislative body for all 32 counties.

In fact, Sinn Fein candidates take an oath to this effect:

> I . . . freely and solemnly declare:
> (*a*) That, if elected, I will not sit in, nor take part in the proceedings of any Parliament legislating or purporting to legislate, for the people of Ireland other than the Parliament of the Irish Republic representative of the entire 32 Counties of Ireland.
> (*b*) That, pending the establishment of the Parliament of the Irish Republic, in all matters pertaining to the duties and function of a Parliamentary representative I will be guided by and hold myself amenable to all directions and instructions issued to me by the Ard Chomhairle (Chief Council) of Sinn Fein.
> (*c*) That, pending the establishment of the Parliament of the Irish Republic, I will, at any time, if called upon to do so, by a majority of the members of the Ard Chomhairle of Sinn Fein, resign my seat as a Parliamentary representative for the constituency of . . .
> (*d*) That I take this pledge voluntarily, of my own free will and in the full knowledge that any breach of (*a*) thereof will be regarded as an act of treachery, to be dealt with as such.

Sinn Fein's argument for one unified island is based on the belief that Ireland is too small an area to be divided; that historically it has been one unit; and that the land boundary between Ulster and Eire not only was indiscriminately drawn but that it was imposed against the will of the majority. Most impartial observers of the Irish scene, particularly the Dutchman, M. W. Heslinga,[1] have pointed out that there is little basis of fact or even precedent for these views. Although only one island of any note (Hispaniola. New Guinea is not considered comparable) is divided into two states, Heslinga points out that, by comparing the lengths of frontiers to the square miles of territory, 'the extent to which Ireland has been broken up by the land boundary is almost equal to the fragmentation of the whole of Europe'

(Iceland and the USSR excluded).[2] He adds that the relationship is approximately the same if the length of the boundary is compared to the population on both sides of it.

The argument that Ireland has historically been one political, economic, and cultural unit does not stand up under examination. The earliest histories of the island show that the land was inhabited by a series of semi-autonomous tribes, each controlling only a part of the island, and all of whom were constantly at war with each other. It was, in fact, only when the British came to dominate the island's political, economic, and social life over the last three centuries that Ireland ever experienced anything in the way of national unity.

The argument that the border was drawn indiscriminately and that it follows no natural barrier has some basis of fact, for there is no doubt that it meanders haphazardly across the face of the land with no apparent logic. But this argument is academic and offers little solace to Sinn Fein's cause since the Party has no desire to re-arrange the boundary; it wishes merely to abolish it.

The argument that the border was imposed against the will of the majority is viewed by both the Roman Catholic nationalists, and the Ulster Protestants from different perspectives. The nationalists, when they refer to the 'majority' who objected to the partition, refer to all the Irish on both sides of the border while the Protestant Ulstermen, when they refer to the 'majority' who favoured partition, refer to the Protestant majority north of the border. Neither side is willing to concede the validity of the other side's claim.

Sinn Fein also objects to what it calls 'British domination' of its land, particularly within Eire. The fact that Britain still controls six counties is proof enough to Sinn Fein that she continues to have imperialistic ambitions for the whole island. Sinn Fein concedes that, on the surface, Britain has withdrawn from the 26 counties but adds that, in fact, she remains surreptitiously, dominating the land as she did for three centuries. MacGiolla claims, for instance, that Leinster House is actually controlled from Threadneedle Street, pointing out that the Irish pound is tied to the price of Sterling and that English money circulates freely in Eire but that Irish money does not circulate freely in England. This economic domination, he said, leads to political and social domination as well. The decisions in Whitehall and Westminster, he added, indirectly affect Ireland and ultimately determine what party is in power in the Dail. In addition, he says that Irishmen, when they move to England, are treated patronisingly in that they can vote in English elections even though they remain Irish citizens. The social threat he feels is so pervasive that it has all but obliterated the independent cultural standards of Ireland. English is universally spoken, except in a few isolated areas in western Ireland (the Gaelic language is now referred to as 'Irish' by the Dublin Government); English law is used in the courts; and, to his horror, Ireland even looks like England. These developments, he says, are all due to England's reluctance to withdraw tactfully from the island and to leave the Irish to their own devices.

The only reason why Ireland was divided in the first place, and the cause of all the friction between Ulster and Eire, is the difference in religion. MacGiolla said he saw no valid reason why a religious minority had the right to break away on its own. He added that when the Protestants did break away, they took with them many Roman Catholic nationalists whose sympathies lay with the South. By gerry-mandering the constituencies and restricting the vote, he claimed these people have been denied the opportunity of being reunited with Eire. If the areas in British Ulster which are predominantly Roman Catholic were allowed to vote themselves back into Eire, he added, the land area of Protestant Ulster would shrink by half, further demonstrating the ridiculousness of the need for a separate state. He also said that the boundary divides the agricultural south from the industrial north which was to neither side's advantage.

Electorally, Tomas MacGiolla and his Sinn Fein Party suffer from the Party's past successes, particularly the 1918 victory when Sinn Fein candidates won 73 of the 105 Irish seats in Westminster. From that high-water mark, Sinn Fein fortunes, in both the 26- and six-county area, have steadily declined. It is not relevant, however, to this present subject to follow the fortunes of Sinn Fein and the IRA in Eire itself; suffice it to say that for the next 30 years after the 1918 victory, Sinn Fein found itself increasingly isolated from the centres of power by its refusal to accept either the Treaty of 1921 or the partition of the previous year. Most of Sinn Fein's strength in the Dail ebbed away with the growth of De Valera's Fianna Fail ('Soldiers of Ireland') Party and Cosgrove's Fine Gael ('United Ireland') Party, the two centre parties in the Dail today. In fact, by 1927, Sinn Fein strength in the Dail had been reduced to five and for the following 30 years they were to have no representation at all.* In the 1930's, Sinn Fein was not only isolated from the political scene but from the IRA as well. The IRA had sided with De Valera in 1932 in a struggle for power with Cosgrove; but this union was not to last. Eventually, the disruptive activities of the IRA forced De Valera to ban it in 1940. From that moment, the IRA has been an illegal organization on both sides of the border, having been previously banned in Northern Ireland at the time of partition.

* In 1957, four Sinn Fein candidates were elected to the Dail, and true to their pledge, refused to take their seats. In the next election in 1961, they were all defeated.

By 1950, a weak and wholly disorganized Sinn Fein Party found itself re-allied with the banned IRA. The Sinn Fein became the political wing of the alliance and the IRA its military wing. Membership in one organization was virtually synonymous with membership in the other, although MacGiolla claims that the overlap was and still is slight. The Party was still contesting seats in the Dail, but it was at this time that it first began to contest the twelve Westminster Parliament seats in Northern Ireland. Its first success came in the 1955 General Election when two of its candidates won in Mid-Ulster and Fermanagh and South Tyrone. Both candidates refused to take their seats. In fact, they were ineligible to do so since both were convicted felons in prison at the time. The Unionists went to court to unseat them. In Fermanagh and South Tyrone, the Unionist was awarded the seat but in Mid-Ulster a second election was held. The Sinn Fein candidate, Tom Mitchell, again won and once more was unseated by the courts. This time the seat was awarded to the second candidate on the ballot – a Unionist – but it was discovered that he, too, was ineligible because he held an office of profit under the Crown. A third election was held in the spring of 1956 and this time the Northern Ireland nationalists put up a candidate in opposition to both Mitchell and the new Unionist candidate. The overall nationalist vote was thus split and the Unionist won a clear victory.

In the 1959 General Election, Sinn Fein performed very poorly primarily because the Roman Catholic nationalists were disgusted with the activities of the IRA. Its vote fell from 152,310 to 63,415. In 1964, it again contested all twelve seats. This time it did a little better. Its total number of votes rose to 101,628 or 17.5 per cent of the total cast in Northern Ireland. This increase was attained despite the intervention of other nationalist candidates and, on the face of it, represents a slight comeback. All 12 seats, however, were held by the Unionists.

The revival of Sinn Fein's political activities in the early 1950s also coincided with a revival of IRA raids along the border. Although IRA activities in Eire, on the border, and in England itself had been carried out sporadically since the day the island was partitioned, they revived in earnest around 1953. Sinn Fein has always approved of the tactics of force and gave its military wing at that time full encouragement to step up its activities. The new wave of border raids were actually initiated by an extremist break-away from the IRA called Fianna Uladh (Ulster Republican Movement). It soon changed its name to Saor Uladh (Free Ulster), the title under which it was to gain its notoriety. Its leader was a native of County Tyrone named Liam Kelly, whom members of the IRA considered to be a 'dangerous amateur'. Kelly felt that the IRA was neither sufficiently aggressive nor militant enough in its pursuit of Irish independence. For three years, from 1953 to 1956, he conducted his own private war in Ulster, independent of the IRA, which included among its other activities a raid for money on the Dungannon Labour Exchange in 1953, an arms raid on Gough Barracks in Armagh in 1954, and a similar raid on the Inniskilling's Depot at Omagh some months later in which eight raiders were arrested – all of them men in their early twenties or younger. The Ulster Government was forced to outlaw this organization in 1955.

Kelly continued his independent activities even after the IRA officially began its campaign in 1956. His most ambitious effort was a hostage raid on the police barracks at Rosslea in 1958 in which two of his men were known to have been killed. However, with the activities of the IRA increasing in volume, Saor Uladh soon faded into the background and was re-absorbed into the main body of the IRA. Kelly himself eventually fled to the United States.

The IRA was forced into the war prematurely and before it had adequate time to prepare itself because Kelly's successes between 1953 and 1956 were drawing many of the IRA's better men away into active battle. There is some evidence that the IRA had planned a large-scale attack on British Ulster at some later date but that Kelly's impetuousness had forced its hand. In any event, the IRA officially entered the fray in December 1956 with the publication of the following proclamation:

OGLAIGH NA h'EIREANN
[Irish Republican Army]

TO THE IRISH PEOPLE

Resistance to British rule in occupied Ireland has now entered a decisive stage. Early today, northern units of the Irish Republican Army attacked key British occupation installations.

Spearheaded by volunteers of the Irish Republican Army, our people in the Six Counties have carried the fight to the enemy. They are the direct victims of British Imperialism and they are also the backbone of the national revolutionary resurgence.

This is the age-old struggle of the Irish people versus British aggression. This is the same cause for which generations of our people have suffered and died. In this grave hour, all Irish men and women, at home and abroad, must sink their differences, political or religious, and rally behind the banner of national liberation.

We call on Irish men in the British armed forces to stand by the motherland and refuse to bear arms against their own countrymen.

We call on members of the RUC and B-Special Constabulary to cease being tools of British Imperialism and either stand on side or join us in the fight against tyranny. We warn them that should they reject this plea they will be adjudged renegades by the Irish people and treated accordingly by the Resistance Movement . . .

The whole of Ireland – its resources, wealth, culture, history and tradition is the common inheritance of all our people regardless of religious belief. The division of this country by Britain, and its subjection to British political control in the north, and to British economic domination of the south, must now be ended for ever. It is up to this generation of Irish men and women to resolve for all time our unity, independence, and freedom from foreign domination. The alternative, if the present situation continues, is extinction as a nation.

The foe will use his considerable resources to divide us by fanning the fires of bigotry and sectarianism – twin enemies of Irish Republicanism. Let us be on our guard; a free Ireland cannot tolerate the one of the other . . .

That then is our aim; an independent, united, democratic Irish Republic. For this we shall fight until the invader is driven from our soil and victory is ours.

ISSUED BY THE ARMY COUNCIL   December 12th, 1956.
IRISH REPUBLICAN ARMY

The border war lasted five full years and in that time the IRA was the instigator of over 600 'incidents' of a major and minor nature. The most active year was 1957 with 341 officially recorded incidents. In 1958, there were only 126 incidents, and by 1960 they had tailed off to no more than 60. For the first two years, the IRA concentrated on destroying government property: telephone relay stations, post-office vans, pillarboxes, electrical transformers, bridges, police barracks, and military installations. But by 1958, it had switched its emphasis to the emergency forces themselves either by ambushing stray members of the Royal Ulster Constabulary and B-Specials* or by raiding police barracks and firing indiscriminately through the doors and windows. By 1961, it was reduced to the stage of setting booby-traps at spots most frequented by the defensive forces, which often resulted in the killing and wounding of innocent civilians.

* There were actually three classes of 'Specials', all organized at the time of partition: The A-Specials, who were the larger and more physically fit, were full-time auxiliary policemen; the B-Specials were the less fit and only took on part-time police work; and the C-Specials who were older men only called out in dire emergencies. The only group remaining in force today are the auxiliary B-Specials. Only Protestants are eligible to become Specials.

The size of the IRA at that time has never been ascertained but it is estimated it numbered no more than a thousand active participants. Their activities, however, kept 5,000 British regulars, 5,000 territorials, 10,000 B-Specials, 3,000 RUCs and 2,000 special security guards on full alert during this period. Officially, a total of six RUCs were killed and 32 men from all the other forces were wounded. The official Ulster records claim six IRA deaths and six wounded, but these figures are probably low. At the height of the crisis in 1958, 187 suspects were interned by the Ulster Government in their Crumlin Road Gaol in Belfast.

The real damage, however, was in two other areas: first was the physical damage to property which some people estimate to have exceeded £1 million; and second, and most serious of all, was the psychological damage done to the minds of the Protestants and Catholics living on the border. The many years of effort by both communities to find a way in which they could both live in peace and friendship had been destroyed and were replaced by the seeds of hate and suspicion. If the aim of the IRA was to re-create the bitterness of partition days, it had done its job well. Even today the bitterness of those five years of strife is evident among the natives in both Eire and British Ulster, particularly among those who lived so close to the border and witnessed the struggle first-hand.

The IRA ceased its activities in early 1962 for a number of reasons, not the least of which was the Ulster Catholics' reluctance to support the IRA. When the IRA began its campaign, it was convinced that the Roman Catholics and nationalists (virtually the same thing) in Northern Ireland would rise up with them to throw the British off the island. It was surprised to find that these people were not prepared to go to war on its behalf. It is true that very few of them collaborated with the Government but, at the same time, they did not give any appreciable help to their countrymen from below the border. It was not so much that they disagreed with the IRA aims – for practically all Ulster nationalists want to see a re-unified Ireland – but what disturbed them most was the unmanly way in which the war was conducted: with ambushes, booby-traps, road mines, and murders. By 1961 these activities had alienated a large section of the Roman Catholic population in the north. It was most visible in the 1959 Westminster elections when all the Sinn Fein candidates were decisively defeated.

Despite the nasty character of the war, a romantic aura has grown up around the IRA's activities. Today, no one south of the border talks about the ambushes, the shot-in-the-back, the killing of innocent people, and the wanton damage to property. According to them, those who died for the IRA and Irish freedom died on a glorious battlefield with 'Come Back to Erin, Mavourneen' on their lips. In some quarters, these men are considered Folk Heroes.

The IRA was also defeated because it lost the sympathy of the Dublin Government. To this day, neither Sinn Fein nor the IRA has regained it. Tomas MacGiolla and 210 of his associates were arrested in 1957 by the Dublin authorities and interned without trial for 20 months at the Curragh Camp. According to MacGiolla, his arrest 'had something to do with IRA activities' (in which he denies ever having been involved).

According to the IRA itself, in its proclamation dated 26 February, 1962, in which it formally announced the cessation of its activities, the causes of its failure were obvious:

> The decision to end the Resistance Campaign has been taken in view of the general situation. Foremost among the factors motivating this course of action has been the attitude of the general public whose minds have been deliberately distracted from the supreme issue facing the Irish people – the unity and freedom of Ireland. Other and lesser issues have been urged successfully upon them and the sacrifices which could win freedom in the political, cultural, social and economic spheres are now stated to be necessary to bolster up the partition system forced on the Irish people by Britain forty years ago. This calculated emphasis on secondary issues by those whose political future is bound up in the *status quo* and who control all the mass media of propaganda is now leading the people of the 26 Counties towards possible commitment in future wars . . .
>
> Terroristic tactics against the civilian population, draconian laws, imprisonment without charge or trial, torture-mills to force 'confessions' from prisoners, long and savage penal servitude sentences, the shooting down of unarmed people at road-blocks and threats of even sterner measures including flogging and hanging have all been employed to maintain British rule in the Six Counties.
>
> The collaborationist role of successive 26 County Governments –acting under British pressure – from December 1956 has contributed material aid and comfort to the enemy. Border patrols by 26 County military and police working in collaboration with the British Occupation Forces were instituted 48 hours after the opening of the Campaign. The press was muzzled and the radio controlled in the interests of British Rule. The methods and eventually the aims and objectives of the Irish Republican Army were misrepresented to the Irish people and to the world by professional politicians of the 26 County State. Top-level conferences with Crown Forces and the continuous supplying of information

to the enemy – secretly at first but later quite openly – were other and lesser known features of collaboration.

Unarmed active service Volunteers found within the 26 Counties were arrested and jailed while armed patrols of the British Forces could cross the Border at will. Jailings of Resistance supporters and even moral sympathisers throughout the 26 Counties followed while quisling Irishmen from the same area were permitted to join the enemy forces. Homes were raided and people followed about by Special political police. The Curragh Concentration Camp was opened and maintained for close on two years with 200 uncharged and untried prisoners. When public opinion forced its closing down, the Prisoners' Dependants Fund was attacked and hundreds of collectors jailed.

When this tactic too was defeated proceedings against IRA Volunteers and their supporters at 26 County District Courts were superseded by the introduction of a Military Tribunal in November last. The savage sentences since imposed for technical offences culminated in the imprisonment of a young IRA scholar from Co. Derry for eight years . . .

The international provisions governing belligerent status including the wearing of means of identification, the carrying of arms openly and being under the control of responsible officers have been observed by the Irish Republican Army but in no case has the enemy recognised the status of the men fighting for their country other than as criminals . . .

From the end of the border war to the present day, the IRA has withered away to the point where it barely exists. Some people claim that the old Saor Uladh has become an 'Irish Mafia' within the organization with a strength of perhaps 250 hardened fanatics who are planning some time in the future to launch a full-scale invasion of Ulster. Recent statements by men claiming to be privy to the inner council's decisions lend credence to the rumour, but they do not bear up under examination. What is left of the IRA today consists primarily of a few rebels, felons, outlaws and cranks who use the IRA name as a cover for their various anti-social activities, many of which have nothing to do with nationalism or the re-unification of Ireland. It is, for instance, a haven for lapsed-Catholic Marxists – those Irishmen who moved to England, lost contact with their Church, joined the Communist Party (which Irish Marxists often call 'a substitute church') because of its authoritarian nature, resigned when they became disenchanted, and then returned to Ireland alienated from both their Church and their people. This process is known in Eire as 'Communism through the back door' and produces some recruits for the

IRA. The Army may initiate a new series of violent outbreaks along the border in the future, but if it does, it is felt that a different breed of men will be at the helm whose objectives may not necessarily have anything to do with the border itself.

The 'moderate' Irish nationalists operate exclusively within the six Ulster counties of Northern Ireland: Antrim, Armagh, Derry, Down, Fermanagh, and Tyrone*. These nationalists cannot be considered a part of a single political party because they have neither party organization nor common policy; but they do act with common purpose when they sit together as the Opposition in Stormont or in the local town councils. Their aims are *basically* the same as Sinn Fein's: they want to re-unite the six British-controlled Ulster counties with the 26 counties of Eire; they claim that the border was imposed against the will of the 'majority'; they claim that, historically, Ireland has been one unit that it is too small to be devided, and so on.

The moderates, however, are more specific than the Sinn Fein in their complaints against English rule. They claim that the Northern Ireland Government is religiously biased, that laws are passed in terms of what good they will do Protestants, that all the good jobs go to Protestants, and that only Protestants are encouraged to get ahead. They accuse the Ulster Protestants of encouraging the divisions that exist between Roman Catholics and Protestants in order to maintain their own power. They claim that the Roman Catholic towns of Derry and Enniskillen have been gerrymandered so that they remain in the control of Protestants; they say that the restricted franchise in local elections (which is limited to ratepayers only) ensures that the poorer Catholics are denied power, and they say that England openly encourages the ruling Protestants by subsidizing them from the Exchequer. These nationalists claim that four of the six counties, if given the opportunity, would opt out of the Union and re-unite with Dublin; but they add, because of the narrow-minded Protestants and their selfish craving for power, the Northern Ireland Government would not allow this to happen.

Unlike Sinn Fein, these nationalists have recognised the existence of British Ulster and her Parliament, Stormont, and for this reason they are considered moderates. No matter how distasteful the fact may be to them, they have acknowledged the partition of the island as an accomplished fact. They do not maintain the fiction that because partition is wrong (to them) British Ulster, therefore, does not legally

* The other three Ulster counties of Cavan, Donegal and Monaghan are part of 26-county Eire.

exist. They feel that the only way this wrong can be righted is to take an active part in the country's political affairs in the hope that changes can be made constitutionally. They base their hopes on sufficiently educating the people in Northern Ireland to the point where they will vote their own six-county country out of existence. As Edward McAteer, the leader of the nationalists in Stormont, put it: 'We are the only political party in the world who want to commit hari-kari'.

These nationalists are at odds with Sinn Fein on two accounts: first, because they feel that their extremist activities do not help to bring the Protestants and Roman Catholics together. They say that border raids, obstructionist tactics, and an inability to face unpleasant facts have done great harm to the nationalist cause. Sinn Fein, in return, claims that the nationalists are not even a party, that they have hopelessly compromised their ideals, and – in a backhanded compliment – that they are supported by the Dublin Government.

The real bone of contention, however, is Sinn Fein's electoral policies. Nationalists claim that Sinn Fein contests Westminster seats even when it realizes its battles are hopeless. If it wins a few seats furthermore, as it did in 1955, its members refuse to sit in Parliament, which to the Ulster nationalists is a wholly negative and pointless policy. Moreover, because Sinn Fein insists on fighting all the Westminster seats, it turns each contest into a three-cornered fight between a Nationalist, a Republican (Sinn Fein) and a Unionist. It thus splits the Catholic vote which ensures that the Unionists remain in power. It also forces the Ulster nationalists to work exclusively in Stormont and not simultaneously in Westminster as they would prefer.

To these nationalists, one of the most annoying facets of Sinn Fein's activities in Ulster is that it is financed in large part by members of the American Clan Na Gael; its members innocently believe they are helping the cause of Irish Freedom by contributing money to Sinn Fein. When those Irishmen (who belong to the Clan) left for America during the first two decades of the century, they took with them the image of Anglo-Irish relations current at the time. Four decades have not altered their outlook at all. Their idea of Ireland today is as firmly fixed on Easter Week as is Sinn Fein's.

Only when the nationalists take their seats in Stormont are they considered to be a political party, for they then assume the position of unofficial opposition to the Northern Ireland Government. The nationalists make the distinction between the existence of British Ulster, which they reluctantly accept, and its permanency, which they do not accept. As a result, they refuse to be considered Her Majesty's Official Opposition because it would give *de facto* recognition to Northern Ireland's permanency. (The sign 'Leader of the Opposition' over their offices in Stormont has 'Leader of the' blanked out. The opposition leader's salary, therefore, goes begging each year.) They prefer the word 'independent' to the word 'official' and insist that they are not even a party but a 'vanguard'.

At the moment, there are nine nationalists in Stormont. They receive support on most questions from an Irish Liberal, a few members of the Republican Labour Party and a few independents, which gives them slightly more than a quarter of the votes in the 52-seat house. Recently, there has been a split between Edward McAteer's and 88-year-old Cahir Healy's more conservative nationalists (who, because they are so conservative, are known as 'Green Tories') and the more liberal nationalists led by Patrick and Thomas Gormley. The Gormley brothers feel that nationalist thought has been too rooted in the past and must adapt itself to current changes and needs. They argue that a more rational approach to politics should replace their old emotional approach. Therefore, they say, the party should change its emphasis from arguing the emotionally explosive merits of partition to arguing the more relevant economic shortcomings of the six counties. The Gormleys, for instance, do not like to see their party forced into an anti-Protestant position every time their old policies are subject to scrutiny; nor do they like the trend of abdicating the nationalist position in Westminster elections to the 'renegade' Sinn Fein Party.

The two brothers are in the process of building a new party, called the National Political Front, complete with charter, policies, branches and members. They hope to draw the young and the technically-inclined into it regardless to which religion they might belong. The Gormleys have the backing of an organization called National Unity which is composed of a small group of intellectuals located at Queens University, Belfast. This group, in conjunction with the Anti-Partition League, provided the initial impetus for the creation of the Front.

Cahir Healy, on the other hand, dismisses this rebellion as an act of spite, pointing out that Patrick Gormley recently lost his bid for the parliamentary party leadership to Healy's man, Eddie McAteer. Healy, an ex-Westminster MP, an ex-Regulation 18b internee during the Second World War, and a life-long nationalist, feels that the party is as adequate as can be under the circumstances and that only by first educating the people and then by working together through the constitutional machinery will the reunion of British Ulster with Eire be achieved. The current posturing by a few malcontents, says Healy, is a waste of time.

Whether the split is indicative of a trend is difficult to say at the moment. There is no question, however, that there are some signs that the younger generation of nationalists are beginning to question the old shibboleths they learned from their fathers. Some of these are undoubtledly being drawn into the National Political Front. So far, however, there have been no indications that the re-thinking in the NPF has been developed to a point where it would accept the *status quo* in Northern Ireland. The Gormleys, for instance, insist that the need to reconsider party policy will in no way affect their primary objective of reunification. When I mentioned that I thought it doubtful that the long-ruling Unionist Party would ever accept them as a serious opposition (capable, perhaps, of one day ruling the six counties) unless they gave up their demands to abolish the State, all the nationalists – practically in unison – expressed the conviction that eventually the Unionists would change their views, not only in the light of the 'justice' of nationalist demands, but also from the pressure that would be brought to bear upon the Northern Ireland Government by the electorate itself. The nationalists feel, moreover, that the discrimination against them as nationalists and Catholics is less the product of necessity to preserve the State itself but more a question of a Protestant minority forcibly imposing its will on a Roman Catholic 'majority'.

Ulster Protestants, on the other hand, reject practically every argument put forth by the nationalists. They claim that, for over 300 years, since the days of the Plantations, Ulstermen have known no other allegiance except to Britain. This loyalty, they say, is based on the similarity of their heritage – social, economic, political and religious – and they detest the thought that they are considered similar to the southern Irish. Ulstermen say they are of Scottish and English stock, who are Protestants, who believe in freedom of expression, freedom of religion, and the right 'to be a Pilgrim'. Ulstermen look with horror upon the Roman Catholic Church in the South, which takes its orders from the Vatican and which controls, they claim, virtually every aspect of an Irishman's life. They point out that the Roman Catholic Church has banned divorce, birth control, and a long list of contemporary literary works (this list is known in Ulster as 'a compendium of required reading'). They say that there is no freedom of expression, no freedom of religion, and no freedom of opportunity in Eire, pointing to the statistics on both emigration and the declining non-Catholic population as evidence. Ulstermen claim, in addition, that the Irish below the border are slothful and rooted in the past. They say their xenophobic desire to revive the Gaelic language – which many Irishmen themselves consider to be a badge of poverty – is indicative of the nationalists' desire to drag them back to Easter Week 1916.

In the eyes of Irish Protestants, therefore, Northern Ireland is a separate nation, distinct in outlook, consciousness, and attitudes from the 26-county Irish Catholics. The boundary that split the island in 1920 was not drawn, they insist, to suit the whims of a 'minority' but a division drawn to separate two nations who have always been distinctly different. They also reject the claim that the island has always been a single economic, cultural and political unit; nor do they believe that it is morally wrong to set up a separate state if it involves the preservation of their own values, standards and religion. Their favourite argument against nationalist allegations is that British Ulster has existed as a unit for over 300 years while Eire is barely older than four decades.

This sense of separateness is so strong that Ulstermen feel that they are, in fact, a nation – not just a slight variation of Eire. Somewhat surprisingly, they feel they are distinct from Great Britain as well. Even though they pledge their loyalty to the Crown, fly the Union Jack, and claim to 'feel British', their ultimate loyalty is to Northern Ireland, although they seldom say it in so many words. The ideological gulf between North and South is, at the moment, almost as wide as it was in 1920 but, at the same time, a slight gulf exists between Ulstermen and their own English allies. It stems from an Englishman's general indifference to Northern Ireland problems and to his ignorance of even the basic situation there (an example: letters which are mailed to 'Belfast, Eire'). In effect, British Ulster is cut off from both friend and foe – completely from the Roman Catholic South and partially from its friends in Britain. This has encouraged a mild form of Ulster Protestant nationalism which is best expressed in the attitude that, in the last analysis, the preservation of Northern Ireland lies not with Westminster but with the Ulster Protestants themselves.

The most fervent expression of Ulster Protestantism is found in the Orange Order, probably the most militant Protestant organization in the world today. Orange Orders exist in every English-speaking country in the world and in a few other Protestant countries as well. Ulster not only gave birth to the Orange Order, but remains today as the centre of its operations and influence. It is estimated, for instance, that, out of a total Ulster Protestant population of 940,000 no less than 200,000 are associated in one form or another with it.

The Order was founded around 1795 'to maintain the laws and peace of the country and the Protestant constitution'. It was organized in the traditions established by older Protestant groups in Ulster such as the Oakboys, Hearts of Steel, and the Peep O' Day Boys whose aims were similar to those of the Orange Order.* Its 'patron saint', of course, is William III of Orange – 'King Billy' – from whom it takes its colours and its inspiration. The anniversary of William's victory at the Battle of the Boyne, 'the glorious 12th of July', brings every Orangeman into the streets of Ulster to show his loyalty to the institution and Protestantism. The Union Jacks are out and men and women of all ages, draped in orange sashes, parade through the towns to the beat of the Lambeg, a large drum that is beaten with sawed-off broomsticks. At the head of the processions march the Protestant politicians and clergy, followed by the Black Preceptories, the Apprentice Boys and ordinary Orangemen.

It is still not possible for a Roman Catholic or a Jew to belong to the Order, and, until recently, there was a ban on mixed marriages. For many years, Orangemen were forbidden to associate with Roman Catholics to the extent of not being allowed to drink beer in a Catholic-owned pub. Although the Order calls itself a 'religious order', its primary function is to act as a society for the protection of Protestants and their interests. For instance, it ensures that any Protestant land up for sale does not fall into Catholic hands and, conversely, when it hears that Catholic land is on the market, it tries through indirect means to buy it. It encourages Protestant employers to hire Protestants and Protestant landlords to rent to Protestants. It has even gone so far as to put up candidates under an 'anti-Partition' or 'Nationalist' label to split the Catholic vote and thus ensure a Protestant victory. The Ulster Catholics, in retaliation are forced to use many of the same tactics to protect their own people. The intransigence of both groups, therefore, guarantees that the two communities remain separated physically as well as spiritually.

The Orange Order is interwoven into the fabric of the Unionist Party to such an extent that it is virtually impossible to tell the two apart. Every member of the Northern Ireland Cabinet in Stormont, for instance, is a member of the Order. All the good government posts go to Orangemen; not only in the Belfast bureaucracy but also in the local county offices. No job of any sensitivity or importance would go to someone not in the Order. Many liberal Protestants,

* The Catholic counterpart to the Orange Order is the Ancient Order of Hibernians. It has neither the militancy nor the numerical strength of the Protestant organization in Ulster and is currently in a period of decline. Its history is obscure but seem to have originated in the old St Patrick Fraternal Order which in turn was an off-shoot of such 17th and 18th century organizations as the Terry Alts, Rockites, Whitefeet, Defenders, Michael Coffeys, and Carders, most of which were referred to collectively as 'Ribbonmen'. Catholic militancy of this nature was often exported with Irish emigration, appearing, for instance, in the United States in the form of the Molly Maguires.

with passive disdain, regard the Orange Order as militant, dogmatic, and out-dated, but they realize that it is still impossible to advance up the political and (to some extent) economic ladder in Northern Ireland without joining it. They also find that it is sometimes necessary to join more reactionary groups as well – those organizations whose memberships overlap with that of the Orange Order – particularly the Black Preceptory and the Apprentice Boys of Derry.*

The Unionist Party, which looks so monolithic from the outside, is actually a blend of all the characteristics and attitudes of the many Protestant sects in Ulster: Presbyterian, Anglican, Methodist, Brethren, Baptist, Congregationalist, etc. The Party's primary duty is not to split this vote, for it represents the cornerstone of Northern Ireland's existence. The Party, therefore, has to be flexible and undogmatic in its approach to problems, attempting to satisfy most of the needs of these groups. Whatever differences may exist within the party – religious, political, economic or social – they are all forgotten whenever the spectre of Roman Catholic nationalism threatens them. This automatic closing-of-ranks explains, in part, why other parties, such as the British Labour Party (which recognizes the permanency of the border) are not given much encouragement to establish themselves in Ulster. Such a party would split the Protestant vote and that, to a Unionist, would be disastrous. It explains, moreover, why the Unionists are forced to be flexible – to be all things to all men – Labourite, Liberal, Conservative, traditionalist, and innovator all rolled into one. They realize that if they cannot satisfy the needs of their own people, there conceivably may come a day when even Roman Catholic domination may seem a fairly plausible alternative.

The consolidation of Unionist power takes place on both a psychological and electoral level. On the psychological level, it has never risen much above beating the Protestant drum to resurrect the fear and hatred of Catholics. It varies in temper from Lord Craigavon's celebrated definition of Stormont – 'A Protestant Parliament for a Protestant people' – to the noted Orange toast of the early 19th century: 'To the Glorious, pious and Immortal Memory of King William III, who saved us from Rogues and Roguery, Slaves

* The most reactionary Protestant sect is the Ulster Protestant Action, whose membership overlaps considerably with the Orange Order's. This group, which claims 10,000 members, is rabidly anti-Catholic and opposes any concessions whatsoever to them. Its greatest strength is in Ulster, but it has loyal supporters in Liverpool (particularly among the Protestant Party), Glasgow, Edinburgh and the United States. Its newspaper, *Ulster Protestant* ('For God and Ulster') concentrates primarily on exposing the sins of Catholics and Catholicism to the extent of excluding Protestant gospel and philosophy.

and Slavery, Knaves and Knavery, Popes and Popery, from brass money and wooden shoes; and whoever denies this Toast may he be slammed, crammed and jammed into the muzzle of the great gun of Athlone, and the gun fired into the Pope's Belly, and the Pope into the Devil's belly and the Devil into Hell, and the door locked and the key in an Orangeman's pocket . . .' There are people within the Unionist Party, however, who are attempting to draw the Party away from this emotional approach to a more rational one, but so far they have had little success. Beating the drum still seems to be the easiest and cheapest method of solidifying the vote.

On the electoral level, solidifying the vote usually means rearranging the electoral boundaries so that they favour the Unionist Party at the expense of the nationalists. It also means restricting the local franchise to ratepayers which denies the vote to many poor Catholics.

No matter with whom I talked within the Unionist Party, I found that very few denied the existence of some form of political discrimination. Most will admit privately that gerrymandering of political districts is a fact of life in Northern Ireland and that it is the Unionist Party that is responsible for it. But they hasten to point out that every government in the world discriminates against an organization that advocates the overthrow of the State itself – the Communist Parties in Britain and America being their favourite examples. They also claim that the gerrymandering only affects their local elections and not their Westminster elections and that if there were any real inequities in the local gerrymandering it would be reflected in the Imperial elections. Unionists will privately acknowledge that gerrymandering is even taken to the lengths of strategically placing Protestants and Catholics in new housing estates in order that the desired electoral imbalance be maintained. But they add that the nationalists overstate their own cause because, when the fog of propaganda has been cleared, there is still a two-thirds majority of Protestants in Northern Ireland; and their representation in Stormont is not much greater than that. They point out that all ruling parties in Great Britain tend to be over-represented and the minority parties under-represented. The only instances where they will admit that gerrymandering is obviously unfair to the Catholics is in Derry City (which Eddie McAteer refers to as the 'Danzig of Ireland') and in Cahir Healy's home town of Enniskillen, where Protestant minorities govern Catholic majorities.

To justify their gerrymandering further, Unionists say that they are not prepared to accept any serious opposition unless they are convinced that their opponents accept the permanency of the Border. Despite the nationalist's claim that gerrymandering is a symptom of

Protestant intolerance of Catholics, the Ulster Protestants insist that it is simply a question of survival.

The most noticeable trend in Ireland today on both sides of the Border is the increasing acceptance of the permanency of partition by more and more Roman Catholic moderates. It was not only visible in the 1959 General Election, where many moderate Catholics turned their backs on the intransigence of Sinn Fein, the IRA, and the nationalists, but is still visible today in the reluctance of most Northern Ireland citizens – Catholic and Protestant alike – to give up the many benefits which have accrued to them under British rule. Most cannot be matched by the Dublin Government. The six counties have a higher standard of living, better old-age and unemployment benefits and a wider diversity of opportunity. British Ulster is not yet self-supporting; it is still subsidized by the Exchequer. But the many benefits available to its citizens, no matter from what source they might come, loom more important today than any argument over 'principles' that seem to many to be 40 years out of date. Ulster Roman Catholics have not yet embraced Unionism – they still vote nationalist out of conscience – but more and more are beginning to question the validity of nationalist claims. They, like the Gormley brothers, have begun to realize that the important questions of the day are economic rather than religious, and that perhaps it is in everyone's best interest to bury the hatchet and to turn their attention to more vital problems.

This tendency is also noticeable on a governmental level. Both the Northern Ireland Prime Minister, Captain Terence O'Neill, and the Irish Taoiseach, Sean Lemass, have made hesitant and sometimes inept gestures towards a new approach to the problem. Captain O'Neill makes it clear that any steps taken to bring the two areas closer together are predicated on the understanding that six-county Ulster intends to remain a part of Great Britain. From what I have heard, Lemass cannot *publicly* accept the Border as permanent for it would still have disastrous political consequences for him and his party. But it has long been felt that the politicians in Leinster House have privately conceded that, at least in the foreseeable future, there is little hope of re-unification. The fact that the Governments are trying to reach a rapprochement, however, is a development which would have been unthinkable ten years ago.

There is also some indication that Roman Catholic voters in Northern Ireland are tired of their second-class citizenship and are willing, for the moment, to accept the fact of partition in the interests of getting on with more important tasks. There are new generations of citizens, both Protestant and Catholic, who do not remember when the country was united and cannot be bothered with the problems of their parents. Much of the hatred on both sides of the religious chasm, however, still rubs off on the young and it is not lessened by the presence of the Orangemen and nationalist militants; but the newer generations have a wider vision than their parents and are tending to leave yesterday's problems to them.

In addition, there are indications that Eire itself is growing out of its insecurity, frustration, Anglophobia, and self-righteousness of the past. It is difficult for any reasonable Irishman to be concerned about a religious quarrel at his back door when, for instance, Irish troops are attempting to maintain the peace in the Congo. In that context, the border problem often appears squalid and petty and most feel that it should be forgotten.

The Unionist Party, although it still embraces a militant anti-Catholic bloc, shows some signs that it is softening its stand as a 'For Protestants Only' party. There is still a slight conspiracy of silence, reinforced by some self-righteousness; but there are growing numbers of young and more liberal members of the Party who reject the sectarianism of the Party and the Orange Order. They are working towards the day when the Unionist Party will be truly representative of all Northern Ireland and not just the Protestant sections of it.

What the future holds for both the Sinn Fein and the nationalists is difficult to predict. If the unfreezing of religious and political attitudes continue, there can be no doubt that they, as well as the extreme Protestant elements, will lose much of their support. Any increase in toleration by the two sides will take years to develop to the point where religion will not be a pervasive factor in Irish politics. During that period, perhaps more moderate groups will move towards the centres of power to concentrate more on the relevant demands of the electorate and less on a cancerous argument (right or wrong as either side may be) that today keeps both areas – Northern Ireland and Eire – from living in harmony.

Perhaps a wind of change will sweep across Ireland in the future, altering the realities of the present political power structure, that will allow the nationalists to come to power. No one, however, foresees the day when this might happen. In the meantime, all the nationalists will continue to live with the dilemma that has plagued them since 1920: that, given the fact that British Ulster exists (Sinn Fein notwithstanding), if they demand that it be reunified with Eire – the only reason for which they exist at present – they maintain the rigid Protestant opposition to them and thus are denied the power to effect reunification; if, however they alter their views and honestly accept the Border as permanent, they may be given a chance to govern, but their very existence as a political force would no longer have any validity.

1. *The Irish Border as a Cultural Divide,* by M. W. Heslinga. Van Gorcum and Company N.V. 1962.
2. Ibid, p. 32.

12 *The Protestant Party*

'Dare to be a Daniel,
Dare to stand alone,
Dare to be a Protestant,
And to hell with the Pope of Rome.'

PROTESTANT PARTY MARCHING SONG.

At first glance, the 40 wards in Liverpool are contested on what most people would call 'political' grounds. That is to say, each of the candidates for the Council, whether he be Tory, Socialist, Liberal or a Communist, seeks victory by appealing to the voter on political issues – better housing, lower rates, wider benefits, or anything else of a similar nature which he feels will draw enough of the votes his way for victory. He organizes his canvassers, cultivates his political contacts, gives interviews to the Press, and tries to ensure that, on polling day, all of the Party faithful will be brought to the polls to vote. In short, these 40 contests would seem to be, on the surface, no different from other local elections (or even Parliamentary elections) throughout Great Britain; and, in practice, most of them are not.

In the two Liverpool wards of Netherfield and St Domingo, however, the situation is slightly different. There, the opposing candidates do not fight each other on political grounds but, rather, on religious ones in the Ulster tradition.

Why this came about can be traced back to the Irish potato famine of 1845–48. At that time, and for the next 75 years, thousands of poor, unskilled, and unlettered Irish Catholic immigrants poured across the Irish Sea in search of a better life in England. They by no means all went to Liverpool, but as the major port of entry for these people, Liverpool seemed to catch the brunt of the onslaught. No accurate record was ever kept of the number of Irish that settled on the banks of the Mersey during those years. There is no doubt, however, that by 1920 the size of the migration to Liverpool in particular had been formidable. Today, for instance, it is estimated that, of the city's population of 748,000, no less than 32 per cent are Irish Catholics.*

* The Roman Catholic Church claims in its 1964 Directory that there are 5,124,180 Roman Catholics in the United Kingdom. This figure, if accurate, would represent slightly less than 10 per cent of the UK population.

As did all poor immigrants in Liverpool in the 19th and early 20th century, they first settled in the slum areas around the docks, the only area afforded them. As more and more Irish streamed into the city, there developed a pocket of Catholicism in the area, completely contained within perhaps a half-mile arc around the docks. Surrounding the Irish on the nearby hills was a solid phalanx of Protestants who viewed the intruders with some distaste. Each group began to push against the other – the Irish because they were overcrowded and needed the room, and the Protestants because they neither wanted the Irish in their midst nor did they want them to aggravate an already poor housing situation in their own areas. Although this pull-and-tug between the Catholic core by the docks and the Protestants on the hillside has been dissipated somewhat by a general dispersal of Catholics throughout the city, the antagonisms caused by it still exist today.

Unfortunately for the more responsible citizens of Liverpool, the advent of the Irish had coincided with the exodus to the surrounding countryside of the prosperous and stable Welsh Methodists who had long provided the city with moderate and enlightened leadership. By 1900, the vacuum had been filled by more intolerant and insecure Protestants who were less prepared to accommodate the needs of the Irish. Furthermore, in a city where the dependence almost entirely on shipbuilding and export-import activities produced an unstable economic situation, the Irish, with their rough ways, their alien religion and their aggressive tactics, were considered a threat to many peoples' very existence. Both the Protestants and the Catholics began to compete for jobs, houses, and political office and, since all three were usually in short supply, there were often bitter clashes between the two groups.

The commonest stories heard and the ones which emphasized the split in the community were those about the competition for jobs, particularly on the docks where the poor Irish and Protestant were most likely to meet. For example, if a gang boss were Irish, he would hire only Irish gangers and, similarly, if he were Protestant, he would hire only those of his own faith. A sign language grew up that would indicate to the gang boss to which religion the job-seeker belonged. If he fluttered his fingers by the side of his cheek in imitation of a fife player, he was a Protestant;* and if he gave the sign of the Cross, he was a Catholic and, as I was told by one Liverpudlian, 'God

* A fife is associated with Protestantism because most Orange Order Lodges have long maintained their own fife and drum corps. The association of one with the other, however, predates the formation of the Orange Orders and is traceable at least to the time of William III of Orange from whence the association probably originated.

help the man who ever made the wrong sign to a gang boss!' The story goes that every morning the workers would line up at the docks for jobs, and in the confusion some ignorant Protestant or Catholic would find himself in the wrong line. 'Got a job for me, Mate?' would ask the Irishman (crossing himself). 'Not bloody likely,' would come the reply from the gang boss (fluttering his fingers). In many cases, such a miscalculation would find the offender being quickstepped to the edge of the pier and thrown into the river.

Competition for jobs was particularly vicious during the Depression years of the 1920s and 1930s. In 1926, for instance, a section of the Mersey Tunnel collapsed during one stage of its construction. The day after the collapse, four priests led 200 or so newly-arrived Irish from the docks to the site of the wreckage at Hatton Garden to dig out the debris. How these people were hired or who was paying them to work was never made clear, but the thousands of unemployed Protestants waiting for jobs on the site were furious that they had been denied the work. They plunged into the gang of Irishmen to precipitate one of the most severe riots in Liverpool history.

Because most of the work in the city has until recently been concentrated on or near the docks, more often than not, that is where most of the clashes occurred. Sometimes they fought over jobs, other times it was over jurisdictional rights, individual privileges, or simply insults. In any event, a punch-up between Protestants and Catholics – complete with spanners, axe handles, and cargo hooks – was not uncommon. There was once a small riot when some Irishmen, unloading a coffin from a boat, noticed on the brass plaque that the dead man was a member of the Orange Order. They refused to carry the coffin any further unless they were paid 'dirt money'.

The competition for the better houses was just as keen and just as bitter. This is not at all surprising: even today, 25 per cent of all houses in Liverpool are considered to be slum dwellings. It is the highest percentage of slums in any major city in Great Britain. A casual walk around the area bordering the docks will give anyone a good indication why the competition was so bitter in the 1920s and 1930s and why it is still so bitter today.

The centre of this particular slum area – the area where Protestant-Catholic antagonisms are greatest – is Great Homer Street ('No Man's Land') which has always been the dividing line between the Catholics on the lower slopes to the west towards the docks and the Protestants to the east on the hills. Scotland Road, parallel to Great Homer Street, is the centre of Catholic strength, while Netherfield Road, half-way up the hill to the east was, until recently, the centre of Protestant strength. On both sides of Great Homer Street – from the docks (the Catholic area) to Heyworth Street on the top of the hill (the Protestant area) – stand perhaps the worst slums of Liverpool. Mrs E. M. Braddock, the Labour Party MP for Liverpool Exchange, once described them as 'bug-ridden, lice-ridden, lousy hell-holes'.[1] The houses, externally, are in various stages of collapse. The woodwork is rotting. The bricks are crumbling, corrugated iron sheets cover many former windows and chimneys lean precariously out of plumb. The streets are full of pot-holes; packs of cats swarm through the area; and on practically every other doorstep sits an old woman staring blankly across the street. Ragged and dirty children play in the vacant lots: screaming in high-pitched excitement, begging from passers-by, throwing brick-shards at the dogs and chasing balls up and down the streets. The whole area has a stench of coal-smoke, urine, and garbage about it that is overpowering.

Farther up the hill to the East, between Great Homer Street and Netherfield Road, some of the slums have been demolished. In their places are 15-storey flats. Originally this was solid Protestant country but since the construction of these new high-rise buildings, it is now mixed – half Protestant, half Catholic.

The Protestants are still firmly entrenched at the top of the hill between Netherfield and Heyworth Roads. Physically, this particular area is in slightly better condition than what is found at the bottom of the hill, but is, nevertheless, still a slum. The Protestants look down in horror at the Catholics who are slowly marching up the hill as they break out of their ghetto to integrate with the Protestants in the 15-storey flats. Great Homer Street, say the Protestants, no longer divides the Protestants from the Catholics; they claim that 'No Man's Land' is now somewhere near their own Netherfield Road.

The reason why this religious intolerance in Liverpool came to be expressed in political parties revolved less around the discrimination in employment on the dock and more over this competition for houses and, inevitably, over the schools for each group's children. The Protestants, most of whom were members of the Conservative Party,* complained that the Irish, most of whom were members of the Labour Party, were using unfair methods to give their own people the pick of the new or better houses. They also claimed that public funds were being used to finance the education of Catholic children – if true, a doubtful practice at best before the passage of the 1944 Education Act. Although discrimination in employment is still an issue, it has taken a back seat to these two major contentious issues – housing and schooling.

* Before 1921, the Conservative Party in Liverpool was known as the Workingmens' Unionist Party.

By the end of the First World War, many anti-Catholics in the then Workingmens' Unionist Party had become sufficiently alarmed at the apparent inroads of Catholicism into Protestant Liverpool that they began to search for more effective ways to combat it. One section of the WUP felt that their own Party leaders were insufficiently militant to thwart the apparent Catholic danger. It occurred to this faction that if anything were to be done to stop the aggressive activities of the Catholics, it would have to be done through a political party outside the Workingmen's Unionist Party. Eventually, all the fears of these Protestants, coupled with their hatred of the Catholics, brought about the formation in 1922 of the Protestant Party. It was founded by the Rev. George Wise, who was to dominate the Party until his death in 1927. The Party headquarters were the Protestant Reformers' Church which Wise himself had established in 1902 in an abandoned Welsh Methodist Chapel. It was destroyed during the Second World War but a mission church, on Hamilton Road in the St Domingo ward, still functions as a focal point for Party activities in the troubled area.

The Party sought support from all Protestants whether they were members of the Orange Order, the new Conservative Party, the Liberal Party, or the growing Labour Party. The aim of the Party was to put up candidates in opposition to Labour Party Catholics, and to oppose, in particular, all housing and education measures that seemed to favour the Catholics.

The Party was never large; in fact, it never even became a city-wide Party. It initially concentrated its activities only in those wards where Protestant-Catholic antagonisms were the most volatile – St Domingo, Netherfield, Vauxhall, Sandhills, Everton and Breckfield – all of which bordered the dock area.

Within the Party itself was an 'activist' group known as 'The Ironsides' founded in 1924 by both Wise and the Rev. H. D. Longbottom, Wise's successor to the Party's reins. Until his death in 1964, Longbottom was the major figure within the Party. He was either a City Councillor or an Alderman for over 38 years and served one term (1950–51) as the City's Lord Mayor. He was one of the most effective debaters in Liverpool, and most of his opponents stood in awe and fear of his verbal ripostes. Because he was physically a small man, he often was the butt of many rude remarks by his opponents who intentionally would confuse his short stature with his name.

The Ironsides, never more than a few thousand strong, were and still are the militant janissaries of the Party. It is a super-secret society within a secret society: the Loyal Orange Order of England which, in turn, is tied in very closely to the Ulster Orange Order. The job of the Ironsides has always been to canvass the Liverpool wards to ensure by whatever means possible that enough votes are produced on polling day, to harass the Catholic militants, and, if necessary, to settle their differences with the Catholics in the streets themselves. For the most part, membership in the Ironsides is limited almost entirely to elderly working-class Protestants who use the organization to vent their social and economic frustrations on the large Irish minority. There are, however, a few young Ironsides but they seem (at least to me) to have joined more as a result of a love for violence rather than as a result of Protestant convictions.

On the Catholic side stood Catholic Action, led at that time and indeed until his death in 1964 by David Logan, MP, a Liverpudlian of Irish extraction who, for many years, represented this troubled area in Westminster. Catholic Action had the active support of all Catholics, most if not all of whom were members of the Labour Party. Its aim was to nominate Catholics within the local Labour Party (never under the CA label) in order that the Catholic sections of the community be better represented on the City Council. The 'activist' group within the CA was the Knights of St Columba, the Liverpool chapter of which was founded by Logan around 1920. The Knights, never much larger in number than the Ironsides, also considered themselves to be a secret society whose aims, quite naturally, were diametrically opposed to those of the Protestant Ironsides.

In recent years, an inner core of militants have grown up within the Knights who influence considerably the activities of the organization. They are known as the 'Sodalities' or the 'Sodality Cells'. Properly speaking, the National Federation of Sodalities of Our Lady (Prima Primaria) is a lay Catholic organization whose purposes, according to the Catholic Directory, are 'to promote the spiritual life, apostolic work and the defence of the Church'. It is actually under the control of the Jesuits (the Society of Jesus) who, in Liverpool at least, are considered to be an ultramontane, militaristic, and strictly disciplined group of priests. Who actually governs the Sodalites is not immediately apparent, although many Protestants believe its leader to be the city's Archbishop, the Most Rev. Dr G. A. Beck, who was once described by a member of the Protestant Party as 'probably the most dangerous of the Romanist dignitaries in this country.' Dr Beck is an acknowledged expert in the field of education and that, in the eyes of Protestant Party members, is sufficient to make him dangerous.

The Jesuits are also involved in the field of education and many Protestants, not all of whom are members of the Protestant Party, complain that their educational zeal often takes them into other fields of endeavour – specifically, they say, the field of politics. Since many of the city's prominent Catholic laymen – which would include some if not all of the Catholic City Councillors – are members of the Sodalities, the Protestants point out that it is inevitable that the Roman Catholic Church has become embroiled in local politics. Many Protestants, particularly those in the Protestant Party, are disturbed by this apparent incursion of the Roman Catholic Church into their own field of endeavour. They add that, because the Jesuits apparently exert so much influence over the lay members of the Sodalities, and because the Sodalities are tied in with the Knights, and the Knights to the CA, and the CA indirectly to the local Labour Party, the Roman Catholic Church can, *ipso facto,* exert some influence on Council decisions. To its own fury, however, the Protestant Party cannot influence anyone because it is cut off from the local Conservative Party and is too small an organization to have any real weight of its own in local affairs. This political impotency is responsible – just as much as the Party's hatred of all Catholics in general – for the organization's shrill attacks upon the Roman Catholic Church.

The six wards of Netherfield, St Domingo, Vauxhall, Sandhills, Everton and Breckfield today have a total electorate of about 55,000 from which they send three elected candidates each to the City Council. The candidates are elected in a three-year cycle, one-third coming up for election every year. The Protestant Party, however, never fought all the contestable seats in the six wards at one time, but skipped from one to the other as they saw the opportunities arise. In time, their activities were reduced exclusively to the wards of Netherfield and St Domingo, the centre spot of the religious conflict. The area, less than half a square mile in area, is a private battleground between the Protestant Party and their real or imagined enemies – most of whom, no matter what their background or position might be, are collectively referred to as either 'Romans', 'Harps', or 'Papists'.

In 1924, the Protestant Party elected two members to the Council; in 1929, they elected four; and in 1932 they elected six, the highest number they were ever to achieve. Out of 120 electoral seats on the Council (there are in addition 40 Aldermen appointed by the Councillors), six never represented very much in the way of political influence, but to quote from the Party's favourite newspaper, the *Ulster Protestant,* their job has always been 'to raise a Testimony against Priestcraft, Popery, Ritualism, Armenianism, Rationalism,

Modernism, and all false cults and religious evils.'* Since 1932, Protestant Party representation on the City Council has averaged in these two wards about three members at any one given time.

The Catholic candidates, proposed and supported by Catholic Action, have always been more difficult to identify since they not only stand as members of the Labour Party, but often stand in wards far removed from those in which the Protestant Party is active. Furthermore, there has never been any CA newspaper, literature, or badge of association which the Protestant Party could use to identify the Catholic candidates.

In the 1930s, the Protestant Party came to an agreement with the Conservative Party that, if the Protestant Party stayed out of other wards, no Tory would stand in opposition to them in the Netherfield and St Domingo wards. Part of the reason why such an agreement was reached was that, for many years, it was virtually impossible for a Catholic to be a member of the Tory Party in Liverpool. This is one of the reasons why the new Irish had no choice but to support the Labour Party. This bias has since broken down among Liverpool Tories, but the agreement to stay out of those two wards in local elections is still in effect today.

During this same period, Archbishop Downey, the Roman Catholic Archbishop of Liverpool at that time, drove the Liverpool chapter of Catholic Action underground, claiming it was not in the interests of the Roman Catholic Church to support a Catholic political party. Catholic efforts to place their men on the City Council, however, did not cease with this edict; it simply became more difficult for the Protestant Party to detect who was who. Eventually, they could only determine the identity of a Catholic either if it were self-proclaimed or if the surname were obviously Irish. Thus their task of 'raising a Testimony' became increasingly more difficult with time.

It is of interest to note that, in the two wards of Netherfield and St Domingo, roughly 75 per cent of the electorate is Protestant. Under these conditions, it would seem that the Protestant Party could control

* *Ulster Protestant,* March 1964, p. 8. This newspaper has a readership throughout the Commonwealth and the United States. Most of the distant Orange Order Lodges who advertise in the paper, particularly those in the United States, have a backs-to-the-wall ring about them: 'No Surrender LLOL No. 144 Millinacket, Maine', and 'California True Blue No. 118 LOL'. The news itself is noteworthy. Quoting at random from the same issue: 'Fascism everywhere, including Nazism, is a product of Catholic Action or Jesuitism'; 'For 18 months Protestant and Catholic youngsters mixed at St David's Youth Club in Plains, Lanarkshire . . .'; and '1964 has also brought to prominence religious leaders who are traitors to the founders of this state. Priest-inviting, pilgrimage-promoting Prelates have replaced gun-running and the message of the Bible with "the Message of Toronto." ', and so on.

all six seats. But, in fact, they cannot because, local elections being what they are, only 20 per cent or so of the electorate bothers to vote. Since the Protestant Party is less organized than the Catholics in the Labour Party (many Protestants, in addition, have always voted for the Labour Party in those two wards), each election is an extremely close one.

For the last 40 years, the Ironsides and Knights, in organized gang-warfare style, have succeeded in keeping the antagonisms very much before the public eye. Both sides have used what some people consider to be the most outrageous tactics against the other, not only in the interests of their own electoral success but also out of sheer malice. Before the war, it was not uncommon for both sides to kidnap unfriendly voters for the day, or to intimidate canvassers as they made their rounds. If an outsider, for instance, moved his family into an alien section, the local votaries would not hesitate to assault them in full view of the neighbours. On March 17th (St Patrick's Day) or July 12th (the anniversary of the Battle of the Boyne) it was, and still is, extremely dangerous for one individual or group to enter the territory of the other. Like military manoeuvres, groups would form on Great Homer Street and advance into 'enemy territory' looking for trouble. If they were caught, little or no mercy was shown. Beatings, muggings and even killings were not unheard of, such was the feeling between the two groups. To control the antagonists, the police were often forced literally to rope off whole areas, forbidding anyone from entering or leaving the area during the period of trouble.

Since the war, the tempo of violence has slackened considerably but, at times, it can flare up again with all the force of pre-war days. For example, in March, 1958, the city's Archbishop, the Most Reverend Dr John (now Cardinal, Archbishop of Westminster) Heenan disregarded the advice of his subordinates and paid a goodwill visit to a Catholic family living on the fringes of the Protestant area. Within minutes of his arrival, over 500 Ironsides were on the site: they stoned his automobile, broke all the windows in the house and threw missiles at anyone who dared show his face in the building. It took the mounted police, who had galloped approximately nine miles from their headquarters to the site, more than two hours to restore order. Likewise as late as 1962, the Ironsides began to harass the Catholics who had moved into the new flats in the mixed area between Great Homer Street and Netherfield Road. As an example of the methods they used, if a Catholic tried to vote or even tried to distribute campaign literature (particularly true in two blocks of flats known as 'The Braddocks'), he ran the risk of defenestration. In fact, one incautious Catholic had both his legs broken when he 'accidentally' fell off a balcony three stories up. To this day, the thought of such a fate has deterred many Catholics in the buildings from exercising their voting rights. Likewise, many Protestant voters in the Catholic areas dare not go to the polls alone. If they go at all, they go with their friends.

The closer one gets to the infected area of Netherfield and St Domingo, the more vocal become the Protestant ministry and laymen, and the more mute become the Catholics. The Protestant clergy, particularly the Rev. George Mason, Longbottom's successor at the Protestant Reformers' Church and Grand Chaplain of the Loyal Orange Order of England, tends to lay all the city's problems at the feet of the Catholics. He points to both Longbottom's pamphlet *Creed and Juvenile Crime** and the present leader of the party's, Mr R. F. Henderson's, pamphlet: *The Roman Catholic School Problem*** as evidence. 'Catholics', he says quite frankly, 'are God-less men of a God-less religion.'

The Protestant Party regulars also see a Catholic behind every inequity or injustice. They see, in particular, a special Papal emissary behind every educational or housing appropriation of the City Council. For example, the Protestant Party claims that Liverpool's decision in 1963 to establish a Comprehensive system of education in the city was a triumph for the Roman Catholic Church. This new educational plan, they say, allows church schools to choose whether or not they will join the system. The Protestant Party believes that none of the Roman Catholic schools will join it because, if they did, the Church would lose control over what is taught in the schools. Perhaps what angers the members of the Protestant Party the most is that the Roman Catholic schools, by remaining outside the system, can still qualify as 'aided' schools. This, they say, allows them to retain their denominational character yet permits them to receive public funds for certain improvements to the school. To the Protestant Party, this new system creates a dual standard of education over part

* *Creed and Juvenile Crime,* by the Rev. H. D. Longbottom, The Wickliffe Press (of the Protestant Truth Society). This pamphlet states that the Catholics are responsible for most of the criminal acts throughout the world in general and in Liverpool in particular. ('We can almost pin-point the schools from which Liverpool's army of youthful criminals comes,' and 'were it not for the presence of the Irish Roman Catholic element in our city we might dispense with three fourths of our police-men, might shut up three fourths of our gaols . . .').

** *The Roman Catholic School Problem,* by R. F. Henderson, Wickliffe Press. This pamphlet states that the Roman Catholics in Liverpool take advantage of public funds to further their own private education ('Public money for church schools but no public control is the principle they adopt. Roman Catholic children should be taught the 'Catholic' religion by 'Catholic' teachers in 'Catholic' schools, with a 'Catholic' atmosphere; and at the public expense . . .').

of which the public has little control yet, at the same time, must partially support with public funds. The Protestant Party has no idea what the Church of England, Quaker, Jewish, and other religious schools plan to do under this new system, but there is no doubt in its mind what the plans are of the Roman Catholic Church. Their complaint seems to be not so much that the Catholics are breaking the law (which they are not) but that the Roman Catholic Church is well organized, and seems to dictate to its followers on the City Council to go after what it wants. The Protestant Party members claim that they are the only ones who realize the true motives of the Catholic Church and that these Catholic activities must be exposed before they are in complete control of the city.

It would be too easy to conclude that the members of the Protestant Party and their allies are simply bigoted people and to let it go at that, but neither the Catholic Church nor its laymen help matters much by their attitudes. It was, for example, extraordinarily difficult for me to talk with most Catholics – including those in the Church – when they realized the subject of my business. When they did see me they seemed to be somewhat less than frank. One man, David Cowley, a Catholic and the Labour (the majority) Party Whip in the Council, denied to me that he knew anything specific about either the problems of religion in housing and schools in Liverpool or those religious problems peculiar to the Netherfield and St Domingo wards. Yet, he and his family run a grocer's shop on Scotland Road.

He would neither confirm nor deny that the Church was actively engaged in politics. However, like many other Liverpool Catholics with whom I talked, he had the habit of using the word 'infiltrate' as a natural part of his vocabulary, particularly when referring to the activities of his Church. The casual use of this word by Catholics only reaffirms in the minds of Protestant Party members what they are convinced are the real motives of the Catholics.

It is apparent that many Protestants and Catholics – particularly in these two wards – still refuse to meet each other half-way. Both eye one another with mutual suspicion, one out of hatred, the other out of self-defence and self-righteousness. It is for this reason that the bland dismissal of the problem as something not worth discussing is subject to question. If one considers the economic prosperity of the city; the growth of new generations who cannot be bothered with such feelings; the removal of some of the slum dwellings; and the advent of the Beatles, Harold Wilson and the current £100 million city-wide face-lifting, then these people are correct. Certainly the prejudices which existed before the war do not exist now to the extent they did then. They are confined to a relatively small area of two wards. But they have been confined to those two wards *for over 30 years* and still they have not died away. The city's attitude has been to ignore the situation hoping that it will disappear with the rise in prosperity. Somewhere along the line they have failed to cure the disease; the symptoms are being torn down but the malady lingers on.

Because this intolerance has failed to die, it has tended to poison the atmosphere throughout the whole city. Even though it is more subtle today, there are signs of it everywhere, not only in the lack of communication that exists between the clergy on the lower levels, but within the City Council itself where, for instance, everyone's religion is still considered to be important. Liverpool, I might add, is the only city which I have visited in England where the combined total of Fascist and CND slogans chalked on walls is insignificant beside the religious imprecations. It is still possible, moreover, to find employment notices that say 'Catholics only' or 'Protestants only'; and the sign language, so long associated with employment in Liverpool, is still used today, not so much in the field of employment alone but rather as general indications of identity, loyalty, and acceptance. One of the best examples of the latent signs of religious strife is that the Scotland Parliamentary Division (David Logan's old seat) may be known in Westminster as a safe Labour seat, but in Liverpool it is known by everyone there as a safe Catholic seat.

The best indication that bigotry is not yet dead in Liverpool, from my point of view at least, was an incident, in which I was an involuntary participant, which took place during one of my visits to the city. On the night before the 1964 City Council elections, I went to a Protestant Party rally in the St Domingo ward as a guest of a Protestant who was a well-known member of the local Labour Party. Catholics, as such, are an anathema to Protestant Party members but an ordinary Protestant who joins the Labour Party is considered by them to be a traitor. Therefore, when we entered the meeting hall, we were not met with any noticeable enthusiasm. The hall was filled with approximately 50 people, most of whom were quite elderly women in shawls. On the platform sat the four speakers: R. F. Henderson, calm, grandfatherly, with hooded eyes; Alexander Harris, Councillor for Netherfield, young-ish with pale skin; Albert Brown, also a Councillor for Netherfield, nervous and moonfaced; and the Rev. George Mason, handsome, nattily dressed in his grey clerical suit, who puffed continuously on his pipe. After a rousing rendition of 'Dare to be a Daniel', my host and I listened in silence as all four spoke in turn against 'the Red and Green Labour Party', against the 'Catholic-dominated Council', and 'The God-less men of a God-less religion'. As each speaker rose to a crescendo of expletives, the enthusiastic audience would bang their canes and umbrellas on the floor with shouts of 'Hear, hear!' and 'Down with Popery!' After approximately two hours of speeches and questions from the floor (one man suggested that, in future elections, the Party campaign on a platform of 'To Hell with the Pope!'), the meeting broke up with the singing of 'God Save the Queen'.

As the two of us were leaving the hall, the women, in particular, began to rail against my host – 'the traitor'. At first they were simply abusive, but at some inexplicable moment and before we had reached the street, their abusive words turned to nasty threats. We both realized it was not time to smile and to take their words in our stride. First we tried to out-walk them, then we broke into a run, and finally we were forced to sprint to our car, being pursued by a squad of cork-shaped old women with drawn umbrellas. Our car was buffeted back and forth, and was assaulted by fists, feet, canes, umbrellas, and spittle. The language from the women was as rough as I have ever heard from any man. We sped away under a shower of stones and brickbats.

1. *The Braddocks,* by J. & E. M. Braddock. McDonald, 1963. p. 70.

13 *The British Political Fringe*

'A man should never put on his best trousers when he goes out to battle for freedom and truth.'

HENRIK IBSEN, *An Enemy of the People.*

After having viewed the British political fringe for over a year, it is unavoidable that, despite my desire to remain neutral to the scene, I came away with a few general reflections of my own.

Perhaps the first point that should be noted is that the British political fringe, so often described as the 'lunatic fringe', is by no means inhabited by madmen. The people who take part in fringe group activities may be eccentric, narrow-minded, intolerant, and even mentally unstable, but none that I ever met would qualify as people dangerous to the public safety. If the term 'lunatic fringe' is to be interpreted as meaning those individuals whose political views do not conform to the currently acceptable norm, then perhaps the title is applicable; but it would also apply to people not normally associated with fringe group activities.

It would also be a distortion of the truth to conclude, as the term 'lunatic fringe' implies, that these people are, on the whole, less intelligent and less capable than the more 'normal' political moderates. Undoubtedly, there are those individuals within the fringe who are dull-witted, slow, mean, and irrational; but there are also men with the intellectual and organizational capabilities approaching those of a Bertrand Russell or an Edward Martell. Some people contend that the talents of these few gifted men are being mis-used or even wasted; but considering that many political changes are born in a seemingly 'lunatic' environment, it can only be mooted whether, in fact, these assets are being wasted.

Although none of the groups surveyed in the previous chapters wield any appreciable political power, they do play a rôle in British society that cannot be overlooked. In the first place, they are a possible source for new ideas. Any group that might develop new ideas – no matter how remote the possibility – should be encouraged to put them forward for evaluation by the public. Perhaps none of the previously-discussed groups have anything of a lasting nature to contribute to Britain or Mankind; on the other hand, perhaps one of them does. It therefore becomes important that they be encouraged to speak up.

Secondly, fringe groups are convenient outlets for the rebellious individuals in society, particularly when the penalties for joining them are not too severe. Certainly everybody would prefer to see these rebels express themselves within the ordinary political and social framework; but, if those outlets are inadequate for them, it is better that they be members of a fringe group than individuals venting their frustrations on the public at large with coshes and bicycle chains. This does not imply that society needs to approve of the venal form some of the fringe groups assume; it does imply, however, that, under the circumstances, it is probably the better choice of a poor bargain.

Finally, many fringe groups act as convenient foils for the public itself on questions it finds difficult to solve. In other words, the community needs vague 'enemies' on which it, too, can vent its frustrations. The enemy may be, of course, the Government in general, Dr Beeching, trade unions, or bankers. In many cases, however, the enemy is a fringe group because it usually stands for ideals that are alien to British ideals. The Fascists and the Communists, for instance, are considered staple enemies; unlike the Government, Dr Beeching, trade unions, and bankers, they are always out of favour.

Perhaps the most noticeable characteristic of the British political fringe is that it gets far more publicity than it deserves. This is due not only to the relatively small size of Great Britain but also to the national character of its news media. A minor incident, for instance, by, say, Mosley in the East End is news to everyone in the country. This point marks the biggest difference between the British fringe and the American fringe. Because America is so large and the news media generally so local in character (with the exception of the radio and television stations of CBS, NBC, and ABC), what, say, George Lincoln Rockwell (the American Nazi) does in Alexandria, Virginia is not ballooned into national importance. His activities may make the Washington, D.C. papers but rarely any others. While most Americans have heard of the John Birch Society, the Ku Klux Klan, the White Citizens' Councils, the Americans for Democratic Action, the Black Muslims, the Congress of Racial Equality, the Communist Party of the United States (which is outlawed), and Norman Thomas' Socialist Party, few Americans have heard of the many other tiny groups constituting the country's fringe.* For the most part, these

* For instance, in the 1960 Presidential elections, no fewer than 14 other candidates stood for President besides John Kennedy and Richard Nixon. They were: C. Benton Coiner, of the Conservative Party of Virginia; Merritt Curtis, of the Constitution Party; Lar Daly, of the Tax Cut Party (Daly is also known as an 'American Firster', a euphemism for an isolationist), who campaigned in an Uncle Sam suit; Dr R. L. Decker, of the old Prohibition Party; Farrell Dobbs of the Trotskyist Socialist Workers Party (in Iowa, it is called the Farmer Labour Party, and in

Continued on following page

groups receive little or no publicity; in fact, so little that most Americans are unaware that such a fringe exists in their country. In Britain, however, most people, even though they may be confused by fringe names and attitudes, are at least aware that they *have* a political fringe.*

Another difference between the American and British fringe is that British fringe groups are more inward looking. That is to say, they seem more interested in events taking place within the fringe arena itself than in the larger, more relevant arena in which the two major parties operate. For instance, the Fascists fight the Communists, the Communists fight the Trotskyists, the Trotskyists fight the anarchists, and the anarchists fight the Fascists. In addition, each group is embroiled in bitter intramural squabbles. Much of their literature, therefore, is directed not to the public at large but in opposition to some other faction within the fringe. Not all fringe groups, however, are preoccupied with the politics of their own arena; some – such as the Freedom Group – still keep their eyes on the national issues. Nevertheless, the tendency is common enough to be noticeable. American fringe groups, obviously subjected to the same pressures – the Ku Klux Klan hates the Congress of Racial Equality and the John Birch Society hates the Americans for Democratic Action – at least give the impression that they are beaming their appeal to the entire American public and that what their opponents do is of little concern to them.

Every British fringe group leader will say that his organization exists to convert the public, or sections of it, to its point of view. This is undoubtedly still true; the fringe groups do not spend *all* their time fighting among themselves. But the extraneous static which emanates from the fringe arena often clouds the messages which are intended for public consumption. With few expections, these leaders will admit that their messages are sometimes unintelligible to the public. However, they place the blame for this not on themselves but on the Government and the Press who, they claim, play up fringe group divisions and play down fringe group objectives. They also claim that

* See Appendix I, II, and III.

Utah, the Socialist Workers and Farmers Party); Orval E. Faubus, the well-known Governor of Arkansas, of the National States Rights Party; Symon Gould, of the American Vegetarian Party; Eric Haas, of the Socialist Labour Party and the Industrial Government Party (in Minnesota); Clennon King, of the Afro-American Unity Party; Henry Krajewski, an independent pig farmer, of the American Third Party; J. Bracken Lee, of the Conservative Party of New Jersey; Whitney Harp Slocumb, of the old-time Greenback Party; William Lloyd Smith, the candidate for an organization known as the American Beat Consensus; and Charles Sullivan, of the Constitution Party of Texas.

the Government and Press discriminate against them because of the persuasiveness of their appeals. Undoubtedly, these people flatter themselves; they tend to ignore the fact that, even if the Government and Press actively promoted these minority points of view, the public would still not heed them. In fact, some fringe groups exist precisely because their messages *are* murky; their supporters are unaware of the groups' true nature.

Perhaps the most universal characteristic of all British fringe groups is the tendency to over-state their cases. Unquestionably, there are some aspects of British life that are intolerable, unfair, and perhaps even wrong. Most fringe groups emerge on to the scene as the result of some inequity, real or imagined; but, once on the scene, the groups generally exaggerate the problem in order to drive home the point. In fact, the exaggeration is often taken to the point where the problem is portrayed as being of catastrophic proportions. Responsible authorities, therefore, hesitate to take their charges seriously; and, to make matters worse, this attitude is often interpreted by the fringe groups as intolerance of any minority opinion.

By over-stating problems, fringe groups often lose their sense of proportion. Those specific aspects of society to which they take exception are assigned a particular importance – usually large – and those problems with which they are not concerned decline proportionately on their scales of valuation. The groups' perspective, therefore, often becomes distorted. They soon become incapable of appreciating the true value of any problem; in fact, their distorted perspective often reaches the point where they find it difficult to believe that anyone, save themselves, possesses intelligence, reason and understanding.

This, in turn, leads to the over-simplification of problems and their solutions. Members of fringe groups claim that problems are simplified in order that the public understand them. But, in reality, this is more an excuse for lack of hard thinking than a plea for simplicity in the interests of comprehension. Solutions to these problems are also simplified, not so much because they feel that the public must understand them, but because a particular problem looms so large in their minds that the repercussions of their solutions on other aspects of society are not considered to be important. For instance, to solve the race problem, some groups propose that all coloured immigrants be shipped back to their own countries. They tend to ignore such questions as: do you force these people to leave, do you send them back if you know they will starve in their own countries, and what are the moral implications of this idea? These groups have no reasonable answer to these questions. Just ship them back, they say, and the problem will be solved.

To build support for their points of view, fringe groups have a tendency to appeal to the weaknesses and prejudices in every man. For instance, they appeal to his insecurity by suggesting that either the Jew, the capitalist, the coloured man, or the bureaucrat is the cause of all his troubles; these scapegoats are convenient excuses for his own personal inadequacies and failings. They also play upon his sense of tradition by suggesting that either kilts, Cymraeg, 'pure English blood', freedom or democracy is on the verge of extinction. They play as well upon his frustrations in a complicated society by proclaiming simplified tomorrows where all men will be 'free', 'equal', or 'independent' – a tomorrow that will bring no worries, hardships, and frustrations.

Perhaps the most devastating criticism levelled at the British political fringe groups as a whole is that they are negative and out-of-date. All members of fringe groups will say, with some justification, that every protest group starts out by being negative and that only once the ills have been recognized does something positive follow. If the job of fringe groups were only to point out certain inequities in British society, then they could justify their existence with some ease (although few of them are very effective at it); but if their job is to propose solutions they would have a more difficult time justifying their existence because the majority of fringe groups are not sufficiently positive – or, more accurately, do not appear to be sufficiently positive – in their approach to problems. Most are nothing more than protest groups. Perhaps the true function of a fringe group is to be negative – the positive solutions which follow the recognition of a particular problem being the concern of some other group outside the fringe arena.

There is certainly some validity as well in the criticism that many fringe groups are out-of-date. They are often viewed as groups who refuse to believe that their own political philosophy, in its 'pure' form, has been rejected by the overwhelming majority of Britons. The expressions most often heard are that they are 'flogging a dead horse' or 'selling second-hand goods'. Therefore, they are accused, with ample justification, of being bull-headed, narrow-minded, and intransigent because they refuse to compromise their 'pure' philosophy. They find it difficult to believe, for instance, that Britain can not only exist but actually prosper by being flexible, pragmatic, reasonable, and democratic. This, to many fringe groups, is heresy. They have never understood the value of compromise; and that, in 1965, makes them out-of-date.

* * *

The general characteristics of the individuals who populate fringe groups vary considerably but can be separated into two distinct classifications: the characteristics of the rank-and-file and those of fringe group leaders.

The most immediately noticeable characteristics of the fringe rank-and-file are embodied in what they themselves call either a 'loser's complex' or a 'fringe mentality'. Generally, these people are pessimistic, defeatist, and cynical; and they have a marked lack of self-confidence. They are, on the whole, less intelligent than their leaders and also less convinced of the 'sacred' nature of the cause. They usually float from group to group quite freely, their dissatisfaction with the society in which they live being reflected in the similar dissatisfaction with the groups to which they temporarily attach themselves. This, of course, is not true with all rank-and-file members: some are intensely loyal, some are idealistic, and some are incurable optimists. These people, however, are in a minority and are overshadowed by the large number of 'losers'.

These people join fringe groups for a variety of reasons: from boredom, from naïveté, for social reasons, because of personal inadequacies, because they have a chip on their shoulder, and even because they believe in the cause. This variety of motives produces a rank-and-file that is extremely unstable and accounts, in part, why they fight so bitterly among themselves and why they tend to be so inward-looking.

Fringe group leaders, on the whole, are not markedly different from ordinary British citizens. They do have a tendency to exaggerate problems, to over-simplify solutions, and to be narrow-minded, self-centred, and uncompromising. But, under the circumstances, they could not be considered another breed of man. However, they do have a few characteristics that distinguish them from their own rank-and-file and the average Briton. In the first place, most of them are not interested in being respectable. They believe that respectability is not only superfluous but, in most cases, a positive hinderance to their work. They will say, for instance, that respectability infers acceptance of the *status quo* and that their organizations, if so labelled, would not draw the people they want. They will add that something labelled respectable does not necessarily mean that it is right, just, or good. As a result, they tend to reject the term out of hand. Some fringe leaders seem to take a vicarious pleasure in being disreputable. Whether this is due to some inner need of the ego or to a conscious policy of shocking the public into listening to their views is not readily apparent. In any event, the public's scorn of their behaviour and attitudes is of little concern to them. Other fringe leaders feel that what is disreputable today may be acceptable tomorrow and vice-versa, basing their conviction not only on the tendency of the public to have a short memory but also on the rather cynical belief that the ordinary Briton is sheep-like – that he will change his views if enough people tell him to.

Those few fringe-group leaders who are concerned about their organizations' reputation face a dilemma that none have ever been able to solve adequately; that is, if on the one hand they choose to be respectable, they realize that few people will pay any attention to their demands. On the other hand, if they choose to be disreputable, they know they will alienate the very people they wish to influence. The secret of overcoming this dilemma seems to be to balance one against the other, never allowing the disreputable aspects to dominate the organization yet, at the same time, never earning the reputation as a toothless tiger. Only a few fringe groups have ever succeeded in balancing the two, the most notable examples being the Freedom Group and Plaid Cymru. The task of balancing the good with the bad is made more difficult because schisms among groups often produce a disreputable faction that clouds the reputation of *all* the other groups in the Movement. This explains why intra-mural bickering is so bitter.

One of the most unusual characteristics of British fringe leaders is that many of them do not want to be successful. There are many reasons for this. For instance, some groups are founded for the sole purpose of gratifying the personal needs of the leader. These needs may not have anything to do with success. The founder may want to be a big fish in a little pond; he may want to be Number One – a position he was denied in the larger political parties; he may have a love of the symbols of power: the authority, the privileges, and the worship he receives from his rank-and-file; or he may have personal inadequacies which he attempts to hide by wrapping himself in a 'position of importance'. He, too, is not immune to the 'loser's complex' or the 'fringe mentality'. Any growth in his organization, therefore, threatens his position as leader by bringing to the fore potential rivals. Because few fringe leaders are endowed with boundless self-confidence, it rarely occurs to them that, if their factions grew, they would become bigger fish in bigger ponds, with more symbols of power, and more adulating rank-and-file, etc.

Often, the very word success becomes an anathema to the fringe group leader. When he reaches this stage, he begins to justify his organization's existence with obscure and confused reasoning. The most often-heard phrase is 'We do not think in terms of success but in terms of . . . ' which is usually followed by a few murky phrases. Some fringe groups have even gone so far as to renounce all pretence of seeking success. Those are the groups who generally confine their activities almost exclusively to the fringe arena itself.

On top of this, many of these leaders will say they do not need to grow. They view their organizations as fulcrums capable, at the proper moment, of toppling the present political structure and replacing it with their own order. This attitude is known within right-wing groups as the 'Hitler complex', among left-wing sects as the 'Lenin complex', and among nationalists as the 'Connolly complex'. Each group secretly believes that it is a contemporary version of the Nazi Party, the Bolshevik Party, or the old Sinn Fein Party. They believe that if Hitler, Lenin, and Connolly could, with a handful of men, bring down the Government in their particular countries (although Connolly did not live to see that day in Ireland), then they, too, have a chance to do the same thing as well. This explains why so many groups are pessimistic and why they predict crisis after crisis, since the Nazis, Bolsheviks, and old Fenians all rode to power on the backs of a crisis.

The British authorities' attitude towards fringe groups is, on the whole, a tolerant one. From time to time they act as if certain fringe groups – particularly Colin Jordan's NSM and the Committee of 100 – were about to take over the reins of government, but such examples are the exception. The Home Office – which includes the police and Scotland Yard – keeps a wary eye on the more volatile fringe groups (most all of whom claim, in a form of fringe group snobbery, that their telephones are tapped) but, at the same time, allow them full freedom to do as they please as long as their activities remain within the law. More important, however, the authorities do more than just tolerate the expression of unpopular views; they actively encourage all people to stand up and say whatever is on their minds. They will not only provide the speaking areas (except under extraordinary circumstances), such as Trafalgar Square, but will at the same time protect the speakers to ensure that they have a chance to air their unpopular views. Freedom of speech, as I viewed it for a year through the 'back door' of British politics, is not some right in which all Britons say they believe but few of whom tolerate or promote at the moment of truth; it is a right that is consciously extended by the authorities to everyone – particularly the political fringe groups – despite the repugnant nature of much of it. It is ironic to think that those fringe groups who most wish to curtail that right are the ones who benefit most from it.

There are also no indications – despite fringe group criticisms to the contrary – that the courts are particularly biased against them. Many fringe groups flatter themselves (particularly the Committee of 100) that their cause is so potent that the course of justice needs to be perverted in order to preserve the current power structure. Most governments have an instinct for self-preservation, not only from a party political point of view but from a nation-wide point of view as well, and they are most likely elected to office because they have this quality. It is only when the State itself is threatened that the Government strikes down these fringe groups, in the same manner it would strike down a threat from the Germans, the French, or the Spanish. Nor is there any evidence to suggest that fringe groups – those that have been subjected to the law – even receive a special brand of British justice. In their tradition of inflating a subject beyond its true worth, some groups will play up what appears to them to be legal inequities, yet they will never mention the many instances of fair play to which they were treated. Undoubtedly, there are some inequities, some free-swinging constables, and some cruel gaolers; however, there have been no signs yet that the fringe groups have been subjected to any more of them than the average British citizen.

The public's attitude towards its own political fringe groups varies considerably. Most Britons agree that, although they do not like what they stand for, they should nevertheless be given every freedom permissible under the law. There are those Britons who are amused by fringe group antics; there are those who find the fringe groups interesting from a sociological or medical point of view; there are others who are confused by the whole picture; and there are those who find the fringe groups to be a general source of irritation. But by far the vast majority of Britons – those who are aware that there is a British political fringe – have come to the conclusion that most, if not all of the groups have little to offer that is relevant to their own problems. They have rejected them and, subsequently, have turned their minds to more important matters.

Appendix I

ORGANIZATIONS PROSCRIBED BY THE LABOUR PARTY

The list was taken from the 1962 Report of the Labour Party, Appendix VIII:

British Soviet Society
British Soviet Frendship Houses, Ltd.
Commonwealth
Communist Party of Great Britain
Labour Research Department
Marx House
Militant Labour League
Scottish U.S.S.R. Society
Women's Parliament
Student Labour Federation
International Youth Council in Britain
World Federation of Democratic Youth
Women's International Democratic Federation
League for Democracy in Greece
British Peace Committee
Socialist Fellowship
Welsh Peace Council
Union Movement
International Women's Day Committee
British Youth Festival
People's Congress for Peace
West Yorkshire Federation of Peace Organizations
World Federation of Trade Unions
The International Union of Students
The International Association of Democratic Lawyers
The International Organization of Journalists.
The World Federation of Scientific Workers
World Peace Council
British-Soviet Friendship Society
British-Polish Friendship Society
British-China Friendship Association
British-Czechoslovak Friendship League
British-Rumanian Friendship Association

The Committee for Friendship with Bulgaria
British-Hungarian Friendship Society
Artists for Peace
Musicians' Organization for Peace
Authors' World Peace Appeal
Teachers for Peace
Scientists for Peace
National Assembly of Women
The Newsletter
Socialist Labour League
Keep Left
Independent Nuclear Disarmament Election Committee

Appendix II

ORGANIZATIONS OUTLAWED IN NORTHERN IRELAND

The list was compiled with the co-operation of the Royal Ulster Constabulary, Belfast:

Irish Republican Brotherhood
Irish Republican Army
Irish Volunteers
Cumann Na h'Ban (the women's section of the IRA)
Fianna Na h'Eireann
Saor Eire
Sinn Fein
'The National Guard'
Fianna Uladh
Saor Uladh
Cumann Poblachta Na h'Eireann (Irish Republican Party)
United Irishman (the newspaper of Sinn Fein and the IRA)

Appendix III

MINOR POLITICAL PARTY CANDIDATES IN THE 1964 GENERAL ELECTION

Below is a list of the numbers of candidates put up by the minor political parties or, as independents, in the 1964 General Election. The size of those organizations not previously mentioned in this book is in all cases not larger than the candidate himself and a handful of friends.

Altogether, these candidates polled 348,905 votes, or 1.3 per cent of the total cast. Only 13 of the 134 candidates listed below saved their deposits. The most votes received by a single minor party candidate was 22,810 (Tom Mitchell, Republican, in Mid-Ulster) and the least received was 88 (R. Vallar, SPGB candidate for Glasgow-Woodside):

Number	*Organization*
36	Communist Party of Great Britain
23	Plaid Cymru
15	Scottish National Party
14	Independent
12	Republican (Sinn Fein)
4	Independent Conservative
3	Independent Loyalist
2	Independent Liberal
2	Independent Nuclear Disarmament Election Committee
2	Patriotic Party
2	Socialist Party of Great Britain
1	Anti-Common Market League
1	Anti-Vivisectionist
1	British and Commonwealth Party
1	British National Party
1	Christian Progressive
1	Christian Socialist
1	Committee Against Revisionism for Communist Unity
1	Farmer's Candidate
1	Fellowship Party
1	Independent Anti-Common Market
1	Independent Conservative Trade Unionist

1	National Democrat
1	New Liberal
1	Radical Liberal
1	Ratepayers' Candidate
1	Republican Labour
1	Social Credit Party
1	Taxpayers' Coalition Party
1	World Government Authority

INDEX

Acland, Sir Richard, 158
Action, 35, 39, 43, 47, 54
Aldred, Guy A., 55fn
Allen, W. E. D., 35
Alternative, The, 41–2, 46
Anarchist Federation in Britain, 150–3
Anarchy, 118, 152
Apprentice Boys of Derry, 219–20
Armand, Emile, 55fn
Association of Jewish ex-Servicemen and Women ('AJEX'), 88, 92–4

Banda, Mike (alias), see Vander Poorten
Banda, Tony (alias), see Vander Poorten
'Battle of Cable Street', 38–9
Beamish, Henry Hamilton, 97–8, 100
Bean, John Edward, 14, 15, 17–22, 31, 33, 44, 48, 57, 62fn, 84–5, 92, 101, 113
Beckett, John, 23fn, 36, 39, 40, 55fn
Bedford, 12th Duke of, 16, 55fn, 158
Behan, Brian, 131, 132, 132fn, 134
'biff boys', 35
Birmingham Nationalist Club, 16
Black Preceptories, 219–20
Blackshirts, 35, 38–9
Board of Deputies, 83–4, 91–3
Boltwood, Charles D., 111–12
'Bomb Shop', The, 114; left-wing literature available at: 115–18
Borsch, Col Friedrich, 25
British Council for Christian Settlement in Europe, 40, 158
British Empire Fascists, 36
British Fascists, 36
British League of ex-Servicemen and Women, 42
British National Fascists, 36
British National Party, 14, 18–24, 42; policies, 18; towards Jews, 21; towards immigrants, 22; tactics, 19, 22–3; split in, 20
British People's Party, 16, 55fn
British Road to Socialism, The, 116, 119–20, 122
British Society for the Removal of Jews to Israel, The, 47fn
British Union of Fascists, 15, 23, 33, 36–40, 54
British Vigilante Action Committee, 42
Briton's Patriotic Society, 42
Britons Publishing Society, 17, 97–105; publications, 99–105
Brockway, A. Fenner, 38, 146, 157
Brooks, W. Austen, 54–58, 61–2, 64
Brown, Albert, 236
Brownrigg, William, 177fn
Bunker, Ted, 145
Burgess, Victor, 43
Bury, A. J. P., 102fn
Bury, P. J. N., 102fn

Cadogen, Peter, 131–2, 134, 142
Cambridge University Nationalist Club, 16
Campaign for Democratic Socialism, 169
Campaign for Nuclear Disarmament, 58, 139, 156–76; leaders of, 160, 163; growth, 160–3; decline, 175–6
Candour, 54, 57, 62–3, 99
Cannon, J. P. M., 127, 130
Catholic Action, 230–2
Central Books Ltd, 113, 116
Chambers-Hunter, W. E. A., 36, 55
Chesterton, Arthur Keith, 36, 39, 40, 54–5, 61, 64, 99, 101
Christie, Stuart, 151, 153
Clan na Gael, 215
Cliff, Tony (alias), see Gluckstein, Ygail
'Cliffites', 139, 142–3
Coates, Ken, 138
Collet's Holdings Ltd, 97, 113–14
Collins, Canon L. John, 160, 164–8, 170–4

Combat, 17, 20–1
Comfort, Alex, 152
Committee of 100, 167, 170–2, 174, 176, 245
Committee to Defeat Revisionism for Communist Unity, 119–26, 140–1
Common Cause, 125fn
Common Wealth, 158fn
Communist Party of Great Britain, 119–26, 128, 130–1
Confederacion National del Trabajo, 154–5
'Conference of Venice', 45–6
'Cotswold Agreement', 25
Cowley, David, 235
Cymru Ein Gwlad, 182

Davis, John, 139–41
Dawson, Peter, 47, 47fn
Dean, Jimmy, 137
Direct Action, 118, 154
Direct Action Committee, 160, 166, 170, 172
Domvile, Admiral Sir Barry, 40, 55fn
Douglas, Clifford Hugh, 106–7, 113
Duff, Peggy, 160
Dunstone, Robert A., 187

Economic League, 125fn, 154
Edwards, Huw T., 182
Edwards, Raymond, 182
18b Detainee's Fund, 42
English Array, 106fn
English Mistery, 105–6
'Europe a Nation', 46, 51
Evans, Arthur H., 121, 123
Evans, David Gwynfor Samuel, 182, 185

Fairhead, John, 139, 141–2
Fascist League, 36
Fascist Movement, 36
Fellowship of Reconciliation, 158
Fianna Uladh, 208
Flockhart, Alfred, 43
Foot, Michael M., 59, 160, 163
Forgan, Robert, 35
Forward Scotland, 197
Fountaine, Andrew, 18, 20–1
Francis-Hawkins, Neil, 36
Freedom Group, 60, 65–81, 94, 240, 244
Freedom Press Group, 152
Fryer, Peter, 131–2, 134
Fuller, Stephen, 187

Gentile-Christian Front, 42
Gittens, Anthony, 17, 98–9
Gittens, Joyce, 98–9
Gluckstein, Ygail, 142
Gollan, John, 123
Goodhall, Keith, 48
Gormley, Patrick, 216–17
Gormley, Thomas, 216–17
Grainger, Martin (alias), see Pallis, C.
Grant, Ted, 137
Greater Britain Campaign, 61fn
Greater Britain Movement, 14, 31
Green, Harry, 87, 89–91
Greene, Leslie Margaret Campbell, 55, 65
Greenshirts, 39–40, 107–8, 111
Grieve, Christopher Murray, 200
Group, The, 131

Hamm, Edward Jeffrey, 43, 46, 49
Hands Off Russia Movement, 157
Hargrave, John Gordon, 39, 106–113
Harris, Alexander, 236
Harris, D. S. Fraser, 55
Hart, Brian, 152–3
Hart, Margaret, 152
Haston, Jock, 127–9
Hawkes, Ken, 154
Healy, Cahir, 40, 216
Healy, Thomas Gerard ('Gerry'), 127–8, 130–7, 143
Hearts of Steel, 218
Henderson, R. F., 234, 236
Heritage Party, 61, 61fn
Hibernians, Ancient Order of, 219fn
Hicks, Wynford, 152–3
'Home Rule for Cumberland', 177fn

Imperial Defence League, 42
Imperial Fascist League, 15, 36, 39, 40, 83
Independent Labour Party, 146–8
'Independent' Scottish Nationalists, 200–1
Industrial Research and Information Service ('IRIS'), 125fn
International Secretariat of Fourth International, 129, 131, 137
International Socialism, 117, 142–3
International Socialism Group, 142–3
'Internationalists', 138–9
Irish 'nationalists', 214–17
Irish Republican Army, 203, 204, 207–13, 222
Ironsides, 229–30, 233

Jeffrey, Robert Key, 63–4
Jones, Dr R. Tudur, 182
Jordan, Françoise Dior, 13, 14, 26, 29–31
Jordan, John Colin Campbell, 13–20, 22–31, 33, 46, 57, 62fn, 82, 84–5, 87, 89, 92, 99, 101, 113; on immigration, 18; on education, 18, 19; on Jews, 24
Jordan, Pat, 138
Joyce, William ('Lord Haw Haw'), 23fn, 36, 39, 40

Kaye, Solly, 88
Kelly, Liam, 208–9
Kerr-Ritchie, Ian, 25–6
Kerrigan, Peter, 131–2
Kidron, Michael, 142–3
Kindred of the Kibbo Kift, 107
Knights of St Columba, 230, 231, 233
Knupffer, George, 101, 101fn

Lauchlan, William, 123
Lawrence, John, 130–1
Lawrence & Wishart Ltd, 113, 116
League of Christian Reformers, 42
League of Empire Loyalists, 16–17, 53–65, 99; General Council, 55; tactics, 58–9; schisms, 61; on anti-Semitism, 61–3
Leese, Arnold Spencer, 15–16, 27, 36, 39, 40, 83–4, 100; on Jews, 15; head-measuring, 101
'Leese House, Arnold', 16, 18, 20, 22, 27–30, 99
Leese, May, 16, 18, 20, 24
Levertoff, Olga, 87, 87fn, 89–90
Levy, Morris, 92
Levy, Sam, 145
Link, The, 40, 158
Logan, David, 230, 236
London Anti-Fascist Committee, 88; see also North and East London Anti-Fascist Committee
Longbottom, Rev. H. D., 229, 234

McAteer, Edward, 215–16, 221
MacCormick, Dr John ('King John'), 190
McCreery, Michael, 119, 122–6
MacDiarmid, Hugh (alias), see Grieve, C. M.
MacDonald, Ian, 192–6
MacGinnis, Joe, 149
MacGiolla, Tomas, 204, 206–7
MacIntyre, Alasdair, 142
McIntyre, Dr Robert, 191–2, 195
McKechnie, Hector George, 43
McShane, Harry, 142
Martell, Edward D., 60, 65–81, 238
Marxist League, 127
Mason, Rev. George, 234, 236
Mebyon Kernow, 185–8
Meibion Glyndwr, 185
Melville, Theo, 139–41
Message From Hargrave, The, 109–12
Militant Group, The, 127
Miners, Hugh, 187–8
Mitchell, Tom, 208
Mitford sisters, 39fn
Moran, 'Tommy', 43
Mosley, Cynthia, 34, 36, 39
Mosley, Diana Mitford, 39
Mosley, Max, 43
Mosley, Sir Oswald Ernald, 6th Baronet, 14–15, 17, 23fn, 32, 33–52, 57, 83, 84–5, 87, 89, 92, 100, 101, 198; early political life, 33–6; with BUF, 36–9; imprisoned, 39–40; post-war views, 41–2, 45–6; post-war electoral efforts, 44–5; on anti-Semitism, 48–9
'Muck and Mysticism', 104–13
Mudiad Amddiffyn Cymru ('MAC'), 183
Muirhead, Roland E., 190–2, 196

National Labour Party, 17, 18, 20
National Party of Europe, 46–7
National Peace Council, 158
National Political Front, 216–17
National Socialist, 13, 24–5, 30
National Socialist League, 23fn
National Socialist Movement, 13, 14, 23–6, 245; policies, 24, 29–30; schism, 26–7; selection of members, 28
New Daily, 67–8, 72–4, 77
New Order Group, 42
New Party, 35–6
Newsletter, The, 117, 131–3
No Conscription Fellowship, 156
No More War Movement, 157
Non-Violence Commission, 159

North and East London Anti-Fascist Committee, 88, 90–2, 95
Northern League, 102–3, 113
'Nottingham Group', 138

Oakboys, 218
Olympia Rally (1934), 37–8
Orange Order, 218–20, 223, 229
Order of the Sons of St George, 42–3
Otter, Laurens, 152

Pablo, Michel (alias), see Raptis, Michael
Pallis, Chris, 131–2, 134–5, 142–3
Patriotic Party, 61fn
Peace News, 113, 115, 138, 147, 157–9
Peace Pledge Union, 40, 157
Peep O' Day Boys, 218
Pirate radios, 59, 183, 195–6
Pirie, Denis, 26
Plaid Cymru, 157, 177–85, 192–3, 244
Posadas, J., 139, 141
Potter, Bob, 143
Protestant Party, 225–37
Protocols of the Learned Elders of Zion, The, 98–100
Public Order Act of 1936, 39

Radio Free Scotland, 195
Radio Free Wales, 183
Ramsay, Captain A. H. M., 40, 100
Raptis, Michael, 129–30, 137
Read, Sir Herbert, 152
Reckitt, Eva Collet, 114
Red Flag, 117, 139, 141
Resurgence, 102fn
Revolutionary Communist Party, 128, 129, 130
Revolutionary Socialist League, 127–8, 137–40
Revolutionary Workers' Party (Trotskyist), British Section of Fourth International, 138–41
'Ribbonmen', 219fn
Richards, Vernon, 152
Right Party, The, 101fn
Roa, Augustin, 155
Roberts, Emrys, 180, 183–4
Robertson, Timothy, 99
Robinson, Jack, 152
Rocker, Rudolph, 55fn, 152
Rockwell, George Lincoln, 25, 28
Row, Robert, 43
Rowe, Frank, 145
Russell, Bertrand, Earl, 156, 158, 160, 165–8, 171, 173–4, 176, 238
Russell, Thomas, 114–15, 118
Ryan, Michael, 43

Sanderson, William, 105–6
Sanity, 115, 164
Saor Uladh, 208–9
Sargent, Rev. William, 82–3, 85–6, 89–91, 95
Schoenman, Ralph, 166
Scott, Rev. Michael, 59
Scottish Covenant Association, 190, 198
Scottish Liberation Army, 196
Scottish National Congress, 196–7
Scottish National Party, 189–91
Scottish Patriots, 198–200
Scottish Provisional Constituent Assembly, 196–8
Scottish Secretariat, 197
Scottish Vigilantes Association, 201–2
Sinn Fein, 203–8, 212, 214–18, 222, 223
62 Group, The, 88–9, 91–3
Smith, H. Norman, 109
Social Credit Party, 39, 105–11
Socialism Reaffirmed Group, 143–4
Socialist Current Group, 144–5
Socialist Fellowship, 130–1
Socialist Labour League, 131–7, 140
Socialist Leader, 117, 147
Socialist Party of Great Britain, 148–50
Socialist Review Group, 142–3
Socialist Standard, 117, 150
Sodalities of Our Lady, National Federation of, 230–1
'Solidarists', 143–4
Solidarity, 117, 143–4
Sollof, Morry, 145
'Specials', A, B, and C, 210fn
Spies for Peace, 174
Spearhead, 19, 20, 25, 26
Syndicalist Workers' Federation, 153–5

Thomas, Emrys, 147
Thomson, Alexander Raven, 36, 43
Tonge, Fred, 88

Trotskyist Movement in Great Britain, History of, 126–31; why it never grew, 145–6
Tyndall, John, 14–15, 22, 24–28, 31, 33, 113
Tyr ha Tavas, 185

Ulster Protestant, 231, 232fn
Ulster Protestant Action, 220fn
Union of British Freedom, 42, 43
Union Movement, 14, 17, 32, 33–52, 83; organization, 49; policies, 41–2; rank-and-file, 47–9
United Socialist Movement, 55fn
'Universal Centre of Light and Liberation', 112

Vander Poorten, Mike, 133
Vander Poorten, Tony, 133
Vanguard, 116, 124
Victory for Socialism, 162

Walters, Avril, 53, 62
War Registers International, 157
Webb, Harri, 182
Webster, William, 17
Week, The, 117, 138
Weller, Ken, 143
Welsh Freedom Army, 183
White Defence League, 16–18
White, George Pawley, 187
Wilson, Gordon, 195
Wise, Rev. George, 229
Wolfe, William C., 195
Wood, Wendy, 191–2, 198–200
Word, The, 55fn
Worker's International League, 127–8
World Jewish Congress, 92–3
World Union of National Socialists, 13–14, 25
World Order of the Whiteman, 14

Yellow Star Movement, 82–95
Young Socialists, 143

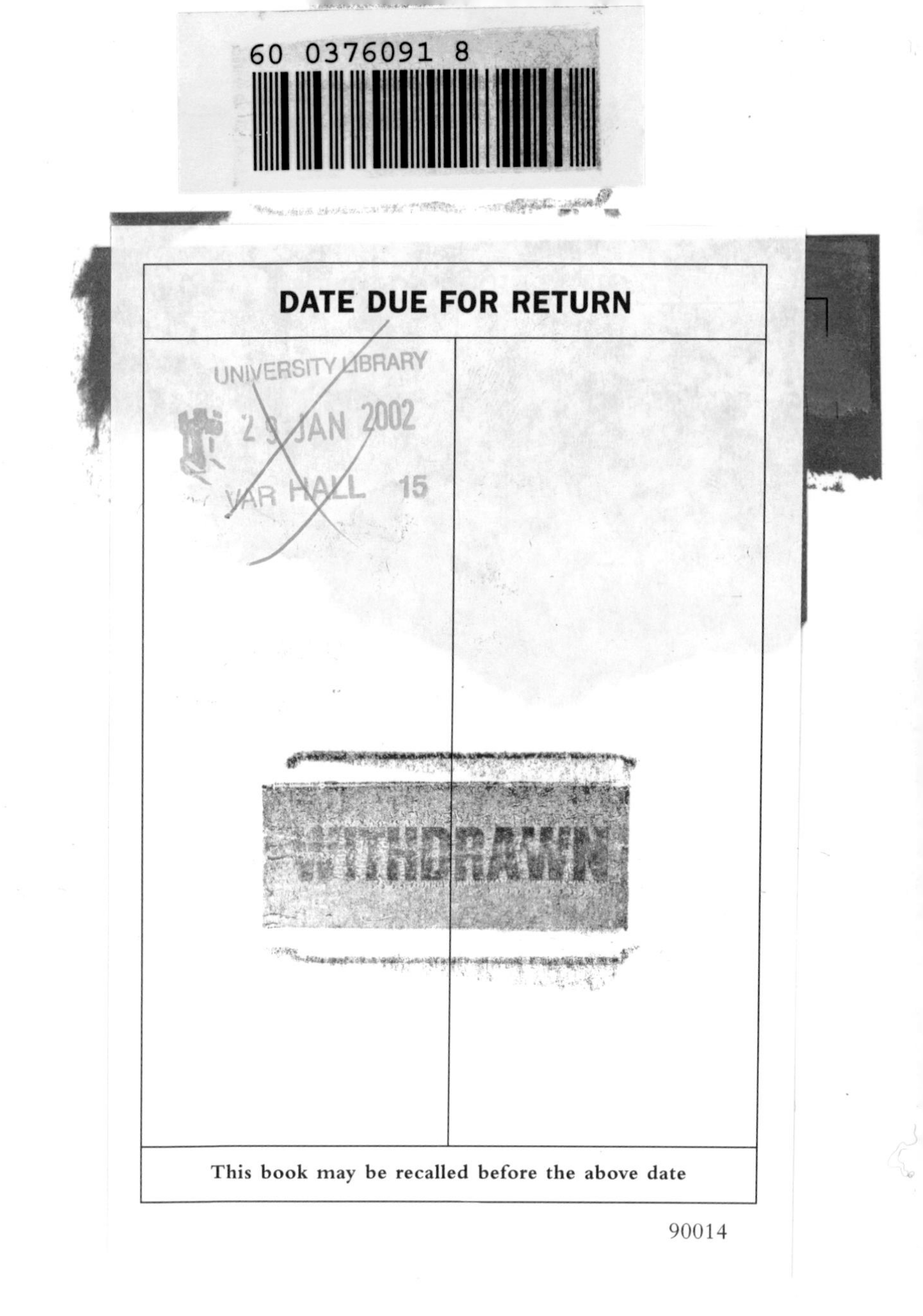

POLITICS IN WESTERN EUROPE TODAY